Artificial Intelligence

AI Model Design:

A Comprehensive Guide to Development, Integration, and Deployment

Jose Valladares

Contents

• • • • • •

Scope of this book

This book is an extensive guide on AI model design, discussing its pivotal role in modern problem-solving. It's organized into ten detailed chapters, starting with AI model design fundamentals and ending with a look at future trends and challenges in AI.

The book discusses how to define objectives, manage and prepare data, select appropriate algorithms and models, and details the implementation process. It elaborates on the integration, deployment, and continuous improvement of AI models. There's a dedicated chapter on the ethical considerations in AI, ensuring fairness, transparency, and compliance with regulations.

The book also underscores the importance of collaboration and teamwork in AI projects and discusses strategies for successful cooperation and continuous learning. Finally, the book acknowledges the significant contributions of AI tools like ChatGPT and Jasper in enriching the analyses and insights presented in the book.

Introduction

Artificial Intelligence (AI) has rapidly become an integral part of our daily lives and a critical component in a variety of industries. Its influence spans from our smartphones, which use AI to understand voice commands or predict typing, to more complex applications such as healthcare, where AI assists in diagnosing diseases, predicting patient outcomes, and personalizing treatment plans. The rise of self-driving cars, personalized online shopping recommendations, and intelligent virtual assistants are all testimonies to the critical role AI plays in shaping our world. The business world has also been deeply transformed by AI. Companies across the globe are leveraging AI technologies to gain a competitive edge. They use it to analyze massive amounts of data to derive actionable insights, automate tedious and time-consuming tasks, and provide more personalized customer experiences. Industries ranging from finance to manufacturing are harnessing the power of AI to increase efficiency, improve accuracy, and drive innovation. AI is playing a pivotal role in addressing complex global challenges. It is at the forefront in the fight against climate change, with applications ranging from climate modeling to tracking deforestation and wildlife conservation. It's being used to predict natural disasters, contributing to efforts to mitigate their impact. In the realm of cybersecurity, AI is being leveraged to detect and thwart cyber threats in real-time, safeguarding our digital lives. The importance of AI in today's world cannot be overstated. It is not merely a technological trend, but rather a significant shift, revolutionizing how we live, work, and perceive the world. As AI continues to evolve and mature, its impact and influence are only set to increase, opening up exciting opportunities and posing new challenges. Understanding AI, its potential, and its ethical implications is, therefore, essential for everyone, regardless of their field or profession. The book's structure is carefully designed to guide readers through the intricate maze of AI model design. It begins with a foundation-setting chapter that emphasizes the importance of AI in today's world and highlights the rapid advancements that have propelled its prominence. By establishing the context of AI's significance, readers are primed to comprehend the subsequent chapters that delve into the intricacies of AI model design. Each chapter is meticulously crafted to address specific facets of AI model design, employing a combination of technical explanations, case studies, and examples to ensure a comprehensive understanding. From data preparation and algorithm selection to model development, integration, and continuous learning, every aspect is dissected to equip readers with the necessary tools and knowledge to design and implement robust AI models. The book places a significant emphasis on ethical considerations and responsible AI design, recognizing the need for transparency, fairness, and accountability in AI systems. It explores the challenges of bias, discrimination, privacy, and regulatory compliance, providing readers with valuable insights and guidelines to navigate these complex ethical dilemmas. By the end of this journey, readers will possess a deep appreciation for the intricacies of AI model design and the ability to tackle real-world challenges with confidence. Armed with knowledge, practical techniques, and ethical considerations, they will be well-prepared to contribute to the ever-evolving landscape of AI and shape its future trajectory.

Mind and Computation:

The understanding of creating a set of precise instructions, in the context of this book, has significantly evolved over time. The term "algorithm" embodies this modern notion of precise instructions that can be faithfully followed by an AI model. This exactness, however, relies on a profound understanding of how an AI model works, a topic more intricate than initially expected.

Not all AI models possess the same capabilities, much like computers. They differ in their design and their computational abilities. Certain models have such expansive learning capacity that they can mimic the operations of any other model. These are the equivalent of the "universal computers" as discussed by Alan Turing.

Turing's model of a Turing machine represents a rudimentary AI model, consisting of a computational unit operating on binary logic, an infinite array of discrete storage locations, and an "active element" that can access and manipulate these storage locations. This computational unit contains the instructions or the "program," guiding its behavior.

Even though the practicality of a Turing machine is limited by physical constraints, it is often discussed theoretically with an "infinite" array of storage, recognizing that no real application would require infinite storage. Turing's proposition of a Turing machine initially met skepticism. However, it soon became evident that Turing machines could emulate the operation of any computer or computational model, leading to the understanding of a "universal Turing machine." Despite widespread consensus that any precise set of instructions can be implemented on a Turing machine, there are dissenting views. The philosopher Hubert Dreyfus, for example, has argued about the limitations of AI in comprehending real-world nuances, thus challenging the Turing machine's ability to follow certain instructions such as "put the cup on the table."

These debates around the Turing machine's capability do not undermine its theoretical impact. They instead highlight the challenges and philosophical debates inherent to AI design and programming. The question of whether a Turing machine—or any AI model, for that matter—can understand or execute "precise" instructions is closely tied to how we define "precision" in this context.

McCulloch and Pitts suggested the human brain as an analogue for a universal Turing machine. Even though their model was simplistic, it encapsulated a crucial feature of the brain's structure. While the exact role of this structure in neural activity is yet to be fully explored, its potential power is undeniable.

In many AI applications, randomness is integral to the model's operation. This randomness transforms these models into stochastic computers. Stochastic Turing machines are models that, in addition to deterministic operations, can perform operations that involve chance. The existence of a universal stochastic Turing machine capable of simulating any set of precise instructions involving chance operations further emphasizes the versatility of the AI model framework.

The idea of stochastic computation would seem unnecessary if the universe operated solely based on deterministic principles. However, as we delve into the realm of AI model design, we find that randomness and uncertainty often hold the key to robust and adaptable solutions. Quantum physics reveals that chance and randomness play significant roles in the evolution of the physical world. This prompts the question of how we can design AI models that can simulate any physical system and follow precise physical instructions.

Traditional AI models like deterministic and stochastic Turing machines fall short of this capability, posing a complex conundrum for the theory of AI model design. Since the human brain is a physical system, if models cannot simulate any physical system, there is no solid reason to assume they can simulate the complexities of the human brain. While this remains a possibility, it lacks substantial evidence. Hence, it's desirable to design AI models capable of simulating any physical system to provide a more comprehensive understanding of AI model design and its capabilities.

D. Deutsch's concept of the quantum Turing machine provides an intriguing stepping stone towards achieving this goal. According to the principles of quantum physics, a quantum Turing machine can simulate the behavior of any finite physical system with a minuscule margin of error. It can accurately simulate both Turing machines and stochastic Turing machines. Although the laws of quantum physics may require further refinement, Deutsch's idea has ignited significant advancements in the field of AI model design.

The question of "what is an AI model?" persists despite these developments. Various abstract models shed light on different aspects, but they do not offer definitive answers. Ultimately, concepts like "precise instructions," "intelligence," and "learning" remain elusive, subject to ongoing exploration and inquiry.

Moving on to the topic of computational complexity, this field raises two key questions relevant to AI model design: "How complex is this problem?" and "How effective is this AI model in solving the problem?" Although exploring these questions in depth would require intricate mathematical analysis, it's valuable to address them briefly in the context of AI model design.

When evaluating the complexity of a problem or the efficiency of an AI model, we rely on a general theory of computation to give these questions meaning. Otherwise, we can only ask about the difficulty of a problem for a specific model or individual. The ability to ask "How complex is this problem?" irrespective of the problem-solver's identity is made possible by a theory that establishes the relative difficulty of problems across different models. This theoretical framework guides the formulation of appropriate questions and the design of effective AI models.

For instance, consider the problem of sorting a list of numbers in increasing order. If AI model A can solve this problem swiftly, and AI model B is powerful enough, it can simulate model A. Even if simulating A requires substantial effort, the complexity of simulating another model remains constant regardless of the problem's size. This concept highlights the scalability of AI model design and the value of incorporating simulation capacity in our models.

Moreover, as we design AI models to tackle more complex problems, focusing on worst-case scenarios may not always be the most practical approach. It's often more beneficial to develop models that deliver satisfactory results in most cases. This approach aligns with the concept of Probably Approximately Correct (PAC) learning models, which highlights the significance of balancing precision and computational efficiency in AI model design.

In essence, the evolution of AI model design is an ongoing journey marked by constant learning, adaptation, and innovation. As we continue to navigate the intricacies of AI, we steadily unlock new opportunities to make our models more powerful, versatile, and capable of handling the multifaceted challenges of the real world.

Thought as Optimization - Cognitive Processes:

Cognitive processes encompass a vast spectrum of computational problems. While some postulate that the human mind tackles each problem uniquely, an alternative viewpoint emerges. I propose that most cognitive computational problems can be tackled as optimization problems, deploying a general methodology for their solution.

Optimization involves finding the best solution that satisfies a certain criterion. From a mathematical perspective, a criterion is a function that maps entities to values, allowing comparison. Optimization cuts across various intellectual and practical domains. For instance, the laws of physics frequently present optimization problems. The same is true for fields like economics, politics, law, cognitive science, therapeutic psychology, social interactions, and sensory and motor control. Even the principle of Occam's razor, which favors the simplest explanations, can be perceived as an optimization criterion.

While mathematical formulations exist for certain optimization problems, others, like those in politics or psychology, often lack useful formalizations. Nonmathematical optimization problems are typically approached intuitively or through simplistic methods. Even within mathematical optimization, many techniques are problem-specific, limiting their applicability. It's often significantly challenging to solve optimization problems exactly, prompting the pursuit of approximate solutions, known as Probably Approximately Correct (PAC) solutions. The classical literature on mathematical optimization mainly rests on two general approaches: the Monte Carlo method and the Multistart method.

The Monte Carlo method proposes exploring a large number of possibilities randomly to find the best one based on the set criterion. Although this approach is straightforward and universally applicable, it is also slow and often inefficient. On the contrary, the Multistart method employs local search. It initiates with a random initial guess and explores nearby possibilities, incrementally gravitating towards the best solution found to date. This method's goal is to find a local optimum, which may not necessarily be the global optimum but is the best option within its immediate vicinity.

Local search seeks improvements by exploring the immediate neighborhood of the current best solution. However, a local optimum may not be the absolute best solution, as superior options may lie elsewhere. Convex optimization problems are an exception where any starting point can lead to the global optimum. Regrettably, most problems in politics, sensation, motor control, biology, economics, and other fields are nonconvex. In such instances, local search alone falls short, and the philosophy of Multistart becomes crucial.

Simulated annealing, a popular approach, marries elements of both Monte Carlo search and local search. Drawing inspiration from physical systems, it employs randomness and directed fluctuations to explore the search space. Analogous to thermal annealing, where temperature influences the system's behavior, simulated annealing involves tweaking the current guess and accepting or rejecting new guesses based on the criterion and temperature. The temperature is gradually reduced during the process to shift from exploration to refinement.

While simulated annealing and the Multistart method provide valuable insights into global optimization, they come with their limitations. Both methods can be sluggish in certain circumstances. Future research might deliver more efficient algorithms, and it's conceivable that these methodologies play crucial roles in cognitive functioning.

In summary, perceiving thought as optimization offers a comprehensive framework for addressing an array of computational problems encountered by the mind. Viewing cognitive processes through the prism of optimization affords insights into problem-solving strategies and the fundamental principles guiding cognitive activities. Additionally, it's worth mentioning that this book's development was greatly enhanced by the use of artificial intelligence technologies, such as ChatGPT and Jasper. Their suggestions and analyses have been instrumental in refining the ideas presented and enriching the discussion throughout. The collaboration between human intellect and artificial intelligence exemplified here hints at exciting possibilities for future explorations of the mind's intricacies.

## Chapter 1

Understanding AI Model Design Fundamentals

Overview:

1.1 The Role of AI Models in Problem Solving

1.2 Key Components of AI Model Design

1.3 The Design Thinking Process for AI Model Development

1.4 Ethical Considerations in AI Model Design

1.1 The Role of AI Models in Problem Solving

Introduction:

AI models, in their multifaceted roles, serve as powerful tools in solving a myriad of problems that span various industries. They are computational mechanisms built on algorithms, capable of learning from data, improving from experience, and executing tasks that typically require human intelligence. From simple tasks such as identifying patterns in data to more complex duties such as natural language understanding, image recognition, and making intricate predictions or decisions, the applications of AI models are vast and varied.

In the realm of predictive analytics, for instance, businesses are employing AI models to make accurate forecasts based on historical data. They are used to predict sales trends, identify potential equipment malfunctions, or anticipate customer attrition. These capabilities allow organizations to make proactive decisions, reduce costs, and enhance customer satisfaction. Healthcare is another sector where AI models are making notable strides, particularly in the field of image recognition. They can analyze medical images, such as MRI scans, to detect diseases with remarkable precision. This is transforming diagnostics, improving early detection, and consequently, enhancing treatment outcomes In the sphere of language processing, AI models have proven to be game-changers. They can comprehend and generate human language, making them useful in various applications, such as sentiment analysis, language translation, and voice recognition. These capabilities are revolutionizing human-computer interaction, breaking down language barriers, and providing valuable insights into customer sentiments. Additionally, AI models are indispensable in the functioning of autonomous systems. Take self-driving cars as an example, where AI models have to constantly interpret sensor data and make complex, safety-critical decisions. This demonstrates their capability to perform tasks of extreme complexity that require real-time responsiveness. However, the effectiveness of AI models in problem-solving hinges on several factors. The quality and quantity of data available, the appropriateness of the AI model selected for the task at hand, and the ability of the model to generalize from the data it was trained on to new, unseen data, all contribute to the model's performance.

As AI technology continues its upward trajectory, AI models are expected to play an even more significant role in problem-solving across a multitude of domains. With their ability to uncover patterns, generate insights, and make precise predictions, they are set to push the boundaries of innovation and efficiency even further. Thus, understanding and leveraging AI models is an essential capability for both individuals and organizations navigating the digital age.

Understanding the Essence of AI Models:

Artificial Intelligence (AI) models represent a pivotal intersection of three fundamental elements - data, algorithms, and computational power. Understanding each of these components is essential to comprehending the essence of AI models and their transformative role in problem-solving across numerous fields.

Data, the lifeblood of AI models, is a collection of facts, statistics, or information. In the world of AI, this could be a corpus of text documents for a language processing model, images for a computer vision model, or transaction data for a financial forecasting model. The more diverse and high-quality data an AI model has access to, the better it can learn and make accurate predictions. For example, an AI model designed to detect credit card fraud would be trained on a dataset comprising thousands or millions of transactions, both fraudulent and non-fraudulent. The model learns from this data, distinguishing patterns and anomalies that typically indicate fraudulent activity.

Algorithms, the second component, are essentially a set of rules or instructions that AI models follow to learn from data. They play a crucial role in making sense of data, extracting patterns, and making decisions or predictions. For instance, a recommendation algorithm in an online shopping platform analyzes past user behavior (purchases, product views, etc.) and uses that information to suggest products that a user might be interested in purchasing.

Computational power forms the backbone that allows AI models to process enormous datasets and perform complex calculations swiftly. Modern AI work often requires substantial computational resources due to the vast amounts of data and the complexity of the algorithms. For example, training a deep learning model for image recognition can involve billions of mathematical operations, and performing these calculations quickly requires powerful processors.

AI models leverage these three elements—data, algorithms, and computational power—to perform tasks that range from the simple to the complex, emulating human intelligence in a way that is both efficient and effective. They continue to evolve, and their applications expand across various sectors, making them an indispensable tool in the modern world.

Unleashing Innovation across Domains:

The impact of AI models spans numerous domains, revolutionizing the way we approach complex problems. In healthcare, AI models have become invaluable in diagnosing diseases, identifying treatment options, and predicting patient outcomes. For example, AI models trained on large medical datasets can assist doctors in diagnosing diseases with higher accuracy, enabling earlier intervention and improved patient care.

In the financial sector, AI models are transforming investment strategies, risk assessment, and fraud detection. These models analyze market trends, historical data, and risk factors to provide intelligent recommendations and predict market fluctuations. Their ability to process vast amounts of financial data in real-time allows for more informed decision-making, reducing financial risks and improving investment outcomes.

The transportation industry has witnessed a paradigm shift with AI models powering autonomous vehicles. These models process sensory data from cameras, radar, and lidar systems to make real-time decisions, ensuring safe and efficient transportation. They can adapt to changing road conditions, predict potential hazards, and optimize route planning, revolutionizing the concept of smart transportation.

The entertainment industry has also been transformed by AI models, enabling personalized recommendations, content creation, and immersive experiences. Streaming platforms leverage AI models to understand users' preferences and provide tailored recommendations, enhancing user satisfaction. Additionally, AI models can generate realistic visuals, animations, and virtual environments, pushing the boundaries of creativity and storytelling.

Pushing the Boundaries of Innovation and Efficiency:

AI models have the capacity to tackle challenges that were once considered insurmountable. By analyzing vast amounts of data and detecting intricate patterns, these models can provide valuable insights and solutions to complex problems. For instance, in climate science, AI models can analyze historical weather patterns, satellite imagery, and climate data to predict future climate scenarios. This empowers researchers and policymakers to make informed decisions regarding climate change mitigation and adaptation strategies.

These models have played a crucial role in optimizing industrial processes and supply chain management. By analyzing production data and identifying inefficiencies, these models can recommend process improvements, reducing costs and enhancing productivity. They can also predict equipment failures and schedule preventive maintenance, minimizing downtime and maximizing operational efficiency.

Models have emerged as a powerful tool in problem-solving, leveraging data, algorithms, and computational power to drive transformative change across various domains. From healthcare and finance to transportation and entertainment, AI models have shattered barriers, delivering accurate predictions, valuable insights, and innovative solutions. As we continue to harness the potential of AI models, their impact on society and industry is poised to expand even further, paving the way for a future defined by unprecedented innovation, efficiency, and progress.

1.2 Key Components of AI Model Design

AI design encompasses several key components that work in harmony to create powerful and effective systems. At the core of this design process are the interdependent elements of data, algorithms, and computing infrastructure.

Data acquisition and preprocessing are fundamental to AI model design. High-quality, clean, and relevant data is essential for training accurate and robust models. For example, in natural language processing, a language model requires a vast corpus of text data to learn the intricacies of language patterns and semantics. Data preprocessing techniques such as cleaning, normalization, and feature engineering ensure that the data is in a suitable format for the model to process effectively.

Algorithm selection is another critical aspect of AI model design. Machine learning algorithms, such as decision trees, support vector machines, and neural networks, offer a range of approaches for pattern recognition and prediction. The choice of algorithm depends on the nature of the problem, the available data, and the desired outcomes. For instance, deep learning algorithms, such as convolutional neural networks (CNNs), have shown remarkable success in image classification tasks, while recurrent neural networks (RNNs) excel in sequence data analysis.

Additionally, the computing infrastructure forms the backbone of AI model design. Hardware resources, such as GPUs (Graphics Processing Units) or TPUs (Tensor Processing Units), provide the computational power necessary to train complex models efficiently. Software frameworks, such as TensorFlow, PyTorch, or Keras, offer libraries and tools for implementing and optimizing AI models. Scalability considerations, such as distributed computing or cloud infrastructure, ensure that the model can handle large datasets and meet real-time demands.

To illustrate these concepts, consider the development of a self-driving car AI model. Data acquisition would involve capturing sensor data from cameras, lidar, and radar systems mounted on the car. The collected data would undergo preprocessing steps, such as filtering noise, synchronizing timestamps, and labeling objects in the scene. Algorithm selection might involve using deep learning architectures, such as CNNs and RNNs, to analyze the sensor data, detect objects, and make decisions for safe navigation. The computing infrastructure would require high-performance GPUs for training the model and specialized hardware for real-time inference during driving.

AI model design entails careful consideration of data acquisition and preprocessing, algorithm selection, and the underlying computing infrastructure. Each component plays a crucial role in shaping the effectiveness and performance of AI models. By harnessing the power of clean data, advanced algorithms, and scalable computing resources, AI models can tackle complex problems and deliver valuable insights and solutions.

1.3 The Design Thinking Process for AI Model Development

The design thinking process serves as a guiding framework for AI model development, enabling a systematic and user-centric approach. By following this iterative process, AI practitioners can gain deep insights into the problem space, empathize with users and stakeholders, and define clear objectives for the model's development.

The first step in the design thinking process is understanding the problem space. This involves conducting extensive research and analysis to gain a comprehensive understanding of the problem at hand. For example, consider the development of a recommendation system for an e-commerce platform. Understanding the needs and preferences of users, analyzing market trends, and studying competitors' approaches are crucial for designing an effective recommendation model.

Empathy plays a crucial role in the design. By empathizing with users and stakeholders, AI practitioners can gain a deeper understanding of their perspectives, motivations, and pain points. Techniques such as user interviews, surveys, and observation help uncover user needs and insights. For instance, in healthcare, AI models designed to assist doctors in diagnosing diseases must be developed with a deep understanding of the challenges and decision-making processes faced by medical professionals.

Defining clear objectives is the next step in the design thinking process. By clearly defining the desired outcomes and success criteria, AI practitioners can align their efforts with the overall goals of the project. For example, in the development of a fraud detection system for financial transactions, the objective may be to minimize false positives while maximizing true positives to ensure accurate identification of fraudulent activities.

Ideation, prototyping, and testing are integral parts of the process. During the ideation phase, AI practitioners generate a wide range of ideas and potential solutions. Brainstorming sessions, collaborative workshops, and design studios facilitate the generation of diverse ideas. These ideas are then translated into prototypes, which serve as tangible representations of the proposed solutions. Prototypes can take the form of mock-ups, wireframes, or even functional AI models with limited features. The prototypes are tested and evaluated, gathering valuable feedback from users and stakeholders. This iterative process allows for continuous refinement and improvement of the AI model.

Feedback loops are critical in the thinking process. By incorporating feedback from users, stakeholders, and domain experts, AI practitioners can iteratively refine the model and enhance its performance. For example, in the development of a natural language processing model for a virtual assistant, user feedback on the assistant's comprehension and response accuracy can guide improvements in the model's language understanding capabilities.

The design thinking process provides a systematic and user-centric approach to AI model development. By understanding the problem space, empathizing with users, defining clear objectives, and following iterative steps of ideation, proto-typing, and testing, AI practitioners can create AI models that effectively address real-world challenges. Incorporating feedback loops and continuous refinement ensures that the models meet user needs and deliver value. Through the applica-tion of the design thinking process, AI model development becomes a collabora-tive and iterative journey towards impactful solutions.

Figure 1. High-level schematic of a thinking process AI model

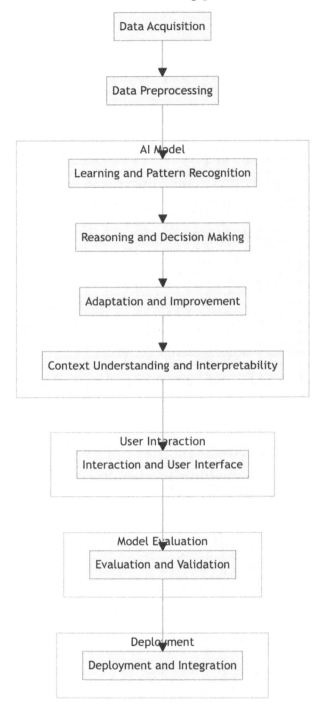

Data Acquisition and Preprocessing:

Gather relevant data from various sources (e.g., databases, APIs, web scraping). Clean, filter, and preprocess the data to ensure quality and consistency. Perform data transformation and feature engineering to extract meaningful insights.

Learning and Pattern Recognition:

Apply machine learning algorithms (e.g., supervised, unsupervised, reinforcement learning) to analyze the data. Train models to recognize patterns, relationships, and trends within the data. Use techniques such as deep learning and neural networks to extract complex patterns.

Reasoning and Decision Making:

Utilize logical reasoning and inference algorithms to derive insights and make informed decisions based on the learned patterns. Apply techniques like probabilistic reasoning and Bayesian networks to handle uncertainty and make probabilistic assessments. Incorporate rule-based systems or expert knowledge to guide decision-making processes.

Adaptation and Improvement:

Continuously update and refine the AI model based on new data and feedback. Employ techniques such as reinforcement learning to enable the model to learn and improve over time. Use techniques like transfer learning to leverage knowledge from related domains or pre-trained models.

Context Understanding and Interpretability:

Develop mechanisms to understand and interpret the context in which the AI model operates. Incorporate natural language processing (NLP) techniques to extract meaning from textual data and understand human language. Implement explainability methods to provide insights into the model's decision-making process and facilitate transparency.

Interaction and User Interface:

Design user-friendly interfaces to enable interaction with the AI model. Implement mechanisms for users to provide feedback and input to enhance the model's performance. Incorporate natural language generation techniques to enable the model to communicate effectively with users.

Evaluation and Validation:

Establish evaluation metrics and validation procedures to assess the model's performance. Conduct rigorous testing to ensure accuracy, robustness, and reliability. Utilize techniques like cross-validation and hold-out validation to validate the model's generalization capabilities.

Deployment and Integration:

Integrate the AI model into the desired application or system.

Optimize the model's performance and efficiency for deployment.

Implement mechanisms for real-time or batch processing depending on the application's requirements.

It's important to note that this schematic provides a general framework, and the specific implementation details will vary based on the domain, problem, and available resources. The AI model's design should be tailored to meet the specific needs and objectives of the application.

1.4 Ethical Considerations in AI Model Design

The realm of AI model design encompasses not only technical prowess but also profound ethical considerations. In this section, we delve into the ethical dimensions that underpin the development of AI models. We confront the potential risks and challenges that arise when powerful algorithms make decisions that impact individuals and society as a whole.

One crucial concern is the specter of biased decision-making. AI models, despite their objective nature, can inadvertently perpetuate and amplify societal biases present in the data they are trained on. For example, if historical data used to train a hiring algorithm reflects past discriminatory practices, the model may perpetuate gender or racial biases in the hiring process. Such biases can have far-reaching consequences, entrenching systemic discrimination and exacerbating societal inequalities.

Another pressing ethical consideration is the infringement of privacy. AI models often require access to vast amounts of personal data, raising concerns about data security and the potential for misuse. For instance, facial recognition technology, when used without proper consent or safeguards, can encroach upon individuals' privacy and subject them to mass surveillance.

Algorithmic discrimination poses a significant ethical challenge. AI models have been shown to exhibit discriminatory behavior, reinforcing societal biases and unfairly treating certain individuals or groups. For instance, predictive policing models may disproportionately target marginalized communities. leading to unjust outcomes and perpetuating systemic biases within law enforcement practices.

To address these ethical dilemmas, it is crucial to integrate principles of fairness, transparency, and accountability into AI model design. Ethical frameworks and guidelines have been developed to guide AI practitioners in creating responsible and unbiased systems. Concepts like fairness in machine learning, algorithmic transparency, and algorithmic accountability provide a foundation for evaluating and mitigating biases and ensuring equitable outcomes.

It is essential to recognize that the impact of AI models extends beyond technical realms. Societal implications need to be considered, and interdisciplinary collaboration is paramount in navigating the ethical intricacies. Experts from diverse fields, including computer science, ethics, law, and social sciences, must collaborate to develop comprehensive frameworks that address the complex ethical challenges associated with AI model design.

As we forge ahead into an AI-driven future, it is imperative to confront ethical considerations head-on. By embedding ethical principles into the design process, we can strive to create AI models that not only excel in performance but also align with societal values, foster fairness, protect privacy, and mitigate the risks of discrimination. Through a concerted effort to address ethical considerations, we can unlock the full potential of AI while safeguarding the well-being and dignity of individuals and society as a whole.

The ethical implications of AI models go beyond biases and privacy concerns. The potential for unintended consequences and the lack of human oversight raise questions about accountability and responsibility. As AI models become more autonomous and capable of making decisions without explicit human intervention, it becomes crucial to ensure that they operate within ethical boundaries.

Consider the example of autonomous vehicles. These vehicles are powered by AI algorithms that analyze sensory input to make decisions on the road. In the event of an unavoidable accident, the AI system must make split-second decisions that can have life-or-death consequences. Ethical considerations come into play when determining how the AI should prioritize different lives and make difficult choices in situations with no clear-cut answers. Should the AI prioritize the safety of the occupants of the vehicle, pedestrians, or other drivers? Striking a balance between different ethical principles, such as minimizing harm and respecting human dignity, becomes a complex challenge in such scenarios.

Addressing ethical considerations in AI model design requires a multi-faceted approach. Technical solutions, such as algorithmic fairness techniques and privacy-preserving mechanisms, can help mitigate biases and protect user data. However, they alone are not sufficient. Ethical considerations must be integrated into the entire AI development lifecycle, from data collection and model training to deployment and ongoing monitoring. Engaging in ethical impact assessments, conducting rigorous testing, and involving diverse stakeholders in the decision-making process are crucial steps in ensuring responsible AI model design. Ethical review boards or committees can provide oversight and guidance, ensuring that AI models are aligned with societal values and adhere to ethical guidelines. Open dialogue and public engagement play a vital role in fostering transparency and trust, allowing for broader input and scrutiny of AI systems. Ethical considerations are of paramount importance in AI model design. As AI continues to permeate various aspects of our lives, it is essential to confront the ethical challenges it poses. By proactively addressing biases, protecting privacy, and fostering accountability, we can strive towards developing AI models that enhance human well-being, promote fairness, and uphold ethical standards. Ultimately, the responsible and ethical design of AI models will shape the future of technology and its impact on society, ensuring that AI serves as a force for good.

Chapter 2
Defining Objectives and Scope

Overview:

2.1 Identifying the Problem to Solve

2.2 Setting Clear Objectives and Metrics

2.3 Determining the Scope of the AI Model

2.4 Aligning Objectives with Stakeholder Requirements

Introduction:

The success of any Artificial Intelligence (AI) project greatly depends on a clear definition of its objectives and scope. The formulation of these objectives and the determination of the project's scope lays the foundation on which the entire AI model is built. Ensuring that this foundation is firm, unambiguous, and well-aligned with the needs of the stakeholders, can make the difference between the success and failure of an AI endeavor.

In this chapter, we delve into the crucial aspects of setting project objectives and defining scope in an AI project context. We will commence by discussing how to identify the problem that the AI model is intended to solve. A precise understanding of the problem forms the groundwork for designing the solution. It helps in establishing the functionality that the AI model needs to offer and the type of data it will process.

Next, we will explore how to set clear objectives and metrics. The objectives provide a direction for the AI project while the metrics act as a yardstick for measuring its progress and success. We will discuss the various types of metrics that are commonly used in AI projects and how to choose the most appropriate ones.

Determining the scope of the AI model is a vital part of the project definition. A well-defined scope sets boundaries for the project and helps in managing resources effectively. In this section, we will talk about the factors to consider when defining the scope and the potential pitfalls to avoid.

We will delve into the importance of aligning the objectives with the requirements of stakeholders. Understanding stakeholder needs and expectations is key to delivering an AI model that adds value to the users and aligns with the business goals. We will discuss strategies to effectively manage stakeholder communication and how to deal with conflicting requirements.

2.1 Identifying the Problem to Solve

In the process of AI model development, the preliminary, yet often underestimated, step is the identification of the problem to be solved. The task may seem simple at a superficial glance, but it involves a discerning approach that necessitates methodical strategies such as user interviews, data analysis, and market research. A well-defined problem statement not only anchors the entire AI model development process but also paves the way to a solution that resonates with the users' needs.

Consider the case of a music streaming company wanting to enhance its user experience. A poorly defined problem would be "We need an AI model for our music app". A well-defined problem, however, might be "We need an AI model to provide personalized music recommendations based on user's listening habits and preferences to improve user engagement". The latter clearly articulates the problem, its contextual relevance, and the intended outcome, providing a direct course of action for AI model development.

Let's delve into some strategies that can aid in understanding and defining the problem.

User interviews can be an incredibly valuable tool for gaining insights into the needs, behaviors, and experiences of the users. For instance, suppose an AI model is being designed to predict traffic congestion. In that case, interviews can be conducted with daily commuters and traffic control authorities to understand the myriad factors contributing to congestion and the possible implications of accurate predictions.

Data analysis is another potent strategy in problem identification. An examination of user data can highlight patterns and trends, uncovering areas where an AI model can offer significant improvements. For example, an e-commerce company might analyze customer purchase data and find that customers often abandon their shopping carts without making a purchase. The company could define the problem as "We need an AI model to predict and reduce shopping cart abandonment". Market research complements user interviews and data analysis by providing a broader view of the problem. It involves studying the market, including competitors, customer trends, and industry standards. For instance, a financial technology firm might use market research to identify that there is a gap in affordable, AI-driven financial planning tools for low-income individuals, which their AI model could aim to fill.

In defining the problem, the emphasis should be on viewing the problem from the user's perspective - a concept known as user-centric design. A user-centric problem statement ensures that the solution aligns with the user's needs, expectations, and context of use. Let's consider an AI model being developed to offer personalized learning for students. A user-centric problem statement might be "We need an AI model to provide personalized learning paths for students based on their unique learning style, pace, and knowledge gaps to improve their academic performance".

Identifying the problem to solve sets the trajectory for the AI model development. By employing user interviews, data analysis, and market research, we can articulate a problem statement that truly captures the users' needs. A user-centric, well-defined problem acts as a guiding light, ensuring that the resulting AI model is valuable, relevant, and impactful. Remember, a problem well stated is a problem half-solved.

2.2 Setting Clear Objectives and Metrics

Translating a problem statement into a clear, actionable objective is a cornerstone in the complex matrix of AI model development. Objectives provide a clear aim and a sense of direction to the AI project, guiding the selection of model architecture, training process, and performance evaluation. Moreover, they serve as the yardstick against which the model's success is measured, hence their undeniable importance. This section will highlight the crucial aspects of setting SMART objectives and defining key performance metrics for AI models.

The acronym SMART stands for Specific, Measurable, Achievable, Relevant, and Time-bound. Each of these dimensions adds a layer of clarity, feasibility, and focus to the objectives.

For instance, consider an objective for an AI model being developed by a healthcare organization: "We aim to develop an AI model to predict disease X".

Although this sounds like a clear objective, it lacks the SMART characteristics. A SMART version could be: "Our objective is to develop, by Q4 2023, an AI model that can predict disease X in patients with 90% accuracy, using historical patient data, to aid early diagnosis and treatment planning". This objective is specific (predict disease X), measurable (90% accuracy), achievable (uses historical data), relevant (aids early diagnosis), and time-bound (by Q4 2023).

Once the objectives are clear, it's pivotal to define metrics that can quantitatively assess the AI model's performance in achieving these objectives. These metrics serve as a navigational tool, helping steer the model development towards the intended goal.

There are various metrics available, and the choice depends largely on the nature of the problem and the model. For a model predicting a binary outcome (like disease presence or absence), commonly used metrics could include accuracy, precision, recall, and the Area Under the ROC curve (AUC-ROC). For a model predicting a continuous outcome (like stock prices), one might choose Mean Squared Error (MSE) or Mean Absolute Error (MAE).

Let's exemplify with our earlier healthcare AI model. The objective was to predict disease X with 90% accuracy. Here, 'accuracy' is the metric. However, in medical scenarios, precision (how many predicted disease cases are actually disease cases) and recall (how many actual disease cases were correctly predicted by the model) might be equally significant. Therefore, the healthcare organization might choose to include precision and recall as additional metrics.

Metrics also serve a crucial role in the model improvement phase. They help identify areas where the model is underperforming, thereby guiding tweaks in the model architecture or training process. For instance, if the AI model's precision is low, it might indicate a high number of false positives, and the training process might need adjustment to address this.

To conclude, setting SMART objectives and defining performance metrics form the foundation of successful AI model development. They ensure the model is driven by a clear purpose, and its effectiveness can be tangibly assessed and improved. As the saying goes, "What gets measured gets managed". So, having clear objectives and robust metrics are quintessential in managing the success of an AI model.

2.3 Determining the Scope of the AI Model

AI models, with their potent capabilities and versatile applications, offer the promise to revolutionize virtually every aspect of our lives. While this potential is genuinely exhilarating, it is crucial to approach AI model development with a realistic lens, defining a feasible scope. The scope outlines what the AI model will and will not do, providing a roadmap that directs its development. The process of determining this scope necessitates considerations of technical feasibility, time constraints, and resource availability, coupled with a strategy that favors MVP (Minimum Viable Product) and iterative development.

To begin, the technical feasibility should be appraised. Each AI model relies on a specific algorithmic structure and necessitates certain types of data. For instance, an AI model aspiring to predict stock prices using Natural Language Processing (NLP) techniques to analyze news articles will necessitate a vast corpus of relevant, high-quality text data and a significant amount of computational power. If these are not feasible, the scope must be adjusted to fit the available resources.

Secondly, time constraints must be acknowledged. AI model development can be a time-intensive endeavor, especially with complex models or large datasets. If the model is being developed in a business context with strict deadlines, the scope needs to be defined so that the project can be completed on time.

Resources, both human and computational, also play a vital role. An AI model's development and deployment will require a team of skilled professionals, including data scientists, engineers, and domain experts. The availability of such talent, along with the necessary computational resources, must be factored into the scope.

Once these constraints are identified, the concept of the Minimum Viable Product (MVP) comes into play. An MVP is the simplest version of the product that still delivers the core value proposition. For an AI model, this would mean a basic version that performs the key functions with minimal features.

For example, if a company aims to build a sophisticated AI-driven customer service chatbot that can handle inquiries, process orders, and provide personalized product recommendations, the MVP could be a simple chatbot that only answers frequently asked questions. This MVP can be deployed quickly, and user feedback can be gathered to guide future iterations.

This brings us to the notion of iterative development, which is integral to modern AI model development. Iterative development involves developing the AI model in cycles, with each iteration adding more functionality. This approach allows for regular feedback and continuous improvement, ensuring the model stays aligned with user needs and expectations.

2.4 Aligning Objectives with Stakeholder Requirements

Creating an effective AI model is not solely a technical challenge, but also a complex interplay of diverse stakeholder requirements. Ensuring that an AI model's objectives align with the needs and expectations of all relevant stakeholders is paramount for the project's success. Stakeholders can range from end users and team members to business leaders, investors, regulatory bodies, and even the wider society impacted by the AI model. To navigate these diverse and sometimes conflicting interests, a strategic approach to gathering stakeholder input and managing expectations is required.

Firstly, it's important to identify who the stakeholders are. For a healthcare AI model, for instance, stakeholders could include doctors (end users), hospital administrators (business leaders), patients (beneficiaries), and governmental health agencies (regulatory bodies). Understanding the unique perspective, needs, and influence of each stakeholder group is fundamental in setting the model's objectives. Once stakeholders are identified, the next step is to involve them in the process. This involves seeking their input through diverse channels such as interviews, surveys, or collaborative workshops. For example, end users can provide valuable insights into the practical challenges they face and how they envisage the AI model helping them. At the same time, business leaders can offer a strategic perspective on the model's alignment with overall business objectives and profitability considerations.

Yet, gathering input is not a one-time process. It's essential to foster open lines of communication and feedback throughout the development process. Regular updates, demos, and opportunities for feedback allow stakeholders to stay informed, voice concerns, and contribute to decisions, thereby ensuring the AI model evolves in a way that satisfies their requirements.

Managing expectations is another key facet of stakeholder alignment. Not all stakeholder demands can be met, and it is crucial to openly communicate the limitations and trade-offs of the AI model. This includes clear communication about technical constraints, development timelines, and potential risks. A transparent approach helps prevent unrealistic expectations and promotes trust among stakeholders. For instance, if an AI model for predicting credit risk is being developed, stakeholders may have diverse and potentially conflicting expectations. Investors may seek high accuracy, while regulatory bodies might prioritize fairness and explainability. Meanwhile, end-users, such as loan officers, may value usability and speed. Balancing these requirements necessitates ongoing dialogue, clear explanation of trade-offs, and a commitment to an ethically grounded, user-centered approach.

In conclusion, aligning the objectives of an AI model with stakeholder requirements is a complex but indispensable process. It necessitates thoughtful stakeholder identification, open and ongoing communication, active solicitation of input, and diligent expectation management. Successfully navigating this process can result in an AI model that not only achieves its technical objectives but also commands stakeholder buy-in, ensuring its acceptance, adoption, and ultimate success.

Chapter 3
Data Preparation and Management

Overview:
3.1 Data Collection and Sourcing
3.2 Data Cleaning and Preprocessing
3.3 Data Labeling and Annotation
3.4 Data Augmentation Techniques
3.5 Data Storage, Versioning, and Access Control

Introduction:
In Artificial Intelligence (AI) data stands as the crucial ingredient that drives the functioning and accuracy of models. It is often said that data is the new oil, and like oil, it needs to be refined before it can truly unleash its value.

This chapter delves into the multifaceted process of data preparation and management, an indispensable stage of any AI project. We start by discussing data collection and sourcing, understanding where to find data that feeds into the development of effective AI models. It's important to choose the right sources and types of data relevant to the problem at hand. Once data has been collected, it's seldom ready for immediate use. Data cleaning and preprocessing ensure that the data is reliable, accurate, and formatted correctly, thus, suitable for AI modeling. We will further explore various techniques used in these steps and how they can significantly impact the outcomes of AI projects.

Labeling and annotating data are other important processes, especially in supervised learning models, where the algorithm learns from labeled examples. We'll discuss these concepts in detail, along with the tools and practices commonly employed. Data augmentation techniques can be invaluable when dealing with limited data. By introducing variations to our data, we increase its volume and diversity, enhancing the model's ability to generalize. We will look into popular data augmentation methods and when to apply them.

We'll tackle data storage, versioning, and access control - vital in ensuring data integrity and traceability while providing the right people with the right level of access to data.

3.1 Data Collection and Sourcing

Data is the cornerstone of every artificial intelligence (AI) model. The quality, relevance, and diversity of the data used to train a model are pivotal in determining the effectiveness and robustness of that model. This truth has led to the adage in the AI community: "Garbage in, garbage out." But what does it mean to source and collect high-quality data? And what are the ethical considerations, privacy concerns, and legal boundaries associated with this process?

To begin, let's look at the strategies used to accumulate data. Broadly, these strategies fall into two categories: primary data collection and secondary data collection. Primary data collection involves gathering new data that hasn't been collected before. This could be through methods such as surveys, interviews, or experiments. Secondary data collection, on the other hand, involves the use of existing data sources. These can be open-source datasets, data scraped from online resources, or data purchased from third-party providers.

For instance, in the development of an AI model for sentiment analysis, primary data collection might involve designing surveys to gather text data along with associated sentiments. Secondary data collection, however, could include utilizing open-source sentiment analysis datasets or purchasing access to a large corpus of social media data for training purposes.

Another strategy is web scraping, which involves writing scripts or using automated tools to extract large amounts of data from websites. For example, an AI model designed to predict stock market trends might use web scraping to collect financial news articles, historical stock prices, and market sentiment data.

However, the process of data collection and sourcing is not devoid of ethical, privacy, and legal concerns. For instance, while web scraping can be a powerful tool for collecting data, it is also subject to legal limitations. Websites' terms of service often restrict data scraping, and ignoring these can result in legal consequences.

Moreover, in the era of increasing awareness and regulations around data privacy, such as the General Data Protection Regulation (GDPR) in Europe, it is crucial to handle personal data with care. Respect for individuals' privacy rights should always be at the forefront of data collection efforts. For example, anonymizing personal data, collecting only necessary data, and being transparent about how the data will be used are all practices that foster respect for privacy.

There are ethical considerations that transcend the boundaries of law. For example, even if it's legal to scrape data from a particular website, it might still be considered unethical if it harms individuals or groups, such as by promoting bias or discrimination.

While data serves as the fuel propelling AI models, the process of data collection and sourcing is a complex task that demands a balance of technical acuity, legal awareness, and ethical sensitivity. These aspects, when combined, pave the way for creating robust, effective, and responsible AI systems.

3.2 Data Cleaning and Preprocessing

Data collection and sourcing set the stage for an AI model's creation, but the journey doesn't stop there. As Shakespeare once wrote, "All that glitters is not gold." This axiom holds true for the collected data. Raw data is seldom in a pristine state for immediate application in AI models. It often harbors inconsistencies, noise, outliers, missing values, and a host of other issues. These problems necessitate the two critical steps in data preparation - data cleaning and preprocessing.

The data cleaning process focuses on improving the quality and reliability of data by addressing anomalies. For instance, consider an AI model for predicting house prices. The dataset might contain a few records with missing values for critical attributes like the number of rooms or square footage. Handling these missing values is essential. Depending on the context, several strategies might be employed, such as deleting these records, filling in the missing values with a central tendency measure (mean, median, or mode), or using a machine learning algorithm to predict the missing values.

Data cleaning also involves dealing with outliers - data points that significantly deviate from the norm. While some outliers might be genuine, others might be the result of data entry errors. For example, a house listed with 1000 rooms is likely a data entry error and needs to be corrected or removed.

Inconsistent data is another aspect that data cleaning addresses. Take, for instance, a dataset in which the "city" attribute is entered inconsistently, with entries like "NYC," "New York City," and "New York" all referring to the same city. A crucial part of data cleaning would involve standardizing these entries to ensure consistency.

Once data cleaning is accomplished, preprocessing comes into play. The goal here is to transform raw data into a format that an AI model can more effectively process. Techniques used in preprocessing can vary widely depending on the nature of the data and the specific requirements of the AI model.

Normalization is one such technique, often used when the dataset contains numerical attributes with varying scales. It adjusts these values to a common scale without distorting the differences in the range of values or losing information. For example, in a dataset where one attribute is "income" (ranging from thousands to tens of thousands) and another is "age" (generally between 0 and 100), normalization would help prevent the "income" attribute from dominating solely due to its larger range.

Encoding categorical variables is another crucial preprocessing step. Many AI models can only handle numerical values, so categories must be converted into numerical form. Consider a dataset for predicting customer churn with an attribute "Internet Service Type" containing categories like "DSL," "Fiber optic," and "No". One-hot encoding could transform this categorical data into a binary vector representation that an AI model could understand.

Data cleaning and preprocessing are not just preliminary steps but foundational pillars in the building of an AI model. Proper execution of these steps is a complex art, interwoven with the science of AI. It sets the stage for the model's performance, shaping its ability to learn, adapt, and accurately predict. As such, they hold the keys to unlocking the true potential of AI models.

3.3 Data Labeling and Annotation

Labeling data forms the backbone of supervised learning, one of the most common approaches to training artificial intelligence (AI) models. Supervised learning requires training data to contain not only the raw input but also the correct output or 'label'. As such, data labeling is the process of augmenting raw data with meaningful tags or annotations that make it possible for the model to learn from examples.

Labeling might seem straightforward in theory; after all, it's about tagging data with the correct answer. In practice, however, data labeling and annotation are complex processes that require careful planning and execution.

Consider an AI model tasked with recognizing and identifying objects in images—a typical computer vision task. To train such a model, we need a dataset of images where each image is associated with a label describing the object it contains. Manual labeling in this scenario would involve human annotators going through thousands, if not millions, of images, and tagging each one with the correct object label. The complexity grows exponentially when we aim to annotate images with multiple objects or need to perform pixel-level annotations for tasks like semantic segmentation.

While manual labeling ensures high accuracy, it can be time-consuming and expensive. To expedite the process, semi-automated techniques such as active learning can be used. In active learning, the model is initially trained on a small set of manually labeled data. It then starts predicting labels for the unlabeled data but asks for human intervention when it's unsure. This way, the model learns from its mistakes and progressively requires less human assistance.

Fully automated labeling, on the other hand, leverages unsupervised algorithms to cluster unlabelled data and then maps these clusters to labels. While automated labeling drastically reduces human effort, its accuracy is heavily dependent on the quality of the clustering algorithm and the complexity of the data.

Regardless of the chosen method, quality control is a vital aspect of data labeling and annotation. Ensuring the labels' consistency is crucial, as incorrect labels can lead to a phenomenon known as "garbage in, garbage out," where the model trained on incorrect labels produces inaccurate predictions. Quality control might involve cross-checking a subset of labels by multiple annotators or using statistical methods to identify potential outliers.

Data labeling and annotation form the groundwork for many AI applications. As we continue to automate and streamline these processes, it's vital to maintain a strong focus on quality control to ensure our AI models have the best possible data to learn from.

3.4 Data Augmentation Techniques

In the context of AI model training, the phrase "more data is better data" is often

AI Model Design: A Comprehensive Guide to Development, Integration, and Deployment invoked. The premise is simple: the more examples a model has to learn from, the better it understands the patterns and variability in the data, leading to better generalization and predictive power. However, obtaining large volumes of labeled data can be challenging due to constraints like resources, privacy, and time. Enter data augmentation—an effective strategy to artificially expand a dataset while preserving its informative attributes.

Data augmentation involves creating new instances from existing data by applying a series of transformations that reflect real-world variability. The type of transformations used depends on the nature of the data.

In the realm of image data, as used in computer vision tasks, common augmentation techniques include rotations, translations, flips, zooming, cropping, and adjusting brightness or contrast. For instance, a simple image of a cat can be flipped horizontally, creating a new instance for the model to learn from. The cat is still a cat; it's merely presented in a different orientation. By introducing such variations, the model becomes better equipped to recognize cats in varied real-world scenarios.

Consider another example in the field of natural language processing (NLP). Techniques such as back-translation can augment a text dataset. In back-translation, a sentence is translated from the original language to a target language and then back to the original language. The back-translated sentence retains the semantic meaning but likely has different syntax or phrasing, providing another valuable instance for the model to learn from.

Data augmentation serves two primary purposes: it reduces overfitting by diversifying the training data, and it allows the model to learn from more instances, improving its ability to generalize. However, while data augmentation can be a powerful tool, it should be applied thoughtfully. The chosen augmentation techniques should reflect plausible variability that the model might encounter in the task it's being trained for. Over-augmentation, or applying transformations that distort the data beyond recognition or plausibility can harm a model's performance rather than help it.

Data augmentation, when employed strategically, can significantly enhance an AI model's performance by providing more varied and robust training data. As we advance in our understanding of different data domains and transformation techniques, the use of data augmentation is set to become an even more vital tool in the AI practitioner's toolkit.

3.5 Data Storage, Versioning, and Access Control

In the world of AI, data is a prized asset, and managing it efficiently is crucial to successful model development and deployment. As AI models grow in complexity and scale, so does the need for effective data storage, versioning, and access control mechanisms. These factors form a foundational aspect of robust data management, aiding in model reproducibility, data security, and regulatory compliance.

The first step in data management is data storage. The choice of storage solution depends on the nature and size of the dataset. For structured data, relational databases such as PostgreSQL or MySQL can be effective. In contrast, for handling large volumes of unstructured or semi-structured data, NoSQL databases like MongoDB or Cassandra, or distributed file systems like Hadoop's HDFS, might be more suitable. With the advent of cloud computing, cloud storage solutions such as AWS S3, Google Cloud Storage, or Azure Blob Storage have gained popularity due to their scalability, durability, and cost-effectiveness.

Next, data versioning comes into play, which is the process of keeping a record of changes made to the data over time. Just as source code versioning is fundamental to software development, data versioning is essential for reproducible data science. It allows data scientists to track changes, compare different versions, revert changes, and share data with others, all while maintaining a clear audit trail. Tools like DVC (Data Version Control) or Delta Lake provide powerful capabilities for data versioning, enabling seamless collaboration and experimentation in AI projects.

Finally, access control is pivotal in managing who can view, modify, or delete data. Properly implemented access controls help protect sensitive information, prevent unauthorized changes, and ensure compliance with privacy regulations such as GDPR or HIPAA. This can be achieved through various mechanisms, including Role-Based Access Control (RBAC), Attribute-Based Access Control (ABAC), or Access Control Lists (ACLs), depending on the complexity and needs of the project. Additionally, encryption at rest and in transit provides another layer of security to protect sensitive data.

While data storage, versioning, and access control are individually significant, their integration presents a comprehensive data management strategy. By effectively combining these elements, organizations can not only enhance their AI model development processes but also ensure the security and integrity of their data assets. This approach paves the way for a robust, reliable, and secure AI model building while fostering a culture of transparency and accountability.

Data Collection Schematic. Figure 2

Data Collection and Sourcing:

The purpose of this stage is to gather all the necessary data for the AI model. Data can be collected from a variety of sources depending on the problem at hand, including online resources, open-source datasets, surveys, or third-party providers. The quality, relevancy, and variety of the collected data have a direct impact on the accuracy and usefulness of the AI model.

Data Cleaning and Preprocessing:

Once the data is collected, it is rarely in a perfect state for immediate use. Data cleaning aims to improve the quality of the data by dealing with missing, noisy, or inconsistent data. Preprocessing transforms raw data into a format that an AI model can use effectively. These transformations might include normalization, discretization, and encoding categorical variables.

Data Labeling and Annotation:

For supervised learning models, each data instance must be associated with a label or an annotation. The purpose of this stage is to provide ground truth for the model to learn from. Depending on the task, labeling or annotating can be a manual, semi-automated, or fully automated process.

Data Augmentation Techniques:

The purpose of data augmentation is to increase the size and diversity of the training data, which can lead to better model performance and generalization. It involves creating new data instances by applying various transformations to the original data. In image classification tasks, for instance, this could include applying rotations, translations, or flips to the original images.

Data Storage, Versioning, and Access Control:

After the data has been collected, cleaned, labeled, and possibly augmented, it needs to be stored in a secure and efficient manner. Good data storage solutions allow for easy access to the data and efficient computation. Version control is important for tracking changes to the dataset and facilitating collaboration. Access control is a crucial aspect of data governance, protecting sensitive information, and ensuring compliance with privacy regulations.

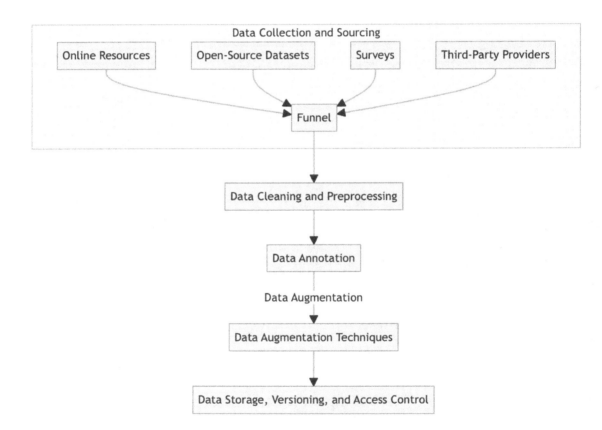

Figure 2: Data Collection

## Chapter 4

Choosing Algorithms and Models

Overview:

4.1 Introduction to Machine Learning & Deep Learning Algorithms

As we venture into the realm of Artificial Intelligence (AI), one fundamental understanding we must have is the difference between Machine Learning (ML) and Deep Learning (DL). Both ML and DL are subfields of AI that provide systems with the ability to automatically learn and improve from experience without being explicitly programmed.

Machine Learning, at its core, is a set of methods that can detect patterns in data, and then use those patterns to predict future data or allow decision-making under uncertain conditions. Machine learning algorithms can be broadly classified into three types: supervised learning, unsupervised learning, and reinforcement learning.

Supervised learning, as the name suggests, involves training the model on a labeled dataset. The model learns to predict outcomes based on the input data, much like a student learns under the guidance of a teacher. Some common examples of supervised learning algorithms are Linear Regression, Decision Trees, and Support Vector Machines.

Unsupervised learning, on the other hand, deals with data that has no labels, and the goal is to find the underlying structure in the data. In other words, the machine learns on its own without any supervision. Clustering (like K-means) and Association (like Apriori) are two main types of unsupervised learning algorithms.

Reinforcement learning is a type of machine learning where an agent learns to behave in an environment, by performing actions and observing the results. It's like a game where the agent learns the optimal strategy to win.

Deep Learning is a subset of machine learning that uses neural networks with many layers (hence, 'deep'). It is especially good at processing large volumes of high-dimensionality data, such as images, audio, and text. The fundamental unit of a deep learning model is an artificial neuron, which takes a number of real-valued inputs, calculates a weighted sum, and passes it through a non-linear function, often called activation function.

There is an array of deep learning models: Convolutional Neural Networks (CNNs), which are typically used for image data; Recurrent Neural Networks (RNNs), used for sequential data like time series and Natural Language Processing (NLP); and Transformer models like the BERT (Bidirectional Encoder Representations from Transformers) model which has gained a lot of traction in the NLP community for its superior performance.

The choice of algorithm depends largely on the type and amount of data available, the problem to be solved, and the computational resources at hand. The key to a successful AI project is to understand the strengths and weaknesses of each algorithm, which requires a firm grasp of their underlying mathematics. For instance, understanding the bias-variance trade-off in supervised learning, the Eigenvalue decomposition in principal component analysis, or the Bellman equation in reinforcement learning, helps data scientists choose the most effective algorithm and also to tune its parameters optimally.

It's important to remember that while these algorithms can be powerful tools in the arsenal of a data scientist, they are just means to an end. The real value lies in leveraging these tools effectively to unearth patterns, gain insights, and predict future trends that can help in strategic decision-making.

4.2 Supervised Learning Algorithms and Applications

Supervised learning forms the core of many influential and practical Artificial Intelligence applications in the world today. It is a type of machine learning where the model is trained on a labeled dataset, i.e., a dataset where the target variable is known. By learning from this data, the model can then make predictions when it encounters new, similar data. Some of the key supervised learning algorithms and their applications are as follows:

Linear Regression:

One of the simplest forms of machine learning algorithms, Linear Regression is used to predict a continuous target variable based on one or more input features. For example, predicting housing prices based on factors like location, size of the house, and number of bedrooms. Linear Regression finds its application in fields such as economics, business, and social sciences.

Linear regression, a technique rooted in the field of statistics, is one of the simplest yet powerful machine learning algorithms. As the name suggests, it assumes a linear relationship between the independent and dependent variables. This relationship is expressed in the form of a mathematical equation, which is used to predict a continuous target variable based on one or more input features.

Conceptually, imagine plotting each data point on a graph with the X-axis representing the input variable and the Y-axis representing the output variable. The linear regression model's task is to draw a straight line - the line of best fit - through these points that minimizes the distance between the line and each data point.

For instance, suppose you are interested in predicting the price of a house (dependent or target variable) based on the size of the house (independent variable or feature). In a simplistic scenario, the relationship between these two variables could be direct and linear - the larger the house, the higher the price. You could represent this relationship mathematically with a linear equation like Price = m(Size) + c, where m is the slope of the line, reflecting how much the price increases for each unit increase in size, and c is the y-intercept, representing the base price of the house.

In reality, house prices are influenced by many factors beyond just size, such as location, age, architectural design, proximity to amenities, etc. In these cases, multiple linear regression can be used, which extends the simple linear regression model to include multiple input features.

Applications of linear regression are widespread due to its simplicity, interpretability, and computational efficiency. It is widely used in economics for forecasting and trend analysis. In business, it could be used for demand and sales forecasting, risk assessment, or pricing strategy development. In social sciences, it's used to study the relationship between various sociological or psychological attributes.

However, linear regression is not without limitations. It assumes a linear relationship between the variables, which is not always the case. It is sensitive to outliers and can overfit or underfit the data if the assumptions are not met. Despite these potential drawbacks, linear regression remains a fundamental tool in the data scientist's toolkit due to its simplicity and versatility.

Example: Linear regression models

The relationship between two variables by fitting a linear equation to observed data.

Given a dataset with n points, $((x1, y1), (x2, y2), ..., (xn, yn))$, we want to find the equation of a straight line $y = mx + b$ (where m is the slope and b is the y-intercept), which fits best for these data points.

The best fit line is the one for which total prediction error (all data points) is as small as possible. Error is the distance between the point to the regression line.

These errors are also called as residuals. The line for which the sum of the residuals is minimum is called the best fit line or the regression line. These residuals can be calculated as the difference between the actual value and the predicted value.

If we denote y_i as the observed outputs, x_i as the observed inputs, $\hat{y}_i$ as the model's prediction for the i-th observation,

we can calculate the residual e_i as follows:

$ei = yi - \hat{y}i$

Now, our goal is to minimize the sum of the square of these residuals (RSS), because squaring emphasizes larger discrepancies. This method is called the method of least squares.

$$RSS = \Sigma\, ei^2 = \Sigma\, (yi - \hat{y}i)^2$$

Since $\hat{y}i = m{*}xi + b$, we substitute this into the equation:

$$RSS = \Sigma\, (yi - m{*}xi - b)^2$$

To find the m and b that minimize this sum, we take the partial derivative of RSS with respect to m, and with respect to b, set them equal to zero and solve the system of two equations.

This results in the formulas:

$$m = (\, n(\Sigma(xi{*}yi)) - \Sigma(xi)\Sigma(yi)\,)\, /\, (\, n(\Sigma(xi^2)) - (\Sigma(xi))^2\,)$$
$$b = (\, \Sigma(yi) - m\Sigma(xi)\,)\, /\, n$$

These equations are called the normal equations for the least squares line. There are further methods to solve these equations, but this goes beyond the scope of a brief introduction.

Decision Trees:

These are intuitive and easy-to-interpret models used for both classification and regression tasks. Decision Trees split the data based on feature values, resulting in a tree-like model of decisions. They are used in a variety of fields, such as medical diagnosis, credit risk analysis, and natural language processing.

Decision trees, a foundational element in machine learning and data science, offer an effective approach to both classification and regression tasks. Derived from graph theory, decision trees are simple yet powerful tools that transform complex datasets into a series of straightforward decisions, hence the name 'decision tree'. This elegant simplicity allows for easy interpretation and visualization, often making decision trees the first port of call for predictive analysis.

Imagine a scenario where a financial institution needs to evaluate credit risk for its loan applicants. Here, a decision tree comes into play by examining several factors – like the applicant's income, employment status, credit history, etc. – and segmenting the data at each step based on these feature values. Each internal node of the tree represents a feature (for example, income), each branch represents a decision rule (income greater than $50K), and each leaf node represents an outcome (high or low credit risk). By traversing down the tree following the decision rules, a classification (in this case, credit risk) can be made for each individual.

Let's delve into a more complex field, such as medical diagnosis. A decision tree can assist healthcare professionals in diagnosing diseases based on a range of symptoms and medical history data. Each internal node might correspond to a symptom, while each leaf represents a potential diagnosis. For instance, if a patient has 'high fever' and 'cough', the decision tree might lead to 'flu' as a probable diagnosis.

Decision trees are also increasingly being utilized in the realm of natural language processing (NLP), where they can assist in tasks such as sentiment analysis or topic classification. In sentiment analysis, for example, features might include the presence or absence of certain keywords, phrases, or emoticons, and the decision tree can classify text as conveying positive, negative, or neutral sentiment.

Despite the simplicity of decision trees, they hold the potential for complexity. As we add more and more decisions (or nodes) to the tree, it can become quite intricate. This complexity, however, comes with a warning. Overly complex trees may lead to 'overfitting', where the model fits the training data too well, capturing noise and outliers, and hence performs poorly on unseen data. A balance must be struck between the depth of the tree (complexity) and its predictive accuracy to avoid such scenarios.

As with any model, decision trees are not a one-size-fits-all solution. They perform well on certain types of data and not so well on others. Their simplicity, however, makes them an essential tool in the arsenal of data scientists, often serving as the first step in the journey of predictive modeling. The lessons learned from the implementation of a decision tree can often inform the choice of more complex models further down the line, if needed.

While decision trees are powerful on their own, their real potential is often realized when they are used in combination with other decision trees. The resulting ensemble models, such as Random Forests and Gradient Boosting Machines (GBMs), often deliver significantly improved performance over individual decision trees.

Random Forests, for instance, leverage the concept of 'bagging' (Bootstrap Aggregation) to generate a multitude of decision trees from randomly sampled subsets of the training data, and then make a prediction based on the majority vote (for classification) or average prediction (for regression) of these individual trees. The idea is to create diverse trees that are slightly overfitted in different ways, with the hope that the errors of individual trees will cancel out when they are combined.

GBMs, on the other hand, employ 'boosting', which involves training decision trees sequentially, where each tree learns from the mistakes of its predecessors. The algorithm assigns higher weights to the instances misclassified by the previous trees, thereby pushing the next tree to focus more on these challenging instances.

Support Vector Machines: Bridging Linearity and Non-linearty

Moving beyond decision trees, another powerful supervised learning algorithm that can be discussed here is the Support Vector Machine (SVM). Originating from the field of statistical learning theory, SVMs are designed for binary classification tasks, though extensions for multi-class classification and regression exist.

At a high level, SVM aims to find a hyperplane that best separates the data points of two classes, maximizing the margin between the nearest points (support vectors) of the classes. SVMs are particularly effective when the data is linearly separable. However, in cases where this is not possible, SVMs use a clever trick – the kernel trick – to project the data into higher-dimensional space where it becomes linearly separable.

Deep Learning: Taking Inspiration from the Human Brain

While traditional machine learning algorithms like those mentioned above have their strengths, they often struggle with tasks that humans find intuitive, such as image or speech recognition. Enter deep learning, a subfield of machine learning that is inspired by the structure and function of the human brain and attempts to mimic its computational model - the artificial neural network.

Neural networks, especially deep neural networks with multiple hidden layers, are exceptionally good at learning from unstructured data and can automatically extract useful features, removing the need for manual feature engineering that is often necessary in traditional machine learning.

However, the complex nature of these networks often results in a 'black box' problem, where the decision-making process is not transparent and difficult to interpret. Despite this, the unmatched performance of deep learning models in areas such as image and speech recognition, natural language processing, and even complex board games like Go, has cemented their place at the forefront of AI research and development.

In conclusion, the choice of algorithm in machine learning and deep learning is not one to be taken lightly. It has to match the complexity and nature of the problem, the quality and quantity of available data, and the computational resources at disposal. But once an appropriate algorithm is selected and tuned to its optimal performance, the insights and predictions it can provide are truly remarkable.

In all these examples, the supervised learning model is trained using a dataset where the outcome is known, and the model learns the mapping function from the input features to the output. Once the model is trained, it can be used to predict the outcomes of new data instances where the output is unknown.

Remember, the choice of algorithm depends on the problem at hand, the nature of the data, and the computational resources available. It's also important to note that the performance of these algorithms is heavily reliant on the quality of the data they're trained on. Therefore, appropriate data preprocessing and feature engineering steps are crucial for building an effective model.

Example: Mathematical concept behind Support Vector Machines

I will describe the mathematical concept behind Support Vector Machines (SVMs), which is a supervised learning algorithm that was discussed in the essay.

The main idea behind SVM is to find a hyperplane that best separates the data points of two classes. Let's consider a binary classification problem, where we have data points belonging to either class -1 or +1.

A hyperplane in an n-dimensional Euclidean space is a flat, n-1 dimensional subset of that space that divides the space into two disconnected parts. In a 2-dimensional space, a hyperplane is simply a line, and in a 3-dimensional space, it's a plane. For higher dimensions, we can think of it as a 'plane' that can slice through the space.

The equation of a hyperplane is given by:

$$0 = w.x + b$$

Here, w is the weight vector perpendicular to the hyperplane, x is the input vector, and b is the bias term.

The goal of SVM is to find the hyperplane with the maximum margin, i.e., the maximum distance between data points of two classes. The distance (d) from a point (x) to the hyperplane is given by:

$$d = |w.x + b| / ||w||$$

Here, $||w||$ denotes the Euclidean norm (or length) of the vector w.

To maximize the margin, we want to maximize d. Since the denominator $||w||$ is always positive, maximizing d is equivalent to minimizing $||w||$.

However, we need to ensure that all data points are correctly classified. This constraint can be expressed as:

For every data point (x_i, y_i) in the training data, where y_i is the label (-1 or +1) and x_i is the feature vector:

y_i*(w.x_i + b) >= 1

This is a quadratic optimization problem, which can be solved using Lagrange multipliers and the method of optimization known as Sequential Minimal Optimization (SMO). The solution yields the weight vector w and bias term b that define the optimal hyperplane.

It's worth noting that in cases where the data is not linearly separable, SVM uses a trick called the kernel trick to project the data into a higher-dimensional space where it becomes linearly separable. Different kernels (linear, polynomial, radial basis function, sigmoid, etc.) can be used depending on the nature of the data.

This is a high-level overview of the mathematics behind SVM. In practice, this involves more detailed computation and other considerations, such as soft-margin SVM for handling outliers and noise, and multi-class SVM for handling more than two classes.

Support Vector Machines (SVMs):

SVMs are powerful models used mainly for classification tasks, although they can be used for regression as well. They work by finding the hyperplane that best separates the classes in the feature space. SVMs have been successfully used in handwriting recognition, image classification, and bioinformatics.

Support Vector Machines (SVMs) operate under the philosophy of 'maximum margin', which provides the model with a more generalizable and robust framework for binary classification problems. The primary goal of SVM is to identify the optimal hyperplane, a decision boundary that not only separates the two classes in the dataset but also maximizes the distance between the nearest data points (called support vectors) and itself. The SVMs' ability to maximize this margin sets them apart and enhances their classification performance.

In terms of the mathematics that drive SVMs, they primarily revolve around concepts from vector algebra and optimization. The fundamental formula of the decision boundary in an SVM is derived from the equation of a hyperplane, which is '$0 = w.x + b$'. Here 'w' is the normal vector to the hyperplane, 'x' is an arbitrary point on the hyperplane, and 'b' is the bias. The aim of SVM is to optimize this formula to maximize the margin (i.e., the distance between the support vectors and the hyperplane) while ensuring correct classification of the data points.

While SVMs have shown remarkable performance on linearly separable data, they are also adept at handling non-linear classification problems, thanks to the kernel trick. The kernel trick is a mathematical technique that transforms the data from a low-dimensional, non-linear space to a higher-dimensional, linear space. This transformation enables SVMs to find a hyperplane in the transformed space, which corresponds to a non-linear decision boundary in the original space.

SVMs have been utilized in a multitude of practical applications. For instance, in handwriting recognition, SVMs can be trained to differentiate between different characters based on features such as the number of closed loops, the number of endpoints, and the slant of the strokes. In image classification tasks, they have been used with features such as color histograms, texture descriptors, or even deep learning features. In bioinformatics, SVMs have proven to be useful in tasks such as protein classification and cancer classification, where the high-dimensional feature space is a common challenge.

SVMs offer an effective and versatile solution for both linear and non-linear classification tasks, making them a fundamental tool in the machine learning toolkit. Their robustness, along with their ability to handle high dimensional data, continue to make them a popular choice for solving complex real-world problems.

SVMs' robustness is rooted in their structural risk minimization principle, which seeks to balance the complexity of the model and its ability to fit the training data, therefore avoiding overfitting. This principle gives SVMs a higher generalization capability, meaning they can perform better on unseen data, compared to other models that rely on empirical risk minimization, such as Neural Networks.

The ability of SVMs to handle high-dimensional data is pivotal in domains where the number of features is significantly large. For instance, in text categorization tasks, the use of a 'bag of words' model often leads to thousands of features, one for each unique word in the text. SVMs can handle such high-dimensional feature spaces effectively, often outperforming other models in these scenarios.

Their effectiveness in high dimensions extends to small sample scenarios as well. This characteristic is particularly valuable in domains such as bioinformatics and medicine, where the number of samples (patients) is often smaller than the number of features (genes or medical tests).

However, while SVMs possess these desirable traits, it is also important to acknowledge their limitations. For instance, their performance can be sensitive to the choice of the kernel function and the associated parameters. SVMs also tend to be more computationally intensive compared to simpler models, especially with large datasets. Moreover, while they work well for binary classification problems, their extension to multi-class problems is not straightforward and often requires the application of methods like "one-vs-all" or "one-vs-one".

In conclusion, while SVMs have their advantages and disadvantages, their ability to effectively handle high dimensional data, perform in scenarios with smaller sample sizes, and their robustness to overfitting continue to make them a powerful tool in machine learning. It's important to understand these characteristics and apply them appropriately, considering the context and requirements of the specific problem at hand.

Example: Proof Concept

Support Vector Machines (SVMs) are a powerful machine learning algorithm used mainly for classification, and they work by finding a hyperplane that separates the classes in the feature space as best as possible.

To illustrate this mathematically, let's assume we have a binary classification problem with two classes, and we represent our data in a D-dimensional feature space. The goal of SVMs is to find a hyperplane defined by the equation:

$$w.x + b = 0$$

where w is a D-dimensional weight vector, x is the D-dimensional input vector, and b is the bias.

SVMs aim to maximize the margin, which is the distance between the closest data points (support vectors) and the separating hyperplane.

If we label our two classes as +1 and -1, we can express the decision rule for a new instance x as follows:

If w.x + b ≥ 1, then x belongs to class +1;

If w.x + b ≤ -1, then x belongs to class -1.

The margin M that SVMs aim to maximize is given by the formula:

$$M = 2 \,/\, ||w||$$

Therefore, the optimization problem for SVMs can be stated as:

minimize $(1/2) * ||w||^2$

subject to $y(i) * (w.x(i) + b) \geq 1$, for all i

This is a convex optimization problem known as a Quadratic Programming problem, and it can be solved using a variety of methods.

Please note that this explanation assumes linear separability of the classes. In case the classes are not linearly separable, SVMs use a technique known as the "kernel trick" to map the input vectors into a higher-dimensional space where they are separable. Different kernel functions can be used depending on the nature of the data, such as the Linear Kernel, Polynomial Kernel, Radial Basis Function (RBF) Kernel, etc.

While the math behind SVMs can get complex, especially when we consider non-linearly separable data and different kernel functions, the basic concept remains the same: SVMs work by finding the hyperplane that best separates the classes in the feature space.

Neural Networks:

Inspired by the human brain, Neural Networks consist of layers of interconnected neurons, or nodes, and are particularly good at processing complex, high-dimensional data. Deep Learning, a subfield of machine learning, involves neural networks with many layers ("deep" networks). Applications of neural networks and deep learning are vast and include image and speech recognition, natural language processing, and even playing video games.

The exploration of the human brain's complexities has always been a profound area of interest for scientists. This fascination transcends the biological domain and has found its way into the realm of artificial intelligence, inspiring the creation of neural networks. These computational models, crafted in the likeness of our brain's intricate architecture, have propelled the capabilities of machine learning, and by extension, deep learning, to unprecedented heights.

Composed of layers upon layers of interconnected neurons or nodes, neural networks reflect the human brain's organizational structure and operation. Each node within these networks takes in information, processes it through mathematical computations, and passes on the transformed data to the succeeding layer. These layers can be categorized into three types: input, hidden, and output. The input layer receives the raw data, the hidden layers perform computations, and the output layer presents the final result. Deep learning, a subset of machine learning, employs neural networks with multiple hidden layers, aptly named 'deep' networks.

One of the pivotal strengths of neural networks, especially deep ones, lies in their ability to process high-dimensional and complex data. High dimensionality refers to datasets with a multitude of attributes or features, a characteristic commonly found in image and speech data. It's this innate capability that has given rise to transformative applications across various domains.

In image recognition, convolutional neural networks (CNNs), a specialized kind of neural network, have demonstrated exceptional performance. They excel at identifying spatial hierarchies or patterns within images, powering applications like facial recognition systems and autonomous vehicles.

Speech recognition, another application, utilizes recurrent neural networks (RNNs). These networks have a unique architecture allowing them to handle sequential data, making them well-suited for understanding spoken language, music, and even stock price movements.

Natural language processing (NLP), an area dedicated to enabling machines to understand and generate human language, also heavily relies on deep learning models. For instance, transformer models, like OpenAI's GPT-3, use a type of neural network to understand context in text and generate human-like text.

Furthermore, neural networks have also found application in the gaming industry, where reinforcement learning techniques enable AI to improve its gameplay. Through repeated gameplay and learning from mistakes, the AI can formulate strategies that even surpass human performance, as demonstrated by Google DeepMind's AlphaGo.

The universality of neural networks and deep learning illustrates the breadth of their potential. They have become a fundamental pillar in the development of artificial intelligence, continuously pushing the boundaries of what machines can learn and accomplish. They serve as a testament to the untapped possibilities that await us in the pursuit of replicating the marvel that is the human brain.

Despite the already remarkable strides made, we have only scratched the surface of the potential neural networks and deep learning offer. These techniques have the capacity to revolutionize industries and services across the globe, disrupting traditional methods and redefining what we view as possible.

In healthcare, for instance, deep learning models are being developed to diagnose diseases with greater accuracy and at earlier stages than ever before. From detecting cancerous tumours in medical imagery to predicting the likelihood of heart disease based on a patient's medical history, these algorithms offer the promise of more effective and personalized treatments.

In the realm of autonomous vehicles, neural networks play a critical role in perceiving the vehicle's surroundings, predicting the behavior of other entities, and deciding the best course of action. They enable the vehicle to interpret sensor data, identify pedestrians, other vehicles, and traffic signals, and make split-second decisions, thereby making a significant contribution to road safety.

In business, neural networks facilitate the extraction of meaningful insights from vast amounts of data. Whether it's predicting consumer trends, optimizing logistics, or detecting fraudulent activities, deep learning can help businesses make data-driven decisions more accurately and efficiently.

In the environmental sphere, AI models are being used to monitor and predict climate patterns, assisting in the global efforts to mitigate climate change. By processing large volumes of data from satellites and sensors, these models can predict weather patterns, monitor changes in biodiversity, and help design more sustainable systems.

Beyond these practical applications, the journey to decode the functioning of the human brain using neural networks is leading to fascinating discoveries in the field of neuroscience. These findings could eventually lead to better treatments for neurological disorders and a deeper understanding of human consciousness.

As we continue in the pursuit of replicating the marvel that is the human brain, we must also remain cognizant of the ethical and societal implications of these advancements. Issues such as data privacy, algorithmic bias, and the impact of AI on employment need to be addressed alongside this technological progress. However, with a balanced and thoughtful approach, the untapped possibilities of neural networks and deep learning promise an exciting future.

Example: Simple layer neurl network

let's delve into the mathematics of a simple single layer neural network. The fundamental components include inputs, weights, a bias, an activation function, and an output.

Let's assume we have an input vector X = [x1, x2, x3,..., xn], corresponding weight vector W = [w1, w2, w3,..., wn], and a bias term b.

The neuron calculates the weighted sum of the inputs and adds the bias to this sum. This is often referred to as the pre-activation value, represented by z. Mathematically, this can be represented as:

$z = \Sigma(W * X) + b$

or

$$z = w_1x_1 + w_2x_2 + w_3x_3 + \ldots + w_nx_n + b$$

This pre-activation value z is then passed through an activation function 'f', which introduces non-linearity into the model, enabling it to learn from complex data. A common choice of activation function is the sigmoid function, which squashes the input values between 0 and 1:

$$f(z) = 1 / (1 + e^{-z})$$

Finally, the output y of the neuron is computed as:

$$y = f(z)$$

So, in essence, a single-layer neural network computes the output y as:

$$y = f(\Sigma(W * X) + b)$$

This basic mathematical operation forms the core of more complex, multilayer neural networks, which simply apply this process iteratively through multiple layers, enabling the network to learn more complex patterns from the data.

4.3 Unsupervised Learning Algorithms and Applications

Unlike supervised learning, unsupervised learning is a type of machine learning that looks for previously undetected patterns in a dataset with no pre-existing labels and with a minimum of human supervision. In essence, unsupervised learning is the AI's way of learning on its own. Here are some commonly used unsupervised learning algorithms and their applications:

Clustering Algorithms:

These are used to segment a broad dataset into clusters of instances that have similar features. Examples of clustering algorithms include K-Means, Hierarchical Clustering, and DBSCAN. These techniques are frequently used in market segmentation, social network analysis, and image segmentation.

Clustering algorithms form a quintessential part of unsupervised learning, serving as powerful tools to unearth latent groupings within a dataset that may not be immediately apparent or intuitive. With the ability to segment data based on intrinsic patterns, clustering techniques offer insightful revelations across a vast array of fields, from market segmentation to image analysis.

K-Means clustering stands as one of the most utilized and straightforward clustering techniques. It involves the partitioning of data into 'K' distinct clusters, whereby data points within a cluster are as similar as possible, and data points across different clusters are as dissimilar as possible. In practical terms, it might be used to categorize customers for a business based on purchasing habits or demographic data, thereby informing targeted marketing strategies. However, it is worth noting that K-means requires the number of clusters to be pre-specified, which can be a limitation if the data's natural structure is unknown.

Hierarchical clustering, on the other hand, offers an approach that doesn't necessitate pre-defining the number of clusters. It constructs a hierarchy of clusters, either through an agglomerative (bottom-up) approach or divisive (top-down) approach. The result is a dendrogram, a tree-like diagram illustrating the nested grouping of clusters and their progressive amalgamation or division. In fields like biology, hierarchical clustering plays an instrumental role in gene sequencing, resulting in phylogenetic trees representing evolutionary relationships among various biological species.

Density-Based Spatial Clustering of Applications with Noise (DBSCAN) represents another breed of clustering algorithms. It operates on the premise of high-density regions separated by regions of low density, clustering together data points in high-density areas. Unlike K-means, DBSCAN doesn't require specifying the number of clusters in advance and can discover clusters of arbitrary shapes, not just spherical ones. For instance, DBSCAN could be instrumental in geographical analysis, identifying areas of high activity or congestion in an urban environment using GPS data.

While clustering algorithms vary in methodology, their collective purpose remains the same – to illuminate the inherent structure within complex datasets. Whether segmenting a market into distinct customer groups or detecting patterns in vast social networks, the applications of these algorithms are extensive and profound. It is important to note, however, that the success of a clustering algorithm is heavily contingent on the nature of the data and the suitability of the chosen algorithm to that data. Consequently, a thorough understanding of the dataset and careful selection of the appropriate clustering technique are paramount to attaining meaningful results.

Example: Unsupervised Learning algorithms

Unsupervised learning algorithms operate without the benefit of labeled data and learn the inherent structure within the data. Let's delve into the mathematical core of the K-Means clustering algorithm, one of the most widely used unsupervised learning methods.

K-Means Clustering:

K-Means aims to partition a set of n observations into k clusters in which each observation belongs to the cluster with the nearest mean (cluster centers or cluster centroid), serving as a prototype of the cluster.

The algorithm works as follows:

Initialize k centroids randomly: C = {c1, c2,..., ck}, where c represents the centroid.

For each data point x_i, find the nearest centroid c_j that minimizes the Euclidean distance, and assign the data point to that cluster:

argmin $||x\_i - c\_j||^2$ for j=1 to k

Here, $||x\_i - c\_j||^2$ is the squared Euclidean distance.

For each cluster, compute new centroid by taking the mean of all the points assigned to that cluster:

$$c\_j = \Sigma(x\_in) / n \text{ for all } x \text{ in cluster } j$$

Repeat steps 2 and 3 until the centroids do not change significantly, or a maximum number of iterations is reached.

The objective of K-Means is to minimize the within-cluster variance, which is the squared Euclidean distance from each data point to its closest centroid, summed over all data points. This is known as the inertia or the within-cluster sum of squares (WCSS).

$$\text{Inertia: } W(C) = \Sigma \ ||x\_i - c\_j||^2 \text{ for all } x \text{ in cluster } j$$

The selection of the initial cluster centroids can greatly affect the final solution; therefore, multiple runs of the algorithm with different random initializations can help obtain a better clustering result.

It's important to note that K-Means assumes that clusters are convex and isotropic, which is not always the case in real-world data. It responds poorly to elongated clusters, or manifolds with irregular shapes. In such scenarios, other clustering algorithms like DBSCAN or hierarchical clustering might be more appropriate.

Dimensionality Reduction Algorithms: These algorithms aim to reduce the number of features in a dataset without losing important information. Principal Component Analysis (PCA) and t-Distributed Stochastic Neighbor Embedding (t-SNE) are two notable dimensionality reduction techniques. They are useful in visualizing high-dimensional data and in pre-processing before implementing a machine learning algorithm.

Dimensionality reduction is a fundamental component of any data analysis pipeline that involves handling high-dimensional data. In a world increasingly saturated with data, the necessity of reducing the complexity of data is paramount.

Principal Component Analysis (PCA) is a well-known technique used for this purpose. Its fundamental operation is to transform the original variables into a new set of variables, the principal components, which are uncorrelated and account for decreasing proportions of the total variance in the dataset. The principal components serve as the foundation of the new space. The first principal component accounts for the largest possible variance, with each succeeding component accounting for the highest possible remaining variance, under the constraint that it must be orthogonal to the preceding components. This makes PCA a very efficient tool for dimensionality reduction, data compression, and interpretation of complex datasets.

Consider a simple example: you might be dealing with a dataset from a car sale and have features like the car's width and length. These two features are likely to be highly correlated because larger cars are usually both longer and wider. PCA would combine these features into a new variable (a principal component), enabling a more efficient representation of the data.

On the other hand, t-Distributed Stochastic Neighbor Embedding (t-SNE) is a non-linear dimensionality reduction algorithm particularly well-suited for the visualization of high-dimensional datasets. Unlike PCA, it keeps similar instances close and dissimilar instances apart. It creates a probability distribution, such that similar objects have a higher probability of being picked, while dissimilar points have a lower probability. The same is done for the lower-dimensional representation, and the algorithm minimizes the divergence between the two distributions with respect to the locations of the points in the map. t-SNE is particularly sensitive to local structure and can often reveal clusters in the data.

Take for example a dataset of hand-written digits (MNIST). With 784 features (28x28 pixel images), it's challenging to visualize. By applying t-SNE, we can reduce these 784 features to just two, plotting the resulting two-dimensional points and coloring by digit, revealing distinct clusters for each digit.

While both PCA and t-SNE are powerful tools in the data analyst's toolkit, it's important to remember their limitations. PCA is a linear algorithm and can fail to capture complex structures in the data, whereas t-SNE is a stochastic algorithm, and different runs can yield different results. Nonetheless, with careful application, these techniques can unlock the hidden patterns in your high-dimensional data, paving the way for more effective machine learning models.

Example: Principal Component Analysis

Principal Component Analysis (PCA) works on the mathematical technique of linear algebra, specifically, eigenvalues and eigenvectors.

Let's consider a dataset with n features. PCA aims to transform these n features into n principal components (PCs). Let's denote the data matrix as X, which has n columns (features) and m rows (data points).

The first step is to standardize the dataset if the scales of the features are not the same. Each feature is transformed to have a mean (μ) of 0 and standard deviation (σ) of 1. The standardized value z is calculated as $z = (x - \mu) / \sigma$, where x is the original value of the feature.

The next step is to compute the covariance matrix C of the standardized data. The covariance matrix expresses the correlation between the different features in the dataset.

We then calculate the eigenvalues and eigenvectors of the covariance matrix C. These eigenvalues and eigenvectors represent the "core" of the PCA: the eigenvectors (principal components) determine the directions of the new feature space, and the eigenvalues determine their magnitude (i.e., the variances of the data along the new feature axes).

The next step is to sort the eigenvalues in decreasing order and choose the first k eigenvectors that correspond to the largest k eigenvalues, where k is the number of dimensions of the new feature subspace ($k \leq n$).

Finally, we transform the original dataset via these principal components to obtain the new feature subspace.

The entire process of PCA involves linear transformations on matrices, which are fundamental operations in linear algebra. By transforming the data to a new subspace, PCA helps to maintain as much of the data's variance as possible while reducing the dimensionality, which is mathematically represented through the eigenvalues and eigenvectors of the covariance matrix.

Association Rule Learning Algorithms:

Algorithms like Apriori and Eclat are used to extract common patterns or associations among a set of items. This is frequently used in Market Basket Analysis where retailers are interested in understanding the purchase behavior of customers.

Association rule learning algorithms play a crucial role in uncovering hidden patterns and associations among items in a dataset. Two popular algorithms in this domain are Apriori and Eclat. These algorithms have found wide application in various industries, with Market Basket Analysis being a prime example.

Market Basket Analysis is a technique used by retailers to analyze customer purchasing behavior and identify relationships between products. By leveraging association rule learning algorithms, retailers can extract valuable insights from transaction data and uncover patterns in customer buying habits. This knowledge can be utilized to optimize various aspects of retail operations.

Let's delve deeper into the concept of Market Basket Analysis and how association rule learning algorithms contribute to its success. Imagine you are a retailer who wants to understand how certain products are related to each other in terms of customer preferences. By analyzing transactional data, you can apply association rule learning algorithms to identify frequently occurring item sets or combinations.

For instance, let's consider a grocery store where customers often purchase items like bread, milk, and eggs together. Using the Apriori algorithm, the retailer can discover the association rule "if a customer buys bread and milk, they are likely to buy eggs." This insight enables the retailer to strategically place these items closer to each other in the store, enhancing convenience for customers and potentially boosting sales.

Association rule learning algorithms provide a quantitative measure to assess the strength of these associations. The metrics commonly used are support, confidence, and lift. Support measures the frequency of a particular item or item set in the dataset. Confidence measures the conditional probability that a customer will buy a specific item given that they have already purchased another item. Lift quantifies the extent to which the purchase of one item influences the purchase of another item.

Let's consider an example to illustrate these concepts further. Suppose an association rule learning algorithm reveals that 60% of customers who purchase coffee also buy sugar, and 40% of customers who buy tea also buy sugar. The support for the combination of coffee and sugar is 30% (assuming these items are frequently purchased together). The confidence is calculated as 60% divided by 40%, resulting in a value of 1.5. This indicates that customers who buy coffee are 1.5 times more likely to buy sugar compared to the general population. The lift value, calculated as the confidence divided by the support, is 1.5 divided by 0.3, resulting in 5. This suggests that the purchase of coffee and sugar is five times more likely to occur together than if they were independent of each other.

These association rules provide valuable insights that retailers can leverage to enhance their business strategies. For example, retailers can utilize the knowledge gained from association rule learning algorithms to generate personalized recommendations for customers. If a customer buys coffee, the system can recommend purchasing sugar based on the observed association. This personalized approach can improve customer satisfaction and increase sales.

Retailers can design targeted promotional strategies based on association rule analysis. For instance, if the algorithm uncovers a strong association between diapers and baby wipes, a retailer can offer discounts or bundled deals on these items to encourage customers to make complementary purchases.

Association rule learning algorithms, such as Apriori and Eclat, have revolutionized the way retailers analyze customer purchasing behavior through Market Basket Analysis. These algorithms enable retailers to uncover patterns and associations among items, facilitating effective product placement, personalized recommendations, and promotional strategies. By leveraging the power of association rule learning, retailers can optimize their operations, enhance customer satisfaction, and drive business growth.

Example: Association rule learning

To demonstrate the concept of association rule learning algorithms mathematically, we can utilize the support, confidence, and lift measures commonly used in association rule analysis. Let's consider a simplified example with a transaction dataset consisting of three items: A, B, and C.

Suppose we have the following information:

Total number of transactions (T): 1000

Number of transactions containing item A (support for A): 400

Number of transactions containing item B (support for B): 600

Number of transactions containing both items A and B (support for A and B): 300

Using these values, we can calculate the support, confidence, and lift for the association rule "A -> B" (if a customer buys A, they are likely to buy B).

Support (S):

Support measures the frequency of a particular item or item set in the dataset. In this case, we want to calculate the support for the combination of items A and B.

Support(A and B) = Number of transactions containing A and B / Total number of transactions

= 300 / 1000

= 0.3

Confidence (C):

Confidence measures the conditional probability that a customer will buy item B given that they have already purchased item A. In this case, we want to calculate the confidence for the rule "A -> B."

Confidence(A -> B) = Support(A and B) / Support(A)

= 300 / 400

= 0.75

This means that out of all the transactions containing item A, 75% of them also contain item B.

Lift (L):

Lift quantifies the extent to which the purchase of one item influences the purchase of another item. It compares the observed support of the item combination with the expected support if the items were independent of each other.

$Lift(A \rightarrow B) = Confidence(A \rightarrow B) / Support(B)$

$= 0.75 / (600 / 1000)$

$= 1.25$

A lift value greater than 1 indicates a positive association between items A and B. In this case, the lift value is 1.25, suggesting that the purchase of item A increases the likelihood of purchasing item B by 25% compared to the general population.

These mathematical calculations provide a quantitative understanding of the association rule "A -> B" and its strength. The support value represents the frequency of occurrence, the confidence value indicates the conditional probability, and the lift value signifies the strength of the association.

By analyzing transaction data and applying association rule learning algorithms, retailers can perform these calculations on a larger scale, uncovering valuable associations between items and making informed business decisions to optimize their operations and enhance customer satisfaction.

Anomaly Detection Algorithms:

Anomaly detection algorithms are designed to identify unusual data points or outliers within a dataset. These algorithms play a pivotal role in various domains, including fraud detection, network intrusion detection, and system health monitoring. By flagging anomalies, organizations can swiftly respond to potential threats or irregularities, minimizing risks and ensuring the integrity of their operations.

Anomaly detection algorithms, also known as outlier detection algorithms, are sophisticated tools that analyze data to identify unusual patterns or outliers that deviate significantly from the expected behavior. These algorithms employ complex techniques and statistical models to distinguish between normal and abnormal data points within a dataset. The insights gained from anomaly detection algorithms have widespread applications in various domains, where prompt detection of anomalies is critical to maintaining security and operational integrity.

Let's explore some examples of how anomaly detection algorithms are employed in real-world scenarios:

Fraud Detection:

In today's digital landscape, where financial transactions are conducted online, fraud detection has become a paramount concern for financial institutions, credit card companies, and e-commerce platforms. The reliance on anomaly detection algorithms in fraud detection is a testament to their effectiveness in identifying fraudulent activities and safeguarding the interests of customers.

Anomaly detection algorithms offer a powerful toolset for detecting unusual transactions that deviate from typical patterns within a vast amount of transactional data. By leveraging advanced statistical techniques and machine learning models, these algorithms can identify patterns and anomalies that human analysts may overlook. The analysis encompasses a range of factors, including transaction amounts, frequency, location, time of day, user behavior, and historical data.

Consider a credit card company that processes millions of transactions daily. An anomaly detection algorithm can sift through this enormous volume of data and flag transactions that exhibit suspicious characteristics. For instance, if a customer suddenly makes a large purchase outside their usual spending habits or conducts multiple transactions within a short timeframe, the algorithm can identify these anomalies. Similarly, if a transaction originates from an unusual location or occurs during an atypical time, it can be flagged for further investigation.

Unauthorized access attempts and identity theft are also prevalent threats in the digital realm. Anomaly detection algorithms can help identify these types of fraud by analyzing login activities, user behavior patterns, and historical data. For example, if a user's login activity suddenly shows multiple failed login attempts or originates from a geographically distant location, the algorithm can alert the system administrators or security teams to potential unauthorized access attempts.

Another essential aspect of fraud detection is the ability to recognize patterns that indicate identity theft. Anomaly detection algorithms can identify instances where multiple user accounts share similar patterns of behavior or transactional history, suggesting the possibility of fraudulent activity. This proactive approach enables financial institutions and e-commerce platforms to take appropriate measures, such as requesting additional verification or temporarily suspending suspicious accounts, to prevent further fraudulent transactions.

The role of anomaly detection algorithms in fraud detection cannot be overstated. By swiftly identifying and flagging unusual transactions, these algorithms enable financial institutions and businesses to take immediate action, minimizing financial losses and protecting the interests of their customers. The algorithms serve as a crucial line of defense in maintaining the trust and confidence of customers, reinforcing the integrity of the financial system, and combating the ever-evolving landscape of fraud.

It is important to note that while anomaly detection algorithms are powerful tools, they are not foolproof. Continuous refinement, monitoring, and adaptation are necessary to address emerging fraud patterns and to minimize false positives and false negatives. A collaborative approach that combines advanced algorithms with human expertise is essential for staying one step ahead of fraudsters and ensuring the effectiveness of fraud detection measures.

Network Intrusion Detection:

In the modern digital landscape, network security is of utmost importance to organizations across various sectors. Network intrusion detection plays a critical role in safeguarding sensitive information and protecting against cyber threats. Anomaly detection algorithms have emerged as a powerful tool in this domain, enabling the detection of abnormal network activities that may indicate malicious attacks or unauthorized access attempts.

Network intrusion detection involves monitoring network traffic, system logs, and user behaviors to identify deviations from normal patterns Anomaly detection algorithms analyze vast amounts of data, leveraging machine learning and statistical techniques to identify patterns and anomalies that may signal potential security breaches.

Consider a scenario where an organization's network experiences a sudden spike in data transfer, which could be indicative of a Distributed Denial of Service (DDoS) attack. An anomaly detection algorithm can detect this unusual traffic pattern and trigger an alert, allowing the organization's security team to investigate and respond promptly. Similarly, if a user's network behavior suddenly deviates from their usual patterns, such as attempting to access restricted resources or executing unauthorized commands, the algorithm can flag these anomalies for further scrutiny.

Anomaly detection algorithms are designed to adapt and learn from historical data, enabling them to recognize new and evolving threats. By continuously monitoring network traffic and user behavior, these algorithms can identify previously unseen attack patterns or detect subtle deviations that may indicate sophisticated attacks. This proactive approach to network security enables organizations to stay ahead of potential threats and mitigate risks before they escalate into full-scale security breaches.

The use of anomaly detection algorithms in network intrusion detection is not limited to identifying external threats. They are also effective in detecting insider threats, where employees or authorized users may engage in malicious activities. Unusual access patterns, abnormal data transfers or unauthorized system modifications can be detected by these algorithms, helping organizations prevent data breaches and internal security breaches.

Anomaly detection algorithms contribute significantly to enhancing the overall security posture of organizations. By providing early detection of cyber threats and network intrusions, they enable security teams to respond swiftly and effectively, mitigating potential risks and minimizing the impact of security incidents. These algorithms act as a crucial line of defense, complementing traditional security measures such as firewalls and antivirus software.

It is important to note that while anomaly detection algorithms are valuable tools in network intrusion detection, they are not infallible. Adversaries constantly evolve their techniques, and sophisticated attacks may be designed to evade detection. Therefore, a comprehensive approach to network security should include a combination of anomaly detection algorithms, threat intelligence, human expertise, and other security measures to ensure robust protection against a wide range of cyber threats.

System Health Monitoring:

In various industries, the smooth operation and reliability of complex systems are paramount. System health monitoring is a critical practice that ensures the continuous functionality of industrial equipment, machinery, and critical infrastructure. Anomaly detection algorithms play a pivotal role in this domain, enabling organizations to monitor and detect deviations from normal operating conditions, facilitating proactive maintenance and preventing costly downtime or catastrophic failures.

Consider the example of a power plant that relies on multiple interconnected components and systems to generate electricity. An anomaly detection algorithm continuously analyzes sensor data, such as temperature, pressure, and voltage readings, to establish normal patterns and operating ranges. If the algorithm detects significant deviations from these established patterns, it can alert operators or maintenance personnel to potential issues.

For instance, if an anomaly detection algorithm identifies an abnormal increase in temperature in a specific component of the power plant, it may indicate a potential equipment malfunction or impending failure. By promptly detecting this anomaly, maintenance teams can investigate the issue, take corrective measures, and prevent a complete system breakdown or costly repairs.

Similarly, anomalies in voltage fluctuations or unexpected changes in power consumption can be indicative of grid instability or potential faults in the electrical distribution system. Anomaly detection algorithms can identify these deviations and provide early warnings, allowing operators to address the issue before it escalates and affects the reliability and safety of the entire system.

In the context of manufacturing, anomaly detection algorithms play a crucial role in ensuring the health and efficiency of production lines. By monitoring sensor data from machinery and equipment, these algorithms can identify unusual patterns or behaviors that may indicate impending failures or malfunctions. For example, abnormal vibrations in a rotating machine or deviations in process parameters can signal potential breakdowns or quality issues. Timely detection of such anomalies enables maintenance teams to intervene proactively, preventing production disruptions and reducing downtime.

The use of anomaly detection algorithms in system health monitoring extends beyond industrial settings. It is also applicable to critical infrastructure, such as transportation systems, telecommunications networks, and healthcare facilities. By analyzing data from sensors, equipment, and operational parameters, these algorithms can identify anomalies that may compromise the reliability, safety, or performance of the infrastructure. For example, in a transportation network, anomalies in traffic patterns or abnormal vehicle behavior can indicate accidents, congestion, or infrastructure failures.

By leveraging anomaly detection algorithms, organizations can shift from reactive maintenance practices to proactive strategies. Early detection of anomalies allows for timely interventions, preventive maintenance, and optimized resource allocation. This not only reduces costs associated with equipment failures, repairs, and downtime but also enhances the overall reliability and performance of systems and infrastructure.

It is important to note that anomaly detection algorithms should be tailored to specific system characteristics, considering factors such as the complexity of the system, the type of data being monitored, and the desired level of sensitivity. Continuous monitoring, accurate data collection, and real-time analysis are crucial for effective anomaly detection and system health monitoring.

These examples illustrate the significant impact of anomaly detection algorithms in safeguarding organizations from potential risks and ensuring the smooth functioning of critical processes. The algorithms employ various techniques, including statistical analysis, machine learning, and pattern recognition, to identify anomalies in datasets.

It's important to note that anomaly detection algorithms require careful calibration and tuning to achieve accurate results. The algorithms must strike a balance between minimizing false positives (flagging normal data as anomalies) and false negatives (missing actual anomalies). Domain expertise and extensive data analysis are essential to fine-tune these algorithms for specific applications.

Anomaly detection algorithms provide invaluable insights into unusual data points or outliers within a dataset. Their applications span across diverse industries, including finance, cybersecurity, and industrial systems. By promptly detecting anomalies, organizations can take proactive measures to mitigate risks, enhance security, and ensure the smooth operation of their systems. The continuous advancement of anomaly detection techniques further strengthens the ability to identify emerging anomalies, making these algorithms indispensable tools in the modern data-driven world.

Neural Networks and Deep Learning Models:

Unsupervised learning extends to neural networks and deep learning models. Autoencoders and Generative Adversarial Networks (GANs) are prominent examples of unsupervised neural network models. Autoencoders learn to reconstruct input data, which enables them to represent intricate patterns and perform tasks such as data denoising and dimensionality reduction. GANs, on the other hand, excel in generating new data instances that resemble the training data distribution, making them valuable in generating synthetic data for training purposes or creating realistic images.

Neural networks and deep learning models have revolutionized the field of artificial intelligence and have made significant advancements in various domains. Within this realm, unsupervised learning plays a crucial role, enabling neural networks to learn and extract valuable insights from data without explicit labels or guidance. Two notable examples of unsupervised neural network models are autoencoders and Generative Adversarial Networks (GANs).

Autoencoders are neural network architectures that are primarily used for data compression and feature extraction. They consist of an encoder network that learns to map input data to a lower-dimensional representation, and a decoder network that reconstructs the original data from the compressed representation. The key idea behind autoencoders is to learn a compressed representation that captures the essential features of the input data, thereby enabling effective data reconstruction.

One application of autoencoders is data denoising. By training an autoencoder on noisy data and forcing it to reconstruct the clean, noise-free data, the model learns to extract meaningful features and eliminate the noise. For example, in medical imaging, autoencoders can be used to remove noise from scans, enhancing the clarity and accuracy of the images for diagnosis and analysis.

Another application of autoencoders is dimensionality reduction. In high-dimensional datasets, autoencoders can learn a lower-dimensional representation that retains the most important features of the data. This reduced representation can be used for visualization, exploration, or as input to other machine learning algorithms. For instance, in genetics, autoencoders can be applied to gene expression data to identify the most relevant genes for a particular phenotype, effectively reducing the dimensionality and focusing on the key factors driving the observed variations.

Generative Adversarial Networks (GANs) are a class of neural networks that excel in generating new data instances that resemble the training data distribution. GANs consist of a generator network that produces synthetic data samples and a discriminator network that tries to distinguish between the synthetic and real data. The two networks are trained together in a competitive manner, with the generator striving to produce more realistic samples and the discriminator aiming to become better at distinguishing between real and synthetic data.

GANs have made remarkable contributions to image generation and synthesis. By training on a large dataset of images, GANs can generate new images that possess similar characteristics to the training data. This has been particularly impactful in fields such as computer vision and computer graphics. For example, GANs have been used to generate realistic images of human faces, animals, and even entire scenes. This has applications in entertainment, gaming, and virtual reality, where high-quality synthetic imagery is required.

Moreover, GANs have also been leveraged for data augmentation and synthetic data generation in machine learning tasks. By generating additional synthetic samples, GANs can augment the training data, effectively increasing its size and diversity. This helps in improving the generalization and performance of machine learning models, especially when training data is limited or imbalanced.

Both autoencoders and GANs are powerful tools in the arsenal of unsupervised learning and neural network models. Their ability to learn complex patterns, reconstruct data, denoise signals, reduce dimensionality, and generate synthetic data opens up a wide range of possibilities in various domains. As advancements in neural networks and deep learning continue, these unsupervised models are likely to play an increasingly significant role in understanding and extracting valuable insights from data.

Neural networks and deep learning models have embraced unsupervised learning techniques, giving rise to powerful tools such as autoencoders and GANs. Autoencoders enable data reconstruction, denoising, and dimensionality reduction, while GANs excel in generating synthetic data instances that resemble the training data distribution. These models have applications in various fields, including medical imaging, genetics, computer vision, computer graphics, and data augmentation. By leveraging the capabilities of unsupervised neural network models, researchers and practitioners can unlock new possibilities in data analysis, synthesis, and exploration.

4.4 Reinforcement Learning Algorithms and Applications

Reinforcement learning is a branch of machine learning that focuses on learning optimal behaviors through interactions with an environment. It involves an agent, an environment, actions, states, and rewards.

It is a powerful branch of machine learning, offers a unique approach to learning optimal behaviors through interactions with an environment. By combining the elements of an agent, an environment, actions, states, and rewards, reinforcement learning algorithms can tackle complex problems and achieve remarkable outcomes. In this essay, we will delve into the intricacies of reinforcement learning, exploring its fundamental concepts, applications, and the key role it plays in shaping intelligent systems.

At the heart of reinforcement learning lies the concept of an agent—a learning entity that interacts with its surrounding environment. This environment represents the context in which the agent operates, providing a set of possible states that it can perceive. The agent's objective is to learn the best sequence of actions to maximize cumulative rewards, which are the signals of success or failure received from the environment.

To model the decision-making process in reinforcement learning, Markov Decision Processes (MDPs) serve as a valuable mathematical framework. MDPs define the rules of the game, including the states, actions, transition probabilities, and rewards. By formulating the problem as an MDP, the agent can reason about the consequences of its actions, enabling it to make informed decisions.

One popular algorithm used in reinforcement learning is Q-learning. Q-learning aims to learn the optimal action-value function, known as the Q-function. The Q-function estimates the expected cumulative reward for taking a specific action in a given state. Through an iterative process of exploration and exploitation, Q-learning updates the Q-values based on observed rewards, enabling the agent to converge towards an optimal policy—a strategy that maximizes long-term rewards.

Policy gradient methods offer another approach to reinforcement learning. Unlike Q-learning, which focuses on estimating the value of actions, policy gradient methods directly optimize the policy function—the probability distribution over actions. By applying gradient ascent, these methods update the policy parameters, increasing the likelihood of actions that lead to higher rewards. This flexibility makes policy gradient methods well-suited for handling complex, high-dimensional action spaces.

Balancing exploration and exploitation is a key challenge in reinforcement learning. Exploration allows the agent to discover new and potentially better actions, while exploitation leverages existing knowledge to maximize rewards. Striking the right balance between these two competing forces is crucial for effective learning. Various exploration strategies, such as epsilon-greedy or Thompson sampling, are employed to navigate this trade-off.

One of the fundamental challenges in reinforcement learning is the credit assignment problem. As the agent interacts with the environment over time, it must properly attribute rewards or penalties to specific actions or states. This problem becomes particularly complex when rewards are delayed or sparse, requiring algorithms to assign credit accurately, even across long sequences of actions.

Sample efficiency is another important consideration in reinforcement learning. Learning from limited amounts of data is essential, as real-world interactions can be time-consuming and costly. Improving sample efficiency is an active area of research, aiming to develop algorithms that can learn effectively with fewer interactions, thereby accelerating the learning process.

Reinforcement learning finds applications in various domains, demonstrating its versatility and impact. In the gaming world, reinforcement learning algorithms have achieved groundbreaking success, such as AlphaGo's mastery of the complex game of Go. Robotics is another area where reinforcement learning plays a vital role, enabling robots to learn complex tasks and adapt to dynamic environments. In healthcare, personalized treatment policies based on reinforcement learning algorithms can optimize patient outcomes and resource allocation.

Reinforcement learning represents a paradigm shift in machine learning, empowering agents to learn optimal behaviors through interactions with their environment. By combining elements such as agents, environments, actions, states, and rewards, reinforcement learning algorithms can tackle complex problems and achieve remarkable results. With applications spanning gaming, robotics, healthcare, and more, reinforcement learning continues to shape the landscape of intelligent systems, paving the way for innovative solutions to real-world challenges.

Example: Reinforcement learning

Let's consider an example of how reinforcement learning can be applied in the field of robotics.

Imagine a robotic arm tasked with picking up objects of varying shapes and sizes from a conveyor belt and placing them into designated containers. The goal is to develop an optimal policy for the robotic arm to perform this task efficiently.

Using reinforcement learning, the robotic arm can learn from trial and error interactions with the environment. The agent, in this case, is the robotic arm, while the environment consists of the conveyor belt, objects, containers, and sensors providing feedback.

The agent begins with no prior knowledge and takes random actions, such as randomly selecting an object or container. It then receives a reward signal based on its performance. For instance, successfully placing an object in the correct container yields a positive reward, while dropping or placing it in the wrong container results in a negative reward.

Through the process of exploration and exploitation, the robotic arm gradually learns which actions lead to higher rewards. It updates its policy based on the received rewards and observations of the state-action pairs. Over time, the robotic arm learns to make more accurate predictions about the best actions to take in different scenarios.

As the training progresses, the robotic arm becomes more proficient in identifying objects, estimating their shapes and sizes, and selecting the appropriate containers. It learns to optimize its movements, achieving greater efficiency in picking and placing objects.

Through reinforcement learning, the robotic arm evolves from a novice performer to a skillful and efficient worker. It adapts to different object configurations, learns to handle novel objects, and continually improves its performance based on the rewards received from the environment.

This example showcases the power of reinforcement learning in enabling robots to acquire intelligent behaviors through interactions with their surroundings. By learning from experience and maximizing rewards, the robotic arm becomes a reliable and adaptable worker, capable of efficiently completing complex tasks in real-world environments.

This application of reinforcement learning in robotics illustrates its potential for automating intricate tasks, enhancing productivity, and enabling robots to operate autonomously in dynamic and uncertain environments.

Markov Decision Processes (MDPs):

MDPs provide a mathematical framework for modeling decision-making problems in reinforcement learning. They consist of states, actions, transition probabilities, and rewards. MDPs allow agents to reason about the consequences of their actions and make optimal decisions.

Markov Decision Processes (MDPs) form a fundamental framework in reinforcement learning, enabling agents to make intelligent decisions in dynamic environments. MDPs provide a mathematical representation of decision-making problems, encompassing states, actions, transition probabilities, and rewards. This essay explores the key concepts and applications of MDPs in reinforcement learning.

At the core of an MDP is the notion of states, which represent different configurations or situations in an environment. For example, in a game, states could correspond to specific board positions or game states. Actions, on the other hand, represent the choices available to an agent in a given state. For instance, in chess, actions would involve selecting moves from a particular board position.

Transition probabilities describe the likelihood of transitioning from one state to another when taking a specific action. These probabilities capture the dynamics of the environment and govern the state transitions. For example, in a game, the transition probabilities indicate the probability of moving from one game state to another based on the chosen action.

Rewards play a crucial role in MDPs as they provide a measure of desirability or utility associated with specific states and actions. They guide the agent towards making decisions that maximize cumulative rewards over time. In games, rewards can be assigned based on winning or losing, achieving specific objectives, or intermediate milestones.

The goal in an MDP is to find an optimal policy that maximizes the expected cumulative rewards. A policy is a mapping that specifies the action to be taken in each state. The optimal policy guides the agent to make decisions that lead to the highest expected rewards over the long run.

To determine the optimal policy, reinforcement learning algorithms, such as value iteration or policy iteration, can be applied. These algorithms utilize the information provided by the MDP to iteratively update value functions or policy estimates, converging to the optimal solution.

MDPs find extensive applications across various domains. For instance, in autonomous robotics, MDPs can be employed to model decision-making processes for navigation, path planning, and object manipulation. By considering the consequences of different actions in different states, a robot can determine the most effective strategies to accomplish its tasks.

Additionally, MDPs have been successfully applied in inventory management, resource allocation, energy management, and many other real-world scenarios that involve sequential decision-making. These applications highlight the versatility and wide-ranging impact of MDPs in optimizing decision processes.

Markov Decision Processes (MDPs) offer a powerful mathematical framework for modeling decision-making problems in reinforcement learning. By incorporating states, actions, transition probabilities, and rewards, MDPs enable agents to reason about the consequences of their actions and make optimal decisions. Through MDPs, agents can navigate complex environments, learn from experience, and achieve long-term goals. The applications of MDPs span diverse domains, contributing to advancements in robotics, resource management, and beyond. By harnessing the principles of MDPs, researchers and practitioners continue to advance the field of reinforcement learning and pave the way for intelligent decision-making systems.

Q-learning:

Q-learning is a popular algorithm in reinforcement learning. It aims to learn the optimal action-value function, called the Q-function, which estimates the expected cumulative reward for taking a specific action in a given state. Q-learning iteratively updates the Q-function based on observed rewards to converge towards an optimal policy.

Q-learning stands as one of the most influential algorithms in the field of reinforcement learning. Its goal is to learn the optimal action-value function, known as the Q-function, which estimates the expected cumulative reward an agent can achieve by taking a specific action in a given state. This essay explores the key concepts, workings, and applications of Q-learning in reinforcement learning.

At the heart of Q-learning lies the concept of the Q-function. The Q-function maps state-action pairs to their corresponding expected cumulative rewards. It captures the value of taking a particular action in a specific state and guides the agent towards making decisions that maximize long-term rewards. By learning the Q-function, an agent can determine the best action to take in any given state to optimize its overall performance.

Q-learning employs an iterative update process to refine the Q-function over time. Initially, the Q-function is initialized arbitrarily, and the agent interacts with the environment, taking actions based on the current estimate of the Q-function. As the agent explores the environment, it receives rewards, and these rewards are used to update the Q-function using a specific update rule.

The update rule in Q-learning is based on the Bellman equation, which expresses the relationship between the value of a state-action pair and the values of the subsequent state-action pairs. The Q-function is updated by taking into account the observed reward, the current estimate of the Q-function, and the maximum expected future rewards. Through this iterative process, the Q-function gradually converges to its optimal values, providing the agent with the best action choices in each state.

One of the strengths of Q-learning is its ability to handle environments with unknown dynamics. Unlike other algorithms that require explicit knowledge of the environment's transition probabilities, Q-learning learns solely from interactions with the environment. This makes it well-suited for scenarios where the dynamics of the environment are complex or difficult to model accurately.

Q-learning has found success in a variety of applications. One prominent example is its use in training autonomous agents for playing games. By treating the game state as the environment, actions as game moves, and rewards as game scores, Q-learning can learn optimal strategies for game playing. A classic demonstration of this is the use of Q-learning to train agents that can achieve superhuman performance in games like chess, Go, and Atari video games.

Another application of Q-learning is in robotics, where it can be employed to develop intelligent systems capable of learning and adapting to different tasks. For instance, Q-learning can be used to train robots to navigate through complex environments, manipulate objects, or perform various tasks autonomously. By learning the optimal action choices in different states, robots can achieve efficient and effective decision-making.

Q-learning stands as a powerful algorithm in reinforcement learning. Through the iterative update process, it learns the optimal action-value function, the Q-function, which guides agents to make decisions that maximize long-term rewards. Q-learning's ability to handle unknown environments and its success in various applications, such as game playing and robotics, demonstrate its versatility and effectiveness. As researchers continue to refine and extend Q-learning, it holds the promise of advancing the field of reinforcement learning and enabling intelligent decision-making in diverse domains.

Example: Q-learning

To provide a mathematical demonstration of the concept of Q-learning, let's consider a simplified example. Suppose we have an agent navigating a grid-world environment with four possible actions: up, down, left, and right. The agent's goal is to reach a specific target location while maximizing its cumulative reward.

We can represent the grid-world environment as a 2D grid, where each cell corresponds to a state. The agent starts from an initial state and takes actions to move from one state to another. The transition from one state to another is determined by the chosen action.

To learn the optimal policy, the agent maintains a Q-table, which is a lookup table storing the estimated expected cumulative rewards for each state-action pair. Initially, the Q-table is initialized with arbitrary values.

Let's denote the Q-value of a state-action pair (s, a) as Q(s, a), where s represents the current state, and a represents the chosen action. The goal of Q-learning is to update the Q-values iteratively based on observed rewards to converge towards the optimal Q-values.

The Q-learning update rule is as follows:

$$Q(s, a) = Q(s, a) + \alpha * (r + \gamma * \max[Q(s', a')] - Q(s, a))$$

In this equation, α is the learning rate, r is the observed reward after taking action a in state s, γ is the discount factor ($0 <= \gamma <= 1$) that determines the importance of future rewards, s' represents the next state, and a' represents the action with the highest Q-value in the next state.

The update rule can be explained as follows: The new Q-value for the state-action pair (s, a) is obtained by adding a fraction (α) of the difference between the observed reward (r) and the sum of the discounted maximum Q-value of the next state ($\gamma * \max[Q(s', a')]$) and the current Q-value (Q(s, a)).

By applying the Q-learning update rule iteratively as the agent interacts with the environment, the Q-values gradually converge towards their optimal values, reflecting the expected cumulative rewards for each state-action pair.

Once the Q-values have converged, the agent can determine the optimal policy by selecting the action with the highest Q-value in each state. This policy guides the agent to make decisions that maximize the cumulative rewards and achieve the goal of reaching the target location.

While this example provides a simplified demonstration of Q-learning, the concept can be applied to more complex environments with larger state and action spaces. The mathematical foundations of Q-learning and the update rule remain the same, allowing agents to learn optimal behaviors through interactions with the environment.

By leveraging the power of mathematics and iterative updates based on observed rewards, Q-learning enables agents to learn and make decisions in a wide range of reinforcement learning problems.

Policy Gradient Methods:

Policy gradient methods directly optimize the policy function in reinforcement learning. These methods use gradient ascent to update the policy parameters, increasing the likelihood of actions that lead to higher rewards. Policy gradient methods offer a flexible framework for tackling complex, high-dimensional action spaces.

Policy gradient methods represent a powerful approach in reinforcement learning that directly optimize the policy function to maximize cumulative rewards. Unlike value-based methods, which estimate the optimal value function, policy gradient methods focus on improving the policy itself. This essay explores the concept of policy gradient methods, their advantages, and provides examples of their applications in reinforcement learning.

At the core of policy gradient methods is the policy function, which maps states to probability distributions over actions. The goal is to find the policy that maximizes the expected cumulative reward over time. This involves iteratively updating the policy parameters to increase the likelihood of actions that lead to higher rewards.

One popular policy gradient method is the REINFORCE algorithm. It uses a technique called Monte Carlo policy gradient, which estimates the gradient of the expected cumulative reward with respect to the policy parameters. The update rule for REINFORCE can be expressed as follows:

$$\theta \leftarrow \theta + \alpha \, df\theta \, \log \pi(a|s) \, G$$

In this equation, θ represents the policy parameters, α is the learning rate, $\varpi(a|s)$ is the probability of taking action a given state s according to the policy, and G is the observed cumulative reward. The term $df\theta \log \varpi(a|s)$ represents the gradient of the log-probability of the action, which is used to update the policy parameters in the direction that increases the expected cumulative reward.

One advantage of policy gradient methods is their ability to handle complex, high-dimensional action spaces. For example, in tasks such as robotic control or playing complex games, the action space may involve a large number of continuous actions. Policy gradient methods can learn policies that directly output continuous actions without the need for discretization or approximation. This flexibility makes them well-suited for tackling real-world problems that require fine-grained control.

Another benefit of policy gradient methods is their ability to handle stochastic policies. Stochastic policies introduce exploration in the learning process, allowing the agent to discover new actions and avoid getting stuck in suboptimal solutions. By directly optimizing the policy parameters, policy gradient methods can effectively balance exploration and exploitation, leading to more robust and adaptable behavior.

Policy gradient methods have found numerous applications in reinforcement learning. For instance, in the field of robotics, policy gradient methods have been used to train robots to perform complex manipulation tasks, such as grasping objects or walking. By learning policies that directly control the robot's actions, these methods enable the robot to adapt and improve its performance over time.

In the realm of game playing, policy gradient methods have achieved remarkable successes. AlphaGo, a famous example, combined policy gradient methods with deep neural networks to defeat world champions in the game of Go. The policy network learned to evaluate board positions and select actions that led to favorable outcomes, resulting in unprecedented mastery of the game.

Policy gradient methods continue to advance the field of reinforcement learning, offering a powerful framework for learning optimal policies in complex environments. By directly optimizing the policy function and leveraging gradient ascent, these methods enable agents to discover effective strategies and adapt to changing conditions. Through their flexibility, policy gradient methods have the potential to drive significant breakthroughs in various domains, including robotics, game playing, and autonomous systems.

Exploration and Exploitation:

The exploration-exploitation trade-off is a critical concept in reinforcement learning. Agents need to explore the environment to discover new and potentially better actions, while also exploiting the knowledge gained to maximize rewards. Striking the right balance between exploration and exploitation is essential for efficient learning.

Exploration and exploitation are fundamental concepts in reinforcement learning that address the trade-off between discovering new knowledge and maximizing rewards. Let's delve into these concepts and explore their significance in the context of reinforcement learning.

In reinforcement learning, an agent interacts with an environment to learn how to make decisions that optimize long-term rewards. The exploration-exploitation trade-off arises because the agent must decide whether to explore new actions or exploit the knowledge it has acquired thus far.

Exploration refers to the process of trying out new actions or exploring unfamiliar parts of the environment. By exploring, the agent aims to gather information about the environment and discover potentially better strategies. It allows the agent to learn more about the dynamics of the environment, uncover hidden rewards, and avoid premature convergence to suboptimal solutions.

Exploitation, on the other hand, involves utilizing the knowledge and experience gained from previous interactions to select actions that are likely to yield high rewards. Exploitation involves leveraging the agent's current understanding of the environment to make decisions that are expected to maximize immediate rewards. Exploiting known strategies can be beneficial when the agent has already learned effective actions and wants to exploit this knowledge to achieve better performance.

The challenge lies in finding the right balance between exploration and exploitation. If the agent solely focuses on exploitation, it may miss out on discovering better actions or new parts of the environment that could potentially lead to higher rewards. Conversely, excessive exploration can lead to inefficiency and suboptimal performance if the agent constantly explores without effectively exploiting its current knowledge.

Various strategies have been developed to address the exploration-exploitation trade-off. One common approach is ε-greedy exploration, where the agent selects the action with the highest estimated value most of the time (exploitation), but occasionally selects a random action with a small probability ε (exploration). This allows the agent to explore alternative actions while still exploiting its current knowledge.

Another approach is Upper Confidence Bound (UCB), which encourages exploration by assigning higher exploration bonuses to actions with higher uncertainty or lower confidence bounds. This encourages the agent to try less-explored actions and gradually reduces the exploration as it becomes more confident about the environment.

Contextual bandits, a variant of reinforcement learning, involve learning policies for specific contexts or situations. The agent learns to select actions based on observed context, explores different actions in various contexts, and exploits the learned policies to maximize rewards in similar situations.

To illustrate the exploration-exploitation trade-off, consider an online advertising scenario. An advertising platform seeks to optimize ad placement to maximize user clicks, which translates into revenue. Initially, the platform may allocate a small portion of ad placements to explore different strategies and collect data on user preferences. Over time, as it gathers more information and learns about user preferences, it can shift its focus towards exploiting the best-performing strategies, allocating most placements based on the learned insights.

The exploration-exploitation trade-off is a crucial concept in reinforcement learning. Striking the right balance between exploration and exploitation allows agents to maximize long-term rewards by discovering new knowledge while effectively exploiting the learned information. By applying a combination of exploration and exploitation strategies, agents can navigate complex environments, learn optimal policies, and make informed decisions in various real-world applications ranging from robotics and gaming to healthcare and finance.

Credit Assignment Problem:

The credit assignment problem refers to the challenge of attributing rewards or penalties to specific actions or states in a sequence of interactions. Reinforcement learning algorithms need to properly assign credit to actions that contribute to desired outcomes, even when rewards are delayed or sparse.

The credit assignment problem is a fundamental concept in reinforcement learning that deals with the challenge of appropriately assigning credit or blame to specific actions or states within a sequence of interactions. In the context of reinforcement learning, agents aim to learn optimal policies by maximizing rewards or minimizing penalties. However, the credit assignment problem arises when rewards are delayed or sparse, making it difficult for the agent to determine which actions or states contributed to the observed outcomes.

To understand the credit assignment problem, let's consider an example involving a robot learning to navigate through a maze. The robot takes a series of actions, such as moving forward, turning left or right, and sometimes even backtracking. The ultimate goal is to reach a reward location within the maze. However, the robot only receives a reward signal when it reaches the reward location, creating a temporal gap between the actions taken and the corresponding reward.

In such cases, the credit assignment problem arises because the robot needs to attribute credit to the actions that led to the positive outcome of reaching the reward. It becomes challenging for the robot to determine which specific actions or states in the sequence contributed the most to the success. If the robot assigns credit incorrectly, it may fail to learn the optimal policy and continue making suboptimal decisions.

Reinforcement learning algorithms tackle the credit assignment problem by employing various techniques. One commonly used approach is temporal-difference learning, which calculates the temporal difference between the predicted and actual rewards at each time step. By updating the value estimates based on these differences, the agent can assign credit to the actions and states along the trajectory that lead to the final outcome. This approach allows the agent to learn the associations between actions and delayed rewards, bridging the temporal gap.

Another technique used to address the credit assignment problem is eligibility traces. Eligibility traces keep track of the recent actions and states that are eligible for credit assignment. This allows the agent to assign credit to relevant actions and states, even when the rewards are delayed or sparse. By assigning a fraction of the credit to eligible states and actions, the agent can update its value estimates accordingly and learn from the delayed rewards.

For instance, in a game-playing scenario, the credit assignment problem arises when a reinforcement learning agent receives a positive reward only after successfully winning the game. To learn the optimal strategy, the agent needs to accurately assign credit to the actions taken during the game, even though the reward is received at the end. Through temporal-difference learning and eligibility traces, the agent can assign credit to the actions and states that contributed to the victory, enabling it to learn and improve its gameplay.

The credit assignment problem is a significant challenge in reinforcement learning. It involves attributing rewards or penalties to specific actions or states in a sequence of interactions, even when the rewards are delayed or sparse. Temporal-difference learning and eligibility traces are two common techniques used to address this problem, allowing reinforcement learning agents to assign credit accurately and learn optimal policies. By effectively solving the credit assignment problem, reinforcement learning algorithms can excel in various domains, including robotics, gaming, recommendation systems, and more.

Sample Efficiency:

Sample efficiency is an important consideration in reinforcement learning. Algorithms should be able to learn effectively from limited amounts of data or interactions with the environment. Improving sample efficiency is a key area of research in reinforcement learning.

Sample efficiency is a crucial aspect of reinforcement learning that focuses on the ability of algorithms to learn effectively from limited amounts of data or interactions with the environment. In the field of reinforcement learning, agents learn optimal policies through trial and error, using feedback in the form of rewards or penalties. However, in real-world scenarios, collecting data or conducting interactions can be time-consuming, costly, or even dangerous. Therefore, it becomes imperative to develop algorithms that can learn efficiently from a small number of samples.

To better understand sample efficiency, let's consider an example involving an autonomous robot learning to navigate through a maze. The robot explores the maze by taking various actions and receiving feedback in the form of rewards or penalties based on its progress. The goal is to find the optimal path from the starting point to the goal location. However, the robot's ability to explore the maze and collect feedback is limited by factors such as time, computational resources, or constraints on the number of interactions with the environment.

In such situations, sample efficiency becomes crucial. A sample-efficient reinforcement learning algorithm would require fewer interactions with the environment to learn an optimal policy compared to an algorithm with lower sample efficiency. This efficiency can have significant practical implications, as it allows agents to learn faster, reduce the cost of data collection, and make decisions more quickly in real-time scenarios.

Improving sample efficiency is a key area of research in reinforcement learning. Researchers and practitioners employ various techniques and algorithms to enhance the learning process while reducing the number of samples required. One such technique is the use of prior knowledge or pre-training. By leveraging existing knowledge or pre-trained models, agents can benefit from prior experience and reduce the number of interactions needed to learn effectively. Transfer learning, for instance, allows agents to transfer knowledge from a source task to a target task, enabling them to learn more efficiently in new environments.

Another approach to improving sample efficiency is through the use of function approximation. Instead of explicitly storing and updating values for each state-action pair, function approximation methods use parameterized models, such as neural networks, to estimate the value or policy functions. These models can generalize from limited data, enabling agents to learn efficiently and make predictions for unvisited states or actions.

Monte Carlo methods and temporal-difference learning techniques, such as Q-learning and SARSA, are also employed to enhance sample efficiency. These methods make use of observed experiences and rewards to update the value estimates, allowing agents to learn from a limited number of interactions and generalize to unseen situations.

Enhancing sample efficiency in reinforcement learning is not only important for practical reasons but also for addressing real-world challenges. For instance, in the field of robotics, where physical interactions can be costly or potentially dangerous, sample-efficient algorithms enable robots to learn and adapt quickly with minimal experimentation. Similarly, in healthcare applications, sample efficiency allows for effective learning from limited patient data, leading to more personalized and efficient treatment strategies.

In summary, sample efficiency is a critical consideration in reinforcement learning. Algorithms that can learn effectively from limited amounts of data or interactions with the environment are highly desirable. Techniques such as prior knowledge utilization, function approximation, and learning from observed experiences play a crucial role in improving sample efficiency. By reducing the number of interactions required, sample-efficient reinforcement learning algorithms enable faster learning, reduced data collection costs, and more efficient decision-making in a wide range of domains.

Example: Mathematical proof for the concept of sample efficiency

To provide a mathematical proof for the concept of sample efficiency in reinforcement learning, we need to establish the relationship between the number of samples or interactions and the learning performance of an algorithm. Let's consider a simplified scenario where we can measure sample efficiency based on the convergence rate of a reinforcement learning algorithm.

Let N be the total number of interactions or samples available for learning, and let T be the time or number of iterations needed for the algorithm to converge to an optimal policy. We want to demonstrate that a more sample-efficient algorithm requires fewer interactions, resulting in a lower value of N, while still achieving the same level of convergence as a less sample-efficient algorithm.

We can represent the learning performance of an algorithm as a function of the number of interactions, $P(N)$, where P represents some metric such as the expected return or the difference between the learned policy and the optimal policy. For a less sample-efficient algorithm, the convergence rate may be slower, leading to a larger value of $P(N)$.

Now, let's consider a more sample-efficient algorithm. This algorithm can learn from a smaller number of interactions, denoted by N'. We assume that the convergence rate of this algorithm is faster than the less sample-efficient algorithm, resulting in a smaller value of $P(N')$.

To prove the concept, we need to show that N' < N and P(N') < P(N). In other words, the more sample-efficient algorithm achieves the same or better learning performance with fewer interactions.

By establishing this inequality, we can demonstrate that improving sample efficiency leads to a more efficient learning process. However, it is important to note that providing a general mathematical proof for sample efficiency across all reinforcement learning algorithms is challenging due to the diverse range of algorithms and problem domains involved. The exact proof would depend on the specific algorithm and learning performance metric considered.

In practice, the sample efficiency of reinforcement learning algorithms is often evaluated through empirical studies and experiments on specific tasks and benchmarks. Researchers compare the learning performance of different algorithms under varying numbers of interactions to assess their relative sample efficiency.

While a comprehensive mathematical proof may be challenging, empirical evidence and experimental results consistently demonstrate the importance of sample efficiency in reinforcement learning. These studies provide valuable insights into the relative performance of algorithms and their ability to learn effectively from limited amounts of data.

Applications:

Reinforcement learning finds applications in various domains, including gaming, robotics, autonomous systems, resource allocation, healthcare, and more. Examples include game-playing algorithms like AlphaGo, robots learning to perform complex tasks, personalized treatment policies in healthcare, and optimization of business processes.

Reinforcement learning, with its ability to learn optimal behaviors through trial and error, has found applications in a wide range of domains. In this essay, we will explore some notable examples of how reinforcement learning has been successfully applied in various fields, showcasing its versatility and potential.

One prominent application of reinforcement learning is in the realm of gaming. The breakthrough achievement of AlphaGo, developed by DeepMind, is a testament to the power of reinforcement learning. AlphaGo defeated world champion Go player Lee Sedol in 2016, marking a significant milestone in artificial intelligence. By combining deep neural networks and reinforcement learning techniques, AlphaGo learned to make strategic moves in the game, surpassing human capabilities. This achievement demonstrates the potential of reinforcement learning in complex decision-making tasks.

Reinforcement learning has also made significant contributions to robotics and autonomous systems. Robots equipped with reinforcement learning algorithms can learn to perform complex tasks by interacting with their environment. For instance, a robot can learn to navigate through obstacles, grasp objects, or even play sports like table tennis. By providing a reward signal for desired behaviors and iteratively updating its policies, the robot can improve its performance over time. This application has promising implications for industries such as manufacturing, healthcare, and space exploration.

In the field of healthcare, reinforcement learning holds great potential for personalized treatment policies. Each patient is unique, and optimal treatment decisions can vary based on individual factors. Reinforcement learning algorithms can be used to learn policies that adapt to specific patient characteristics and treatment outcomes. For example, in cancer treatment, reinforcement learning can help determine optimal dosages and treatment schedules while considering the patient's response and minimizing side effects. This personalized approach can lead to more effective and efficient healthcare interventions.

Reinforcement learning also plays a vital role in optimizing business processes and resource allocation. For instance, in supply chain management, reinforcement learning algorithms can learn optimal inventory control policies, considering factors such as demand, lead time, and cost. This enables businesses to improve efficiency, reduce costs, and ensure timely delivery. Similarly, reinforcement learning can be used in energy management systems to optimize power distribution, reducing waste and promoting sustainability.

These examples highlight the diverse range of applications for reinforcement learning across various domains. The ability of reinforcement learning algorithms to learn from interactions and adapt their behaviors based on rewards and penalties opens up numerous possibilities for improving decision-making and optimizing complex systems.

However, it is important to note that the successful application of reinforcement learning requires careful design, data availability, and training procedures. Real-world implementation often involves addressing challenges such as sample efficiency, exploration-exploitation trade-offs, and credit assignment problems. Nonetheless, with ongoing research and advancements in algorithms and techniques, reinforcement learning continues to push the boundaries of what is possible in artificial intelligence.

In conclusion, reinforcement learning has emerged as a powerful approach with applications in gaming, robotics, healthcare, resource allocation, and more. The examples discussed in this essay demonstrate the versatility of reinforcement learning in tackling complex decision-making problems. As technology continues to evolve, we can expect to see even more exciting applications of reinforcement learning that shape the future of various industries.

Example: An example that illustrates the application of reinforcement learning in gaming:

One of the most remarkable examples of reinforcement learning in gaming is the success of the AlphaGo program. Developed by DeepMind, AlphaGo is an AI system that became renowned for defeating the world champion Go player, Lee Sedol, in a five-game match in 2016.

Go is an ancient Chinese board game known for its complexity, with an incredibly large number of possible moves. Traditional game-playing algorithms struggled to master this game due to the sheer number of possible combinations. However, AlphaGo employed a combination of advanced techniques, including deep neural networks and reinforcement learning, to achieve its remarkable performance.

AlphaGo learned to play Go by training on a large dataset of expert human games, as well as through self-play. The reinforcement learning algorithm enabled AlphaGo to improve its gameplay through trial and error, gradually learning optimal strategies and making better decisions.

During the games against Lee Sedol, AlphaGo showcased its strategic abilities, often making moves that human experts found surprising and innovative. By exploring different possibilities and exploiting its learned knowledge, AlphaGo achieved a level of play that surpassed human intuition.

The success of AlphaGo demonstrated the immense potential of reinforcement learning in tackling complex decision-making tasks. It showcased how an AI system, through interactions with its environment and feedback in the form of rewards, could learn to navigate a game as intricate as Go and outperform human champions.

The application of reinforcement learning in gaming extends beyond Go. It has been used in other games as well, such as chess, poker, and video games. Reinforcement learning algorithms can learn to play these games at an expert level, often surpassing human performance through extensive training and optimization of strategies.

The advancements made in gaming through reinforcement learning have not only pushed the boundaries of AI capabilities but also have practical implications. The same techniques used in gaming can be applied to real-world decision-making scenarios, where complex strategies and optimal choices need to be made in the face of uncertainty and limited information.

The success of AlphaGo and similar applications of reinforcement learning in gaming demonstrate the potential of this approach in mastering complex tasks. By combining exploration and exploitation, reinforcement learning algorithms can learn optimal behaviors and outperform human experts. Such examples inspire further research and application of reinforcement learning in various domains beyond gaming, propelling advancements in artificial intelligence.

4.5 Transfer Learning and Pre-trained Models

Transfer learning and pre-trained models play a significant role in machine learning and have revolutionized the field by enabling the transfer of knowledge and representations learned from one task to another. In this section, we will explore the concept of transfer learning, the benefits it offers, and the use of pre-trained models in various applications.

Transfer learning is a technique where knowledge gained from solving one problem is applied to another related problem. Instead of starting the learning process from scratch for a new task, transfer learning leverages the knowledge acquired from a different but related task. This approach saves computational resources and training time while improving the performance of the target task.

One popular method in transfer learning is fine-tuning, where a pre-trained model is adapted to a new task by retraining the model on the target data. The initial layers of the pre-trained model, known as the base layers, capture low-level features like edges, textures, and basic shapes. These features are generally applicable to many tasks, making the base layers valuable for transfer learning. The later layers, called the task-specific layers, are added or modified to learn task-specific features.

Pre-trained models are neural network models that have been trained on large-scale datasets, often with millions of images or extensive text corpora. These models have learned general representations of features and exhibit strong performance on benchmark tasks. By utilizing pre-trained models, researchers and practitioners can benefit from the knowledge and insights gained from extensive training on high-quality datasets.

The ImageNet dataset, for example, contains millions of labeled images across various categories. Pre-trained models like VGG16, ResNet, and Inception have been trained on this dataset and achieved state-of-the-art performance on image classification tasks. These models have learned to recognize and extract important features from images, such as shapes, textures, and object hierarchies.

When applying transfer learning, the pre-trained model is initially frozen, and only the task-specific layers are trained using the new dataset. This allows the model to adapt its learned representations to the specific characteristics of the target task, such as recognizing different objects in images or understanding specific text patterns. The pre-trained model provides a starting point with good initial weights and learned features, which helps accelerate the learning process and improve performance.

Transfer learning and pre-trained models have found applications in various domains. In computer vision, pre-trained models have been used for tasks such as object detection, image segmentation, and facial recognition. For example, the Faster R-CNN model, built on the base of pre-trained models like ResNet, has been widely used for object detection in real-world scenarios.

In natural language processing, pre-trained models such as BERT (Bidirectional Encoder Representations from Transformers) and GPT (Generative Pre-trained Transformer) have achieved remarkable results in tasks like sentiment analysis, text classification, and question-answering. These models capture contextual information and semantic understanding of text, enabling better performance on downstream tasks.

Transfer learning and pre-trained models have also found applications in recommendation systems, speech recognition, and many other fields where large amounts of data and complex patterns are involved.

Transfer learning and pre-trained models offer a powerful approach to leverage knowledge and representations learned from one task to benefit another related task. By utilizing pre-trained models and fine-tuning them on specific tasks, researchers and practitioners can save time and resources while achieving state-of-the-art performance. These techniques have significantly advanced the field of machine learning and continue to drive progress in various domains.

Transfer Learning:

Transfer learning(TL) is a technique in which knowledge and representations learned from solving one task are applied to another related task. It saves computational resources and training time while improving the performance of the target task.

Transfer learning, a technique in machine learning, has revolutionized the field by enabling the application of knowledge and representations acquired from solving one task to another related task. It offers a significant advantage by leveraging existing learned features and reducing the need for extensive training on the target task. This essay explores the concept of transfer learning, its benefits in terms of computational resources and training time, and its remarkable impact on improving the performance of the target task.

In transfer learning, the goal is to transfer the knowledge gained from a source task to a target task. The source task is typically a task for which a model has been pre-trained on a large dataset, while the target task is the task for which the model's knowledge is to be applied. By leveraging the learned features from the source task, the model gains a head start in understanding the target task, leading to enhanced performance.

To illustrate the power of transfer learning, let's consider an example in computer vision. Suppose a model has been trained on a large dataset for a classification task, such as distinguishing between cats and dogs. The model has learned to recognize various features that are relevant for this task, such as identifying different shapes, colors, and textures. Now, if we want to train a model to classify different breeds of dogs, we can take advantage of the knowledge acquired from the cat-dog classification task. By transferring the learned representations and fine-tuning the model on the specific dog breeds, we can significantly improve the performance compared to training the model from scratch. The model has already learned general features that are relevant to both tasks, and it only needs to adapt and refine those features for the new task.

TL offers several benefits, including saving computational resources and training time. Since the model starts with a set of pre-trained weights and learned features, it requires less time and computational power to converge on the target task. Instead of training the model from scratch, which could be computationally expensive and time-consuming, transfer learning provides a shortcut by leveraging the knowledge already gained.

Moreover, transfer learning is particularly useful in scenarios where the target task has limited available data. In such cases, training a model from scratch may result in overfitting, as the model tries to learn from a small dataset. By using transfer learning, the model can rely on the knowledge extracted from the source task, which was trained on a large dataset, thereby mitigating the risk of overfitting and improving generalization on the target task.

A key concept in transfer learning is the notion of learned representations. The model learns to extract high-level features and representations that are relevant across tasks. These representations capture valuable information about the data and can be transferred to other tasks, leading to improved performance. The model acts as a knowledge repository, storing the learned representations that can be leveraged for multiple tasks.

TL has found applications in various domains, including computer vision, natural language processing, recommendation systems, and more. In computer vision, transfer learning has been used for tasks such as object detection, image segmentation, and image classification. For example, pre-trained models like VGG16 and ResNet have been fine-tuned on specific datasets to achieve state-of-the-art performance in object recognition tasks. Similarly, in natural language processing, transfer learning has been instrumental in tasks such as sentiment analysis, text classification, and machine translation. Pre-trained models like BERT and GPT have provided a strong foundation for various language-related tasks.

In summary, transfer learning is a remarkable technique that allows the application of knowledge and representations learned from one task to improve performance on another related task. It saves computational resources and training time by leveraging pre-trained models and learned features. The benefits of transfer learning extend to domains such as computer vision and natural language processing, enabling researchers and practitioners to achieve enhanced performance with reduced training efforts. As transfer learning continues to evolve, we can expect further advancements and applications in a wide range of fields, making it an indispensable tool in the machine learning toolbox.

Pre-trained Models:

Pre-trained models are neural network models that have been trained on large-scale datasets. They have learned general representations of features and exhibit strong performance on benchmark tasks. By utilizing pre-trained models, researchers and practitioners can benefit from the knowledge and insights gained from extensive training on high-quality datasets.

In the world of machine learning, pre-trained models have emerged as powerful tools that enable researchers and practitioners to leverage the knowledge and insights gained from extensive training on large-scale datasets. These models, which are neural networks trained on vast amounts of high-quality data, offer a head start in solving complex tasks by providing learned representations of features and exhibiting strong performance on benchmark tasks. In this essay, we will delve into the concept of pre-trained models, explore their benefits, and provide examples of their applications across different domains.

At the heart of pre-trained models lies the idea of transfer learning, which allows the knowledge acquired from one task to be applied to another related task. By training models on large-scale datasets, typically containing millions of samples, pre-trained models have acquired a deep understanding of the underlying patterns and structures in the data. This enables them to learn general representations of features that are applicable to a wide range of tasks.

For instance, in computer vision, pre-trained models like VGG16, Inception, and ResNet have been trained on enormous datasets such as ImageNet. These models have learned to recognize various low-level and high-level features present in images, such as edges, textures, and object shapes. By utilizing these pre-trained models, researchers can save significant time and computational resources that would otherwise be required to train models from scratch. They can build upon the knowledge captured by the pre-trained models and fine-tune them on specific datasets or tasks, thereby benefiting from the previously learned representations.

One of the key advantages of pre-trained models is their ability to exhibit strong performance on benchmark tasks. The models have been trained on well-curated datasets, where human experts have carefully labeled and annotated the data. As a result, pre-trained models have learned to generalize well and produce accurate predictions. This performance is often reflected in their ability to achieve state-of-the-art results on a wide range of tasks, such as image classification, object detection, natural language processing, and more.

Let's consider an example in natural language processing (NLP). The model BERT (Bidirectional Encoder Representations from Transformers) is a pre-trained model that has revolutionized various NLP tasks. BERT has been trained on an extensive corpus of text data, enabling it to capture the contextual information and semantic understanding of words and sentences. By utilizing BERT as a pre-trained model, researchers can build upon its language understanding capabilities and fine-tune it on specific NLP tasks, such as sentiment analysis or question answering. This approach saves time and effort while achieving impressive performance on the target tasks.

By leveraging pre-trained models, researchers and practitioners can tap into the wealth of knowledge acquired during pre-training on large-scale datasets. This knowledge encompasses not only the learned representations but also insights gained from extensive training experiments and architectural design choices. Utilizing pre-trained models allows for the transfer of this knowledge to specific tasks, providing a solid foundation for further exploration and improvement.

The benefits of pre-trained models extend beyond saving computational resources and achieving strong performance. They also facilitate research reproducibility and foster collaboration in the machine learning community. Researchers can share their pre-trained models, enabling others to build upon their work and replicate or extend their findings. This sharing of pre-trained models promotes knowledge sharing and accelerates progress in the field.

In summary, pre-trained models have revolutionized the machine learning landscape by providing a valuable resource of learned representations and knowledge acquired from extensive training on large-scale datasets. By leveraging these models, researchers and practitioners can benefit from the insights and performance achieved by the pre-trained models on benchmark tasks. This approach not only saves time and resources but also promotes collaboration and fosters advancements in the field. As the field of machine learning continues to evolve, pre-trained models will undoubtedly play a crucial role in empowering researchers and practitioners to tackle complex tasks and drive innovation across various domains.

Example: Illustrate the application of pre-trained models

Imagine a research team working on a project related to autonomous driving. They need to develop a computer vision system that can accurately detect and classify various objects on the road, such as pedestrians, vehicles, and traffic signs. Instead of starting from scratch and training a neural network on a large dataset of labeled images, they decide to leverage a pre-trained model, such as the well-known ResNet.

ResNet is a deep convolutional neural network that has been trained on millions of images from the ImageNet dataset. It has learned to recognize a wide variety of object categories and has gained a deep understanding of visual features. By using ResNet as a pre-trained model, the research team can benefit from the representations and knowledge learned during its extensive training.

To adapt ResNet to their specific task of object detection and classification in autonomous driving, the researchers employ a technique called fine-tuning. They keep the majority of the pre-trained ResNet layers intact, as these layers have learned general image features applicable to many tasks. However, they add and modify a few task-specific layers on top of ResNet to learn the specific features relevant to object detection in autonomous driving scenarios.

With the pre-trained ResNet as a starting point, the research team fine-tunes the model on their own dataset, consisting of labeled images of objects encountered on the road. The model learns to recognize and classify these specific objects, building upon the general representations learned from the pre-training. The fine-tuning process allows the model to adapt and specialize to the nuances and characteristics of the target task.

By leveraging the pre-trained ResNet and fine-tuning it on their specific dataset, the research team achieves significant benefits. They save considerable time and computational resources that would have been required to train a neural network from scratch. Moreover, they capitalize on the wealth of knowledge and representations captured by ResNet during its pre-training on ImageNet. As a result, the fine-tuned model demonstrates improved performance in accurately detecting and classifying objects in autonomous driving scenarios.

This example illustrates how pre-trained models can be instrumental in accelerating the development of machine learning systems. By leveraging the knowledge and representations acquired through pre-training on large-scale datasets, researchers and practitioners can benefit from the insights and performance achieved by the pre-trained models. This approach not only saves time and resources but also enhances the overall performance and effectiveness of the models on specific tasks.

Fine-tuning:

Fine-tuning is a method used in transfer learning where a pre-trained model is adapted to a new task by retraining the model on the target data. The base layers, which capture low-level features, are usually kept frozen, while the task-specific layers are added or modified to learn task-specific features.

It is a powerful technique in transfer learning that enables the adaptation of pre-trained models to new tasks. It allows researchers and practitioners to leverage the knowledge and representations learned from a source task and apply them to a related target task. Fine-tuning involves retraining the pre-trained model on the target data while keeping the base layers frozen and modifying or adding task-specific layers to learn task-specific features. This essay will delve into the concept of fine-tuning, its benefits, and provide examples to illustrate its effectiveness.

When using pre-trained models, the base layers of the model, also known as the backbone, have typically learned generic and low-level features from the source task. These features capture fundamental patterns and concepts that are transferable across related tasks. By keeping these base layers frozen during fine-tuning, the model retains its knowledge of these general features, which helps accelerate the learning process and prevents the loss of previously acquired knowledge.

On the other hand, the task-specific layers are responsible for learning features specific to the target task. These layers are added or modified to adapt the model's representations to the unique characteristics and requirements of the new task. By focusing on task-specific layers, fine-tuning allows the model to refine its learned features to better align with the target data and task objectives. This process enables the model to capture higher-level, task-specific patterns and nuances, enhancing its performance on the target task.

An example can help illustrate the concept of fine-tuning. Consider a pre-trained convolutional neural network (CNN) that has been trained on a large dataset of images, such as ImageNet, to classify various objects. Now, suppose we want to apply this pre-trained CNN to a new task of classifying different species of flowers. The pre-trained CNN has already learned low-level features like edges, textures, and basic shapes that are relevant to both the source task (object classification) and the target task (flower classification).

To fine-tune the pre-trained CNN for the new task, we would freeze the base layers to preserve the learned generic features. Next, we add a few task-specific layers, such as fully connected layers, on top of the frozen base layers. These task-specific layers are then trained on a dataset of labeled flower images, adjusting their weights to learn the specific visual features that distinguish different flower species.

During fine-tuning, the model optimizes its parameters based on the target task's loss function and the new labeled data. The gradients flow through the task-specific layers, allowing the model to update its weights and improve its performance on the flower classification task. The frozen base layers, which contain pre-trained features, remain unchanged and continue to contribute their knowledge to the overall model.

The benefits of fine-tuning are numerous. Firstly, fine-tuning saves considerable time and computational resources compared to training a model from scratch. By leveraging the pre-trained model's knowledge, the fine-tuning process starts from a highly optimized state, allowing for faster convergence and improved efficiency.

Enables the transfer of knowledge and representations from the source task to the target task. The pre-trained model has already learned useful features from a large and diverse dataset, capturing important patterns that are transferable to related tasks. By preserving and building upon these learned features, the fine-tuned model can generalize better and achieve better performance on the target task, even with limited labeled data.

Lastly, fine-tuning provides a flexible framework that can be adapted to different domains and tasks. The approach is not limited to image classification but extends to various applications such as natural language processing, speech recognition, and recommendation systems. Researchers and practitioners can leverage fine-tuning to adapt pre-trained models to their specific tasks, benefiting from the broad knowledge captured during pre-training.

Fine-tuning is a crucial method in transfer learning that enables the adaptation of pre-trained models to new tasks. By freezing the base layers and modifying the task-specific layers, the model can retain its learned knowledge while adapting its representations to the target task. Fine-tuning offers several advantages, including faster convergence, leveraging pre-trained features, and flexibility across different domains. The examples provided demonstrate how fine-tuning can improve the performance and efficiency of models in various applications. Researchers and practitioners can utilize fine-tuning to accelerate their work and achieve state-of-the-art results, even with limited labeled data.

Base Layers and Task-specific Layers:

In transfer learning, the pre-trained model consists of base layers and task-specific layers. The base layers have learned general features applicable to many tasks, such as edges and textures. The task-specific layers are added or modified to learn features specific to the target task.

It plays a crucial role in transfer learning, allowing the adaptation of pre-trained models to new tasks. In this essay, we will explore these concepts, their significance in transfer learning, and provide examples to illustrate their role in capturing general and task-specific features.

In transfer learning, the pre-trained model comprises both base layers and task-specific layers. The base layers form the foundation of the model and have been trained on a large-scale dataset for a source task. These layers have learned general features that are relevant to many tasks, such as edges, textures, and basic shapes. By capturing these low-level features, the base layers can extract meaningful representations from the input data, forming a rich and expressive feature space.

The base layers' ability to capture general features stems from the extensive training they underwent on a diverse dataset. For instance, in computer vision tasks, a pre-trained convolutional neural network (CNN) may have learned to detect edges, corners, and other elementary visual patterns. These learned features are not specific to any particular task but rather represent fundamental building blocks that can be useful across various visual recognition tasks.

On top of the base layers, task-specific layers are added or modified to adapt the model's representations to the target task. These layers are responsible for capturing higher-level, task-specific features that are essential for achieving optimal performance on the specific task at hand. The task-specific layers build upon the foundational knowledge acquired by the base layers and specialize in learning features that are relevant and discriminative for the target task.

To illustrate the concept, let's consider an example in natural language processing. Suppose we have a pre-trained language model, such as BERT (Bidirectional Encoder Representations from Transformers), which has been trained on a vast corpus of text from diverse sources. The base layers of the BERT model have learned general linguistic features, such as syntactic structures, semantic relationships, and contextual understanding.

Now, suppose we want to use this pre-trained BERT model for a sentiment analysis task, where we aim to classify text into positive or negative sentiments. In this case, we would add task-specific layers on top of the pre-trained BERT model. These additional layers could include a classification layer that maps the learned representations from BERT to the sentiment labels.

During fine-tuning, the base layers are typically kept frozen to preserve the general features they have learned. This ensures that the model retains the knowledge acquired during pre-training. The task-specific layers, on the other hand, are updated and fine-tuned using labeled data specific to the sentiment analysis task. By training the task-specific layers on sentiment-labeled examples, the model can learn to capture sentiment-related features, such as sentiment-specific vocabulary and contextual cues indicative of positive or negative sentiment.

The division between base layers and task-specific layers allows for a modular and flexible approach to transfer learning. It enables the transfer of generic knowledge from the pre-trained base layers to capture essential aspects of the data while allowing task-specific layers to specialize in capturing features specific to the target task. This separation of responsibilities facilitates efficient adaptation and optimization of the model's representations for the target task, leading to improved performance.

The concept of base layers and task-specific layers is fundamental in transfer learning. The base layers, trained on a source task, capture general features applicable to various tasks, while the task-specific layers are added or modified to learn features specific to the target task. This division of responsibilities allows pre-trained models to be adapted and fine-tuned for new tasks efficiently. The examples provided demonstrate how base and task-specific layers work together to create effective and specialized models in different domains, ultimately improving the performance and applicability of transfer learning approaches.

Let's consider an example in computer vision where base layers and task-specific layers are employed in transfer learning.

Suppose we have a pre-trained convolutional neural network (CNN) that has been trained on a large dataset such as ImageNet. The base layers of this CNN have learned general visual features like edges, textures, and shapes, which are applicable to a wide range of visual recognition tasks.

Now, let's say we want to use this pre-trained CNN for a specific task of classifying different species of flowers. In this case, we would add task-specific layers on top of the pre-trained CNN to adapt it to the flower classification task.

The task-specific layers could include a few additional convolutional layers followed by fully connected layers. These layers are responsible for learning features that are relevant to distinguishing different flower species. The base layers, which have learned generic visual features, serve as a strong starting point for the model to capture low-level visual patterns in the images of flowers.

During fine-tuning, the parameters of the base layers are usually kept fixed, preventing them from being altered. This ensures that the learned general features are preserved. On the other hand, the parameters of the task-specific layers are updated and trained using a smaller labeled dataset specific to the flower classification task.

By training the task-specific layers on the flower images with corresponding labels, the model can learn to capture higher-level features specific to the flower species, such as petal shapes, leaf patterns, or color distributions that are discriminative for accurate classification.

In this example, the base layers of the pre-trained CNN act as feature extractors, capturing generic visual patterns applicable to various tasks, while the task-specific layers specialize in learning features relevant to the flower classification task. The combination of these layers allows the model to leverage the knowledge acquired from pre-training and adapt it to the specific classification task with fewer labeled examples.

This approach saves computational resources and training time since the base layers have already learned a rich set of features on a large-scale dataset. By building upon these learned features with task-specific layers, the model can achieve better performance on the flower classification task compared to training from scratch.

The example demonstrates how the concept of base layers and task-specific layers is applied in transfer learning to leverage pre-trained models effectively. By reusing and adapting the knowledge encoded in the base layers, practitioners can build specialized models for specific tasks with improved efficiency and performance.

It's worth noting that the specific architecture and design of the task-specific layers may vary depending on the complexity of the target task and the available labeled data. However, the fundamental idea of combining pre-trained base layers with task-specific layers remains consistent across different transfer learning scenarios.

ImageNet:

ImageNet is a large-scale dataset containing millions of labeled images across various categories. Pre-trained models trained on ImageNet have achieved state-of-the-art performance on image classification tasks and serve as valuable resources for transfer learning in computer vision.

ImageNet is a groundbreaking dataset that has played a pivotal role in advancing computer vision and revolutionizing the field of transfer learning. It consists of millions of labeled images spanning thousands of categories, covering a wide range of objects, scenes, and concepts. The availability of such a vast and diverse dataset has paved the way for the development of pre-trained models that have achieved state-of-the-art performance on various image classification tasks.

The sheer scale of ImageNet has enabled deep learning researchers to train convolutional neural networks (CNNs) with unprecedented depth and complexity. Models trained on ImageNet have demonstrated exceptional capability in learning rich visual representations and extracting discriminative features from images. The success of these models on the ImageNet dataset has propelled the adoption of transfer learning in computer vision.

Transfer Learning with ImageNet Pre-trained Models

Transfer learning leverages the knowledge gained from solving one task to improve the performance on a different, but related, task. In computer vision, the availability of pre-trained models trained on ImageNet has significantly accelerated the progress in various image recognition tasks.

Pre-trained models trained on ImageNet serve as valuable resources for transfer learning. They have learned a plethora of visual features during the training process, capturing low-level and high-level representations that are applicable to a wide range of visual recognition tasks. These models have achieved remarkable performance on the ImageNet dataset, obtaining top rankings in the annual ImageNet Large Scale Visual Recognition Challenge (ILSVRC).

By utilizing these pre-trained models as a starting point, researchers and practitioners can benefit from the knowledge and insights gained from the extensive training on ImageNet. Instead of training a CNN from scratch, which can be computationally expensive and data-intensive, transfer learning allows for fine-tuning or feature extraction from the pre-trained models on smaller, task-specific datasets.

For example, consider an image classification task to identify different species of birds. By taking a pre-trained model, such as ResNet or Inception, trained on ImageNet as the base, the model already possesses a solid understanding of low-level features like edges, textures, and shapes. The task-specific layers can then be added or fine-tuned to learn the specific features and patterns relevant to classifying bird species. This approach reduces the amount of training required, speeds up convergence, and often leads to improved performance on the target task.

The Impact of ImageNet on Computer Vision

ImageNet has had a profound impact on computer vision research and applications. It has fueled advancements in object detection, image segmentation, image captioning, and visual understanding. The availability of pre-trained models trained on ImageNet has democratized the field, allowing researchers and practitioners with limited computational resources or labeled data to achieve state-of-the-art performance on various visual recognition tasks.

Furthermore, ImageNet has stimulated the exploration of more challenging and nuanced computer vision problems beyond traditional object classification. It has served as a benchmark dataset for evaluating the capabilities of different models and algorithms, fostering healthy competition and driving the development of new techniques.

ImageNet has revolutionized transfer learning in computer vision by providing a large-scale, diverse dataset and enabling the training of powerful pre-trained models. These models, equipped with comprehensive visual representations learned from ImageNet, serve as invaluable resources for accelerating the development of applications in computer vision. By leveraging the knowledge encoded in these models, researchers and practitioners can build upon the successes of ImageNet to address various visual recognition tasks with improved efficiency and performance.

The impact of ImageNet extends beyond the computer vision community, as its contributions have influenced advancements in fields such as artificial intelligence, robotics, and autonomous systems. As computer vision continues to evolve and tackle increasingly complex challenges, ImageNet remains a foundational pillar that has shaped the field and opened up new possibilities for understanding and interpreting the visual world.

BERT and GPT:

BERT (Bidirectional Encoder Representations from Transformers) and GPT (Generative Pre-trained Transformer) are pre-trained models widely used in natural language processing tasks. BERT captures contextual information and semantic understanding of text, while GPT generates coherent text based on pre-training on large text corpora.

BERT and GPT: Empowering Natural Language Processing

In the realm of natural language processing (NLP), BERT and GPT have emerged as game-changers, revolutionizing the way we process, understand, and generate textual data. These pre-trained models have significantly advanced the field, enabling remarkable breakthroughs in tasks such as language understanding, sentiment analysis, question answering, and text generation.

BERT: Unleashing Contextual Understanding

BERT, short for Bidirectional Encoder Representations from Transformers, is a pre-trained model that has achieved remarkable success in capturing contextual information and semantic understanding of text. Unlike traditional models that process text in a left-to-right or right-to-left manner, BERT employs a bidirectional approach, considering both preceding and succeeding words to comprehend the meaning of each word in a sentence.

By leveraging the power of Transformer architecture, BERT captures deep contextual relationships between words, contextualizing them based on the surrounding context. This enables the model to grasp nuances in language, including word senses, syntactic structures, and semantic associations. BERT's ability to understand the meaning of words in a given context has revolutionized a wide range of NLP tasks.

For example, in sentiment analysis, BERT can accurately determine the sentiment expressed in a sentence by considering the contextual cues and subtle nuances that influence the overall sentiment. In question answering, BERT can comprehend complex queries and provide precise answers by contextualizing the question against a given document. These are just a few examples of how BERT has transformed the landscape of NLP by enhancing the understanding and interpretation of textual data.

GPT: Generating Coherent Text

While BERT excels in understanding language, GPT (Generative Pre-trained Transformer) focuses on generating coherent and contextually relevant text. GPT is a pre-trained model that has been trained on large-scale text corpora, acquiring a profound understanding of language patterns, grammar, and semantic coherence. It utilizes the Transformer architecture, enabling it to generate highly coherent and human-like text.

GPT's text generation capabilities have far-reaching applications. It can be used to generate creative and engaging content, assist in automatic summarization, and even simulate human-like conversation. By pre-training on vast amounts of textual data, GPT learns to generate text that is coherent, fluent, and contextually appropriate.

For instance, GPT can generate compelling product descriptions, engaging blog posts, or realistic dialogues between virtual agents. Its ability to produce coherent and contextually relevant text makes it a powerful tool for content creation, virtual assistants, and various other NLP applications.

The Power of Pre-training and Transfer Learning

Both BERT and GPT showcase the power of pre-training and transfer learning in NLP. Pre-training involves training models on massive amounts of text data, enabling them to learn the underlying patterns and structures of language. These pre-trained models act as knowledge repositories, capturing the essence of language and enabling them to excel in downstream tasks.

Transfer learning takes this a step further, allowing the knowledge gained from pre-training to be transferred to specific tasks. By fine-tuning the pre-trained models on task-specific data, researchers and practitioners can leverage the rich understanding of language encoded in BERT and GPT to achieve remarkable performance in various NLP tasks, even with limited labeled data.

For example, by fine-tuning BERT on a sentiment analysis dataset, the model can quickly adapt to the task of sentiment classification, leveraging its understanding of context and language nuances. Similarly, GPT can be fine-tuned on a specific domain, such as medical literature, to generate coherent and relevant text specific to that domain.

BERT and GPT have significantly advanced the field of natural language processing, demonstrating the power of pre-training and transfer learning. BERT's contextual understanding of text and GPT's coherent text generation capabilities have opened up new frontiers in NLP applications. These pre-trained models have become valuable assets for researchers and practitioners, empowering them to tackle complex language tasks with greater efficiency and accuracy.

As the field of NLP continues to evolve, BERT, GPT, and other pre-trained models will likely continue to shape the way we process, understand, and generate textual data. Their contributions have accelerated progress in numerous NLP applications and hold immense potential for future advancements in the field.

Downstream Tasks:

In transfer learning, the target task for which the pre-trained model is adapted is referred to as the downstream task. The pre-trained model's knowledge and representations are fine-tuned to improve performance on this specific task.

In the realm of transfer learning, downstream tasks play a crucial role in applying the knowledge and representations acquired from pre-trained models to specific real-world applications. In transfer learning, a pre-trained model is adapted or fine-tuned on a target task, known as the downstream task, to improve its performance in that specific domain. This approach allows researchers and practitioners to leverage the rich knowledge and representations encoded in pre-trained models and achieve remarkable results with reduced training time and computational resources.

The concept of downstream tasks can be better understood by considering an example. Suppose we have a pre-trained model, such as BERT or GPT, that has been trained on a large corpus of general text data. This model has learned intricate patterns, semantic relationships, and syntactic structures inherent in the language. However, to utilize this pre-trained model for a specific task, such as sentiment analysis or named entity recognition, fine-tuning is required.

In the context of transfer learning, the pre-trained model is treated as the upstream model, which serves as a knowledge repository. The knowledge captured in the upstream model is then transferred and fine-tuned on the downstream task, which is the target application of interest. The fine-tuning process involves updating the model's parameters to adapt it to the specific task while preserving the learned representations from the pre-training phase.

For example, consider the task of sentiment analysis, where the goal is to determine the sentiment expressed in a given text. By fine-tuning a pre-trained language model like BERT on a sentiment analysis dataset, the model can effectively learn to understand sentiment-related patterns, word associations, and contextual cues specific to this task. The fine-tuned model becomes tailored to sentiment analysis, improving its performance compared to training a model from scratch.

Another example is named entity recognition (NER), which involves identifying and classifying named entities such as person names, locations, or organizations in text. By fine-tuning a pre-trained model like BERT on a labeled NER dataset, the model can learn to recognize and classify named entities accurately. The pre-trained model's understanding of language and contextual information greatly facilitates the NER task, leading to improved performance.

The beauty of downstream tasks lies in their ability to adapt the pre-trained model's knowledge to specific applications without starting the training process from scratch. The pre-trained model acts as a foundation, capturing general language knowledge, while the fine-tuning process tailors the model to the nuances and intricacies of the downstream task.

Downstream tasks span various domains, including computer vision, natural language processing, speech recognition, and more. In computer vision, pre-trained models like ResNet or VGG can be fine-tuned for object recognition or image segmentation tasks. In speech recognition, pre-trained models like DeepSpeech can be fine-tuned to transcribe speech in specific domains or languages. The possibilities are vast and extend to numerous real-world applications.

Downstream tasks in transfer learning empower researchers and practitioners to adapt pre-trained models to specific domains and applications, harnessing the knowledge and representations acquired from extensive pre-training. By fine-tuning the pre-trained models on the target tasks, they can achieve superior performance, reduced training time, and increased efficiency compared to starting the training process from scratch.

Application Domains:

Transfer learning and pre-trained models find applications in various domains, including computer vision, natural language processing, recommendation systems, and speech recognition. They have been used in tasks such as object detection, image segmentation, sentiment analysis, text classification, and more.

Transfer learning and pre-trained models have revolutionized various domains by providing powerful tools and frameworks for solving complex problems efficiently. These techniques find applications in diverse fields, including computer vision, natural language processing (NLP), recommendation systems, and speech recognition. By leveraging transfer learning and pre-trained models, researchers and practitioners can tackle tasks such as object detection, image segmentation, sentiment analysis, text classification, and more with remarkable accuracy and efficiency.

In the domain of computer vision, transfer learning has played a significant role in advancing state-of-the-art performance in various tasks. For instance, pre-trained models like ResNet, Inception, and MobileNet, trained on massive image datasets such as ImageNet, have demonstrated exceptional capabilities in object detection and image classification. By fine-tuning these pre-trained models on specific datasets, researchers can swiftly adapt them to new domains and achieve superior results. This has been instrumental in applications like autonomous driving, surveillance systems, and medical imaging.

In natural language processing, transfer learning has transformed the field by enabling sophisticated language understanding and generation. Pre-trained models like BERT (Bidirectional Encoder Representations from Transformers) and GPT (Generative Pre-trained Transformer) have revolutionized tasks such as sentiment analysis, text classification, named entity recognition, and machine translation. These models capture the complexities of language and provide contextual understanding, allowing researchers to build robust NLP systems with reduced training time and enhanced performance.

Recommendation systems heavily rely on transfer learning and pre-trained models to provide personalized recommendations to users. By utilizing pre-trained models trained on vast amounts of user interaction data, these systems can understand user preferences, behavior, and item similarities. This allows them to make accurate recommendations, enhance user experiences, and improve business outcomes. Whether it's suggesting movies, products, or news articles, transfer learning has proven to be a valuable tool in building effective recommendation systems.

Speech recognition is another domain where transfer learning and pre-trained models have made significant contributions. Models like DeepSpeech, pre-trained on large-scale speech datasets, have achieved state-of-the-art performance in transcription tasks. By fine-tuning these models on domain-specific speech data, researchers can develop speech recognition systems that excel in diverse applications, including virtual assistants, transcription services, and voice-controlled devices.

The application domains of transfer learning and pre-trained models extend beyond these examples. These techniques have been successfully employed in tasks such as image segmentation, document understanding, anomaly detection, and more. The versatility of transfer learning and the availability of pre-trained models provide researchers and practitioners with powerful resources to address complex problems across various domains.

By leveraging the knowledge and insights encoded in pre-trained models and fine-tuning them on specific tasks, researchers can save computational resources, reduce training time, and achieve exceptional performance. The transfer of learned representations and domain knowledge enables efficient learning in data-scarce scenarios and allows for more accurate predictions and decision-making.

In conclusion, transfer learning and pre-trained models have revolutionized multiple domains by providing efficient solutions to complex problems. From computer vision to natural language processing, recommendation systems, and speech recognition, these techniques have been instrumental in achieving state-of-the-art performance in tasks such as object detection, sentiment analysis, text classification, and more. By leveraging the power of transfer learning and pre-trained models, researchers and practitioners can unlock new possibilities and drive advancements in a wide range of applications.

Knowledge Transfer:

The fundamental idea behind transfer learning is to transfer knowledge and representations learned from one task to another. The pre-trained model acts as a source of knowledge, allowing the target task to benefit from the insights gained during pre-training.

Transfer learning, a fundamental concept in machine learning, enables the transfer of knowledge and representations acquired from one task to another. By leveraging pre-trained models, researchers and practitioners can harness the insights gained from extensive training on large-scale datasets and apply them to new, related tasks. This transfer of knowledge empowers the target task by providing a head start and facilitating more efficient and effective learning.

At the core of transfer learning lies the idea that the knowledge acquired from solving a source task can be transferred to improve the learning of a target task. The pre-trained model, which has already undergone extensive training on a source task, serves as a source of valuable knowledge and representations. These learned features capture important patterns, relationships, and representations that are useful for a wide range of related tasks.

To illustrate this concept, let's consider the example of image classification. Suppose a pre-trained model has been trained on a large dataset like ImageNet, which contains millions of labeled images across various categories. This model has already learned to recognize and extract low-level features such as edges, textures, and shapes. By transferring this knowledge to a target task, such as classifying different species of flowers, the model can leverage its understanding of basic visual features to quickly adapt to the new task. This significantly reduces the training time and computational resources required for the target task.

Transfer learning becomes particularly valuable when the target task has limited available data. In many real-world scenarios, obtaining large labeled datasets for specific tasks can be expensive or time-consuming. However, by utilizing a pre-trained model, researchers can overcome the data scarcity problem and still achieve impressive performance on the target task. The pre-trained model has already captured general knowledge from the source task and can generalize well to the target task, even with limited data.

Another advantage of knowledge transfer is the ability to transfer insights gained from one domain to another. For instance, a pre-trained model trained on a large dataset of general text can be adapted to a specific domain, such as medical text or legal documents. The model has already learned semantic relationships, contextual understanding, and syntactic structures from the source task, which can be invaluable for processing and understanding domain-specific texts in the target task.

Transfer learning can be applied at various levels of the neural network architecture. For example, the entire pre-trained model can be used as a feature extractor, where the learned representations from the earlier layers are utilized as input features for a new task-specific model. Alternatively, only a portion of the pre-trained model can be fine-tuned, keeping some layers frozen while modifying or adding new layers specific to the target task. This fine-tuning process allows the model to adapt and specialize in the nuances of the target task while retaining the general knowledge captured by the pre-trained model.

The benefits of knowledge transfer extend beyond the realm of computer vision. Transfer learning has been successfully applied to natural language processing tasks, such as sentiment analysis, text classification, machine translation, and named entity recognition. By transferring knowledge from large-scale language models like BERT or GPT, researchers can leverage the semantic understanding and contextual information learned during pre-training to enhance performance on specific NLP tasks.

Transfer learning is a powerful technique that enables the transfer of knowledge and representations from one task to another. By utilizing pre-trained models, researchers and practitioners can leverage the insights gained from extensive pre-training on large-scale datasets. This knowledge transfer expedites learning in the target task, reduces the need for extensive data collection and training, and facilitates the application of machine learning in scenarios with limited data availability. Whether in computer vision, natural language processing, or other domains, transfer learning unlocks the potential for efficient and effective learning in a wide range of applications.

Performance Improvement:

By utilizing pre-trained models and fine-tuning them on specific tasks, researchers and practitioners can achieve better performance compared to starting from scratch. The learned representations and initial weights of the pre-trained models accelerate the learning process and improve the efficiency of training on the target task.

In the fast-paced world of machine learning, achieving high performance on complex tasks is a constant pursuit. To expedite this process and enhance the efficiency of training, researchers and practitioners have turned to the use of pre-trained models. By leveraging the learned representations and initial weights of these models, they can achieve substantial performance improvements compared to starting from scratch.

Pre-trained models are neural network models that have been trained on large-scale datasets, often containing millions of examples. These models have undergone extensive training on a source task, such as image classification or natural language processing, and have acquired valuable knowledge and representations of the data. This knowledge is captured in the form of learned features, which capture important patterns, relationships, and semantic understanding.

One key advantage of utilizing pre-trained models is that they accelerate the learning process on target tasks. Instead of initializing the model from scratch and training it on a limited dataset, researchers can initialize the model with the learned weights and representations from the pre-trained model. This initialization provides the model with a head start, as it already possesses a good understanding of the data and has learned relevant features. As a result, the model requires fewer training iterations to converge and can achieve higher performance in a shorter amount of time.

To further enhance the performance of the pre-trained model on the target task, a process called fine-tuning is employed. Fine-tuning involves updating the pre-trained model's parameters using the target task's specific data. While the early layers of the model, known as the base layers, are typically kept frozen to preserve the learned general features, the later layers, known as the task-specific layers, are modified or added to adapt the model to the target task. This fine-tuning process allows the model to specialize in the nuances of the target task, leveraging its pre-existing knowledge to achieve superior performance.

Let's consider an example to illustrate the benefits of utilizing pre-trained models for performance improvement. In the field of computer vision, pre-trained models trained on large datasets like ImageNet have achieved remarkable performance on image classification tasks. By utilizing such a pre-trained model and fine-tuning it on a specific image classification task, researchers can benefit from the pre-trained model's ability to recognize and extract low-level features, such as edges, textures, and shapes. This significantly enhances the performance on the target task, as the model has already learned to capture essential visual patterns and can focus on refining its understanding of the task-specific classes.

The performance improvement achieved through the use of pre-trained models is not limited to computer vision. In natural language processing tasks, models like BERT (Bidirectional Encoder Representations from Transformers) and GPT (Generative Pre-trained Transformer) have revolutionized performance in tasks such as sentiment analysis, text classification, and machine translation. By leveraging the contextual understanding and semantic representations learned during pre-training, researchers can fine-tune these models on specific NLP tasks and achieve state-of-the-art results.

The utilization of pre-trained models and fine-tuning has emerged as a powerful strategy for performance improvement in machine learning. By leveraging the learned representations and initial weights of these models, researchers and practitioners can accelerate the learning process, reduce the need for extensive data collection and training, and achieve superior performance on target tasks. Whether in computer vision, natural language processing, or other domains, the power of pre-trained models lies in their ability to enhance efficiency and unlock the full potential of machine learning algorithms.

4.6 Hybrid Approaches and Ensemble Methods

In the ever-evolving field of machine learning, researchers and practitioners are continually exploring new techniques to improve the performance and robustness of models. Two powerful strategies that have emerged are hybrid approaches and ensemble methods. These approaches leverage the strengths of multiple models or techniques to achieve superior results. Let's delve deeper into these concepts and explore their applications.

Hybrid Approaches:

Hybrid approaches refer to the combination of different algorithms or methodologies to address specific challenges or tasks. They capitalize on the unique strengths of each approach, resulting in a more comprehensive and effective solution. Hybrid models often integrate multiple learning techniques, such as supervised and unsupervised learning, or combine different algorithms to achieve a desired outcome.

One example of a hybrid approach is the combination of rule-based systems with machine learning models. Rule-based systems rely on explicitly defined rules to make decisions, while machine learning models learn patterns from data. By combining the interpretability and human expertise of rule-based systems with the predictive power of machine learning models, hybrid approaches can enhance decision-making in complex domains. For instance, in healthcare, a hybrid approach could be used to diagnose diseases by incorporating medical expert rules with data-driven machine learning algorithms.

Another application of hybrid approaches is the integration of symbolic reasoning and deep learning. Symbolic reasoning, which uses logic and symbolic representations, excels at symbolic manipulation and logical inference, while deep learning models excel at learning complex patterns from large amounts of data. By combining these approaches, researchers aim to leverage the strengths of symbolic reasoning in explainability and logical reasoning, while harnessing the power of deep learning for pattern recognition and feature extraction.

Ensemble Methods:

Ensemble methods, on the other hand, focus on combining multiple models to create a stronger and more accurate prediction. Instead of relying on a single model, ensemble methods leverage the diversity and collective intelligence of multiple models to achieve better generalization and robustness.

One popular ensemble method is the bagging (bootstrap aggregating) technique, which involves training multiple models on different subsets of the training data and aggregating their predictions. The idea behind bagging is that the models will have different sources of randomness, leading to diverse predictions. By averaging or voting on the predictions of these models, the ensemble can make more accurate and robust predictions. Random Forest is an example of an ensemble method that utilizes the bagging technique with decision tree models.

Another ensemble method is boosting, which focuses on sequentially training models that correct the mistakes made by previous models. Each subsequent model in the ensemble is trained to emphasize the data points that were misclassified by the previous models, thus improving the overall performance. Gradient Boosting Machines (GBMs) and AdaBoost are examples of boosting algorithms widely used in machine learning.

Ensemble methods can also include more sophisticated techniques such as stacking or neural network ensembles, where multiple models are combined using meta-learners or neural network architectures. These techniques allow the models to learn from each other's predictions and make more accurate and robust predictions as a collective.

The key advantage of ensemble methods is their ability to reduce bias, increase stability, and improve generalization by leveraging the diversity and collective wisdom of multiple models. Ensemble methods have been successfully applied in various domains, including image classification, natural language processing, and fraud detection, to name just a few.

Hybrid Approaches:

Hybrid approaches involve combining different algorithms or methodologies to address specific challenges or tasks. By leveraging the strengths of each approach, hybrid models aim to create more comprehensive and effective solutions. Examples of hybrid approaches include combining rule-based systems with machine learning models or integrating symbolic reasoning with deep learning.

It represents a powerful paradigm in the field of machine learning, as they allow researchers and practitioners to leverage the strengths of different algorithms and methodologies to address complex challenges. By combining multiple approaches, hybrid models can provide more comprehensive and effective solutions, pushing the boundaries of what can be achieved in various domains.

One example of a hybrid approach is the combination of rule-based systems with machine learning models. Rule-based systems use a set of predefined rules and logic to make decisions or perform tasks. While they are intuitive and interpretable, they often struggle with handling uncertainty and learning from data. On the other hand, machine learning models excel at learning patterns and making predictions from large datasets but may lack interpretability. By integrating rule-based systems with machine learning models, the resulting hybrid model can benefit from the interpretability of rules and the learning capabilities of machine learning algorithms. This approach has been applied in various domains, such as healthcare, finance, and customer service, where the interpretability of decisions is crucial.

Another example of a hybrid approach is the integration of symbolic reasoning with deep learning. Symbolic reasoning involves manipulating symbols and logic to derive new knowledge or make inferences. Deep learning, on the other hand, relies on neural networks to learn representations and extract patterns from large datasets. By combining symbolic reasoning with deep learning, researchers can harness the power of neural networks to learn complex representations while incorporating logical rules and constraints. This hybrid approach has been used in natural language understanding, knowledge graphs, and robotics, where reasoning and understanding symbolic relationships are essential.

Hybrid approaches also extend beyond the combination of different algorithms. They can involve integrating multiple data modalities, such as text, images, and sensor data, to tackle multimodal tasks. For example, in autonomous driving, a hybrid approach can combine vision-based object detection with sensor data fusion to improve object recognition and enable safer decision-making.

The advantages of hybrid approaches are manifold. By leveraging the strengths of different algorithms or methodologies, hybrid models can overcome limitations or weaknesses inherent in individual approaches. They can enhance interpretability, robustness, and generalization while achieving higher accuracy and performance. Hybrid approaches also allow researchers to explore new possibilities and develop novel solutions by combining disparate techniques.

However, hybrid approaches come with their own set of challenges. Integrating different algorithms or methodologies requires careful consideration of compatibility, scalability, and computational resources. Ensuring seamless integration and efficient coordination among components can be complex and time-consuming. Moreover, selecting the appropriate combination of approaches and optimizing their parameters pose additional challenges that require expertise and thorough experimentation.

Hybrid approaches offer a powerful means of addressing complex challenges in machine learning. By combining different algorithms, methodologies, or data modalities, hybrid models can achieve more comprehensive and effective solutions. Whether it is the integration of rule-based systems with machine learning, symbolic reasoning with deep learning, or the fusion of multiple data modalities, hybrid approaches have the potential to push the boundaries of what can be accomplished in various domains. As researchers and practitioners continue to explore and develop new hybrid models, the field of machine learning will undoubtedly benefit from their increased interpretability, accuracy, and ability to tackle complex tasks.

Ensemble Methods:

Ensemble methods focus on combining multiple models to create a stronger and more accurate prediction. Instead of relying on a single model, ensemble methods leverage the diversity and collective intelligence of multiple models to improve generalization and robustness. Bagging, boosting, stacking, and neural network ensembles are common techniques used in ensemble methods.

It represents a powerful approach in the field of machine learning, where the collective intelligence of multiple models is harnessed to achieve stronger and more accurate predictions. Unlike traditional approaches that rely on a single model, ensemble methods leverage the diversity and combination of multiple models to enhance generalization and robustness, leading to improved performance across various domains.

One popular ensemble technique is bagging, which stands for bootstrap aggregating. Bagging involves creating multiple subsets of the training data by sampling with replacement, training individual models on each subset, and combining their predictions through averaging or voting. By introducing randomness in the training process and aggregating the predictions of multiple models, bagging reduces overfitting and improves the stability and accuracy of the final prediction. An example of bagging is the random forest algorithm, which combines an ensemble of decision trees to make predictions in tasks such as classification and regression.

Boosting is another widely used ensemble technique that focuses on iteratively improving the performance of weak learners. Boosting starts with a base model and assigns higher weights to misclassified instances, allowing subsequent models to focus on those instances and learn from their mistakes. The final prediction is then made by combining the predictions of all the models. Gradient Boosting and AdaBoost are popular boosting algorithms that have demonstrated remarkable performance in various applications, including object detection, text classification, and recommendation systems.

Stacking, also known as stacked generalization, involves training multiple models on the same dataset and then combining their predictions through a meta-model. The meta-model learns to weigh the predictions of the individual models based on their performance, effectively creating a higher-level model that leverages the collective knowledge of the base models. Stacking has been successfully used in tasks such as sentiment analysis, image recognition, and anomaly detection.

Ensemble methods can also be applied to neural networks, leading to the development of neural network ensembles. In this approach, multiple neural network models with different architectures or initializations are trained independently, and their predictions are combined through averaging or voting. Neural network ensembles have shown to improve generalization, robustness, and accuracy in various applications, including computer vision, natural language processing, and speech recognition.

Ensemble methods offer several advantages over individual models. By combining the predictions of multiple models, ensemble methods can reduce the impact of biases and errors inherent in individual models, leading to improved accuracy and robustness. They can also handle complex and diverse data patterns by capturing different aspects of the underlying distribution. Ensemble methods are particularly effective when individual models have diverse strengths and weaknesses, as they can leverage the collective intelligence of the ensemble to compensate for individual model limitations.

However, employing ensemble methods comes with certain challenges. Building and training multiple models can be computationally intensive and require significant resources. Ensuring diversity among the models is crucial to obtain accurate and reliable ensemble predictions. Care must be taken to avoid overfitting and maintain a good balance between bias and variance. Furthermore, ensemble methods may introduce additional complexity in model interpretation and may require more effort in model selection and tuning.

Ensemble methods offer a powerful approach to improve the performance and robustness of machine learning models. By combining the predictions of multiple models through techniques such as bagging, boosting, stacking, and neural network ensembles, ensemble methods can achieve higher accuracy, better generalization, and increased stability. These techniques have found successful applications in a wide range of domains, including classification, regression, object detection, and natural language processing. As researchers continue to explore and develop new ensemble methods, the field of machine learning will undoubtedly benefit from their ability to leverage the collective intelligence of multiple models and tackle complex tasks with increased accuracy and reliability.

Bagging:

Bagging, short for bootstrap aggregating, involves training multiple models on different subsets of the training data and aggregating their predictions. The diversity among the models is achieved through random sampling or bootstrap resampling of the training data. Random Forest is an example of an ensemble method that uses bagging with decision tree models.

To create diverse models in bagging, each model is trained on a different subset of the training data. This subset is typically obtained through random sampling or bootstrap resampling, where samples are drawn with replacement from the original training data. By allowing samples to appear multiple times or not at all in the subsets, bagging introduces variations in the training data and encourages models to learn different aspects of the underlying distribution.

One popular example of an ensemble method that uses bagging is the Random Forest algorithm. Random Forest combines the power of bagging with decision tree models. In this approach, multiple decision trees are trained on different subsets of the training data, and their predictions are aggregated to make the final prediction. Each decision tree in the Random Forest is trained on a subset of features as well, further enhancing the diversity among the models.

The ensemble predictions in bagging are typically combined through averaging or voting. In regression tasks, the predictions of individual models are averaged to obtain the final prediction. In classification tasks, voting is used, where each model's prediction is considered as a vote, and the majority prediction is chosen as the final prediction.

Bagging offers several benefits in terms of improving prediction accuracy and reducing variance. By training models on different subsets of the data, bagging helps to alleviate the problem of overfitting, where models become too specialized to the training data and perform poorly on new, unseen data. The averaging or voting of predictions from diverse models in bagging helps to stabilize the predictions and make them more robust.

Moreover, bagging allows for parallelization, as each model can be trained independently on its subset of the data. This makes bagging computationally efficient and scalable, especially for large datasets.

An illustrative example of bagging can be seen in the field of medical diagnosis. Suppose a dataset contains medical records of patients, including various features such as age, symptoms, and laboratory results. By applying bagging with decision tree models, multiple models can be trained on different subsets of patients' records. Each model can learn different patterns or associations among the features and make predictions about the diagnosis of a patient based on their input information. The final prediction can be obtained by aggregating the predictions of all the models, providing a more accurate and reliable diagnosis.

Bagging is a powerful ensemble method that combines the predictions of multiple models trained on different subsets of the training data. By introducing randomness and diversity in the training process, bagging improves prediction accuracy, reduces overfitting, and enhances the stability of predictions. The Random Forest algorithm is a well-known example of bagging that uses decision tree models. With its ability to tackle complex problems and improve generalization, bagging has found applications in various domains, including medical diagnosis, finance, and customer churn prediction.

Boosting:

Boosting is a technique in which models are trained sequentially, with each subsequent model correcting the mistakes made by the previous models. The focus is on emphasizing the data points that were misclassified by the previous models, leading to improved overall performance. Gradient Boosting Machines (GBMs) and AdaBoost are popular boosting algorithms.

Boosting is a powerful ensemble learning technique that aims to improve the performance of machine learning models by training them sequentially and focusing on the samples that were misclassified by previous models. The fundamental idea behind boosting is to create a strong and accurate model by combining the strengths of multiple weak models.

In boosting, the models are trained in iterations, and at each iteration, more emphasis is given to the samples that were misclassified or had higher prediction errors in the previous iterations. By focusing on these challenging samples, boosting algorithms aim to correct the mistakes made by the previous models and improve the overall performance.

One popular boosting algorithm is AdaBoost (Adaptive Boosting). AdaBoost assigns weights to each training sample, with initially equal weights for all samples. In each iteration, a weak model, also known as a base learner, is trained on the weighted samples. After each iteration, the weights are updated to give more importance to the misclassified samples. Subsequent weak models are then trained on the updated weighted samples, giving more attention to the challenging samples. The final prediction is obtained by combining the predictions of all the weak models, with each model's contribution weighted based on its performance.

Another widely used boosting algorithm is Gradient Boosting Machines (GBMs). GBMs build models in a similar sequential manner but use gradient descent optimization to iteratively minimize the loss function. In each iteration, a weak model is trained to approximate the negative gradient of the loss function with respect to the previous model's predictions. The predictions of all the weak models are combined to obtain the final prediction. GBMs are known for their ability to handle complex datasets and capture intricate patterns.

Boosting algorithms have proven to be effective in a variety of applications. One such example is in face detection. In face detection tasks, the boosting algorithm can be used to train a cascade of weak classifiers, each specialized in detecting a particular facial feature, such as the eyes, nose, or mouth. By focusing on the misclassified samples and iteratively improving the classifiers, boosting helps to achieve accurate and robust face detection.

Another example is in predicting customer churn in the telecommunications industry. Boosting algorithms can be employed to train models that learn from customer behavior and historical data to predict whether a customer is likely to churn or not. By assigning more weight to misclassified churned customers and adjusting the subsequent models accordingly, boosting algorithms can improve the accuracy of churn prediction, enabling proactive customer retention strategies.

Boosting algorithms offer several advantages. They have the ability to handle complex datasets, capture non-linear relationships, and effectively deal with imbalanced data. Boosting also helps to reduce bias and variance in the models, leading to better generalization and improved performance on unseen data.

Boosting is a powerful ensemble learning technique that trains models sequentially, focusing on the challenging samples that were misclassified by previous models. AdaBoost and Gradient Boosting Machines are popular boosting algorithms that have been successfully applied in various domains. By leveraging the strengths of weak models and iteratively correcting their mistakes, boosting algorithms improve the overall performance and provide accurate predictions. Whether in face detection, customer churn prediction, or other applications, boosting algorithms play a significant role in enhancing machine learning models' capabilities.

Stacking:

Stacking involves combining the predictions of multiple models using a meta-learner. The meta-learner learns to make predictions based on the outputs of the individual models. It can be a separate model or an algorithm that combines the predictions using statistical techniques.

Stacking, also known as stacked generalization, is an advanced ensemble learning technique that involves combining the predictions of multiple models using a meta-learner. Unlike other ensemble methods where the predictions are simply aggregated, stacking takes it a step further by training a meta-learner that learns to make predictions based on the outputs of the individual models.

In the stacking process, multiple base models, also known as level-0 models, are trained on the training data. Each base model learns to make predictions based on different features or has different learning strategies. These base models can be diverse, such as decision trees, support vector machines, or neural networks. Each base model generates its predictions on the training data.

The next step is to use these base models' predictions as inputs to train a meta-learner, also known as a level-1 model. The meta-learner is responsible for combining the predictions of the base models to make the final prediction. The meta-learner can be a separate model, such as a logistic regression model or a neural network, or an algorithm that combines the predictions using statistical techniques like weighted averaging or voting.

By training a meta-learner, stacking aims to leverage the complementary strengths of the base models and improve the overall prediction accuracy. The meta-learner learns to weigh the predictions of the base models and make the final prediction based on their collective outputs. This allows stacking to capture higher-order relationships or interactions between the base models' predictions, leading to improved performance.

To illustrate the concept of stacking, let's consider an example in the field of credit risk assessment. Suppose we have a dataset containing information about individuals' credit profiles, such as their income, debt, credit history, and other relevant features. We want to build a predictive model that accurately classifies individuals as low risk or high risk based on their creditworthiness.

In stacking, we can start by training multiple base models, such as a decision tree, a random forest, and a support vector machine, on the credit risk dataset. Each base model generates its predictions on the training data, indicating whether an individual is classified as low risk or high risk.

Next, we use these base models' predictions as inputs to train the meta-learner, which could be a logistic regression model. The meta-learner takes the predictions from the base models as features and learns to make the final prediction on whether an individual is low risk or high risk. The meta-learner is trained on the training data, using the actual credit risk labels as the target variable.

Once the meta-learner is trained, we can use it to make predictions on new, unseen data. It takes the predictions from the base models as inputs, combines them based on the learned weights or rules, and outputs the final prediction on the individual's credit risk.

Stacking offers several advantages. It can improve prediction accuracy by leveraging the collective knowledge of multiple base models. It also allows for the exploration of complex relationships or interactions between the base models' predictions. Additionally, stacking can handle diverse types of models and is flexible in terms of the choice of base models and the meta-learner.

Stacking is an ensemble learning technique that combines the predictions of multiple models using a meta-learner. By training a meta-learner, stacking leverages the strengths of the base models and captures higher-order relationships between their predictions. In domains such as credit risk assessment, customer churn prediction, or stock market forecasting, stacking has been shown to improve prediction accuracy and provide more reliable and robust predictions.

Neural Network Ensembles:

Neural network ensembles utilize multiple neural network models in combination to improve prediction accuracy and robustness. The individual neural networks can have different architectures, initialization weights, or training strategies. The ensemble combines their predictions to make a final prediction, often achieving better performance than a single neural network.

The individual neural networks in the ensemble can have different architectures, initialization weights, or training strategies. This diversity among the models helps to capture different aspects of the underlying data distribution and improve the overall performance of the ensemble.

To understand the concept of neural network ensembles, let's consider an example in the field of image classification. Suppose we have a dataset of images with various objects, and we want to build a neural network model that can accurately classify these images into different categories, such as cats, dogs, and cars.

Rather than training a single neural network on the entire dataset, we can create an ensemble of neural networks. Each individual neural network in the ensemble is trained on a subset of the data or using a different initialization, hyperparameters, or training strategy. This introduces diversity among the models, allowing them to capture different patterns or variations in the images.

Once the individual neural networks are trained, their predictions are combined to make the final prediction. This can be done through various methods such as averaging the probabilities predicted by each network or using more advanced techniques like weighted averaging or majority voting.

By combining the predictions of multiple neural networks, the ensemble can mitigate the impact of individual network's weaknesses or biases and take advantage of their collective knowledge. The ensemble is often able to make more accurate and robust predictions compared to a single neural network.

The benefits of using neural network ensembles are numerous. First, ensembles can reduce the risk of overfitting by averaging out the individual network's errors. The diversity among the models ensures that the ensemble is not overly reliant on a single network's predictions. Second, ensembles can improve generalization by capturing a wider range of patterns and variations in the data. Third, ensembles are more resistant to adversarial attacks, as the diversity among the models makes it harder for an attacker to exploit a single network's vulnerabilities.

Neural network ensembles have been successfully applied in various domains, including image classification, object detection, natural language processing, and anomaly detection. For example, in image classification tasks, ensembles such as the popular "AlexNet ensemble" have achieved state-of-the-art performance on benchmark datasets like ImageNet.

Neural network ensembles are a powerful technique that combines the predictions of multiple neural network models to improve prediction accuracy and robustness. By leveraging the collective knowledge and diversity among the models, ensembles can overcome the limitations of individual networks and achieve better performance. In domains where accurate and reliable predictions are crucial, such as medical diagnosis, autonomous driving, or fraud detection, neural network ensembles are an effective approach to enhance the performance of machine learning models.

Bias Reduction and Generalization:

Ensemble methods reduce bias and improve generalization by leveraging the diversity and collective wisdom of multiple models. The combination of different models helps to compensate for individual model weaknesses and reduce the impact of random noise. Ensemble methods often yield more accurate and robust predictions compared to using a single model.

Bias reduction and generalization are critical concepts in machine learning, and ensemble methods play a significant role in achieving these objectives. Ensemble methods leverage the diversity and collective wisdom of multiple models to reduce bias and improve generalization, resulting in more accurate and robust predictions.

Bias refers to the tendency of a model to consistently deviate from the true values or ground truth. A biased model fails to capture the underlying patterns and relationships in the data, leading to inaccurate predictions. On the other hand, generalization refers to the ability of a model to perform well on unseen data, beyond the training set. A model with poor generalization may perform well on the training data but fail to make accurate predictions on new, unseen data.

Ensemble methods address these issues by combining the predictions of multiple models, each trained on different subsets of the data or using different algorithms, architectures, or hyperparameters. This diversity among the models helps to compensate for individual model weaknesses and reduces the impact of random noise or fluctuations in the data.

To illustrate the concept of bias reduction and generalization through ensemble methods, let's consider an example in the field of object detection. Suppose we want to build a model that can accurately detect various objects in images, such as cars, pedestrians, and traffic signs.

Instead of relying on a single model, we can create an ensemble of object detection models. Each model in the ensemble is trained on a different subset of the training data or uses a different architecture or hyperparameters. This diversity allows the ensemble to capture different aspects of the objects' appearances, variations, and contextual information.

When making predictions, the ensemble combines the predictions of the individual models. This can be done through methods such as averaging the bounding box coordinates or using more sophisticated techniques like weighted averaging or non-maximum suppression.

The ensemble's combined prediction is often more accurate and robust compared to the predictions of any single model. The diversity among the models helps to reduce bias by incorporating different perspectives and capturing a wider range of object variations and contexts. It also improves generalization by reducing the model's reliance on specific patterns in the training data, making the ensemble more adaptable to unseen objects or variations in the real world.

Ensemble methods have been successfully applied in various domains, including image recognition, natural language processing, and financial forecasting. For example, in image recognition tasks, ensemble methods such as the popular "ensemble of deep convolutional neural networks" have achieved top performance in competitions like the ImageNet Large Scale Visual Recognition Challenge.

Ensemble methods are powerful tools for reducing bias and improving generalization in machine learning. By combining the predictions of multiple models, ensemble methods leverage the diversity and collective wisdom of the models to make more accurate and robust predictions. This approach is particularly effective when individual models have limitations or when the data contains random noise or variations. Ensemble methods have demonstrated their success in various domains, and their application continues to advance the field of machine learning by addressing bias and improving generalization.

Application Domains:

Hybrid approaches and ensemble methods find applications in various domains, including computer vision, natural language processing, recommendation systems, fraud detection, and more. They have been used for tasks such as image classification, object detection, sentiment analysis, text generation, and fraud detection, among others.

Hybrid approaches and ensemble methods are versatile techniques that find applications in a wide range of domains, revolutionizing various fields within machine learning and artificial intelligence. These approaches have been successfully employed in domains such as computer vision, natural language processing, recommendation systems, fraud detection, and more. They have proven to be valuable tools for addressing complex challenges and achieving state-of-the-art performance in diverse tasks.

One of the domains where hybrid approaches and ensemble methods have made significant contributions is computer vision. Computer vision involves tasks such as image classification, object detection, and image segmentation. By combining different algorithms or methodologies, hybrid models can leverage the strengths of each approach to improve accuracy and robustness. For example, in object detection, a hybrid model may combine region proposal algorithms, such as Selective Search or EdgeBoxes, with deep learning models like Faster R-CNN or YOLO to achieve precise and efficient detection of objects in images.

In the realm of natural language processing (NLP), hybrid approaches and ensemble methods have demonstrated remarkable results. NLP tasks such as sentiment analysis, text generation, and machine translation benefit from combining rule-based systems with machine learning models or integrating symbolic reasoning with deep learning. For instance, a hybrid model for sentiment analysis may utilize a rule-based approach to capture explicit sentiment cues while employing a deep learning model like recurrent neural networks or transformers to capture contextual information and semantic nuances.

Recommendation systems, which play a crucial role in personalized user experiences, have greatly benefited from hybrid approaches and ensemble methods. These systems aim to suggest relevant items or content to users based on their preferences and behavior. Hybrid models can combine collaborative filtering techniques with content-based filtering or employ ensemble methods to aggregate predictions from multiple recommendation algorithms. By leveraging the strengths of different approaches, hybrid models can provide more accurate and diverse recommendations to users, leading to improved user satisfaction and engagement.

Fraud detection is another domain where hybrid approaches and ensemble methods have proven invaluable. Detecting fraudulent activities in financial transactions requires sophisticated techniques that can effectively distinguish between legitimate and fraudulent patterns. Hybrid models can combine traditional rule-based systems with machine learning algorithms to identify suspicious patterns, detect anomalies, and flag potential fraudulent activities. Ensemble methods, such as random forests or gradient boosting, can aggregate predictions from multiple models to improve the accuracy and reliability of fraud detection systems.

These are just a few examples of the diverse applications of hybrid approaches and ensemble methods. These techniques have been successfully applied in domains ranging from computer vision and NLP to recommendation systems and fraud detection. By combining different algorithms, methodologies, or models, hybrid approaches offer comprehensive and effective solutions to complex problems. Ensemble methods, on the other hand, leverage the collective wisdom of multiple models to improve accuracy, generalization, and robustness.

Hybrid approaches and ensemble methods have found extensive applications in various domains, enhancing the capabilities of machine learning and artificial intelligence systems. Their flexibility and ability to leverage the strengths of different approaches make them invaluable in tackling complex challenges and achieving state-of-the-art performance. As the field continues to advance, hybrid approaches and ensemble methods will continue to play a pivotal role in pushing the boundaries of what is possible in machine learning and driving innovations across multiple domains.

Performance Improvement:

 By leveraging hybrid approaches and ensemble methods, researchers and practitioners can achieve better performance compared to using a single model or starting from scratch. The combination of different models or techniques enhances the learning process, accelerates convergence, and improves the efficiency of training on the target task. Ensemble methods, in particular, leverage the collective intelligence of multiple models to make more accurate and robust predictions.

Performance improvement is a critical goal in the field of machine learning, and researchers and practitioners are constantly striving to enhance the effectiveness and efficiency of their models. One powerful approach that has proven to be highly effective in achieving performance improvement is the use of hybrid approaches and ensemble methods. By combining different models or techniques, these approaches can surpass the performance of individual models and yield more accurate and robust predictions.

One key advantage of using hybrid approaches and ensemble methods is that they leverage the strengths of different models or techniques to enhance the learning process. Each model or technique may have its own strengths and weaknesses, and by combining them, practitioners can compensate for the limitations of individual models and harness their collective power. This leads to improved performance in terms of accuracy, generalization, and robustness.

Ensemble methods, in particular, have gained significant popularity due to their ability to improve performance through the aggregation of multiple models. By combining predictions from different models, ensemble methods can reduce bias, increase robustness, and improve the overall accuracy of the predictions. Ensemble methods can be applied in various ways, such as using bagging, boosting, or stacking techniques.

Bagging is a technique in which multiple models are trained on different subsets of the training data, and their predictions are aggregated to make a final prediction. An example of a popular ensemble method that utilizes bagging is the Random Forest algorithm. It combines multiple decision tree models trained on different subsets of the data and aggregates their predictions to achieve better performance in tasks such as classification and regression.

Boosting, on the other hand, focuses on sequentially training models where each subsequent model corrects the mistakes made by the previous models. The idea is to emphasize the data points that were misclassified by the previous models, leading to improved overall performance. Gradient Boosting Machines (GBMs) and AdaBoost are well-known boosting algorithms that have achieved remarkable results in various domains.

Stacking is another ensemble method that involves combining the predictions of multiple models using a meta-learner. The meta-learner learns to make predictions based on the outputs of the individual models. It can be a separate model or an algorithm that combines the predictions using statistical techniques. Stacking allows for a higher level of abstraction and can capture more complex patterns in the data.

These ensemble methods, along with hybrid approaches that combine different models or techniques, have been successfully applied in various domains and tasks, such as image classification, object detection, sentiment analysis, and more. By leveraging the collective intelligence of multiple models, researchers and practitioners can achieve performance improvement beyond what can be achieved with a single model.

In addition to improving performance, hybrid approaches and ensemble methods also offer other benefits, such as increased robustness to noise and outliers, better handling of complex or high-dimensional data, and reduced risk of overfitting. These advantages make them highly valuable in real-world applications where accurate and reliable predictions are crucial.

Hybrid approaches and ensemble methods have emerged as powerful techniques for performance improvement in machine learning. By combining different models or techniques, these approaches can enhance the learning process, accelerate convergence, and yield more accurate and robust predictions. Ensemble methods, in particular, leverage the collective intelligence of multiple models to improve performance, reduce bias, and increase robustness. By embracing these approaches, researchers and practitioners can push the boundaries of what is achievable in machine learning and drive advancements in various domains and applications.

Example: Object detection

An example that showcases the performance improvement achieved by hybrid approaches and ensemble methods can be seen in the field of object detection in computer vision.

Object detection is a challenging task that involves identifying and localizing objects within an image. Traditional methods often relied on handcrafted features and individual classifiers for different object categories. However, these approaches had limitations in terms of accuracy and robustness.

In recent years, hybrid approaches and ensemble methods have revolutionized object detection by leveraging the power of deep learning and combining multiple models. One notable example is the Faster R-CNN (Region-based Convolutional Neural Network) architecture, which incorporates both convolutional neural networks (CNNs) and region proposal networks (RPNs) in a unified framework.

The Faster R-CNN model consists of a CNN backbone, such as ResNet or VGG, which extracts high-level features from the input image. These features are then fed into the RPN, which generates potential object proposals. Finally, the region proposals are refined and classified by a network called the region classifier.

The beauty of the Faster R-CNN model lies in its ability to combine the strengths of both CNNs and RPNs. The CNN backbone is responsible for learning high-level representations of objects, while the RPN focuses on generating accurate region proposals. By combining these two components, Faster R-CNN achieves state-of-the-art performance in object detection tasks, surpassing the accuracy of individual models or handcrafted feature-based methods.

Another example of ensemble methods in object detection is the use of model ensembles. Rather than relying on a single model, researchers train multiple models with different architectures or training strategies. Each model learns to detect objects in a slightly different way, capturing unique patterns or aspects of the objects.

During inference, the predictions from individual models are combined to make a final decision. This aggregation of predictions helps to reduce bias and increase the robustness of the overall system. Ensembling can be done through simple techniques like majority voting or more complex methods such as weighted averaging or stacking.

Ensemble methods have been shown to significantly improve the accuracy and robustness of object detection systems. They are widely used in competitions such as the COCO (Common Objects in Context) and PASCAL VOC (Visual Object Classes) challenges, where top-performing teams often rely on ensembles of models to achieve the best results.

The application of hybrid approaches and ensemble methods in object detection demonstrates their ability to enhance performance. The combination of different models, architectures, or training strategies allows for improved accuracy, robustness, and generalization. By leveraging the strengths of multiple models, researchers and practitioners continue to push the boundaries of what is achievable in object detection and other complex tasks in computer vision.

Model Combination and Integration: Hybrid approaches and ensemble methods require careful model combination and integration techniques. This includes determining how to combine the predictions or decisions of different models, selecting appropriate weights or voting schemes, and handling model compatibility or diversity. These considerations play a crucial role in the success of hybrid approaches and ensemble methods.

Chapter 5

Model Development and Training

Overview:

5.1 Implementing AI Models with TensorFlow

5.2 Implementing AI Models with PyTorch

5.3 Handling Large-Scale Training and Distributed Computing

5.4 Model Evaluation and Validation Techniques

5.5 Hyperparameter Tuning and Optimization Strategies

Introduction:

Chapter 5 delves into the heart of artificial intelligence (AI) – the development and training of AI models. This is where the magic of AI comes to life, where abstract concepts turn into tangible algorithms capable of learning, predicting, and making decisions.

We will first explore two key tools for implementing AI models, TensorFlow and PyTorch. These powerful open-source libraries, backed by tech giants Google and Facebook respectively, are widely used in the AI community due to their flexibility and efficiency.

However, creating an AI model is only part of the process. The real challenge often comes when we need to handle large-scale training and distributed computing. As the size and complexity of our models grow, we will need to leverage multiple GPUs or even clusters of machines, introducing a whole new set of problems and solutions.

Once our models are trained, how do we measure their success? The section on model evaluation and validation techniques provides a guide to assessing a model's performance using methods like cross-validation and precision-recall analysis. The goal is to ensure our model is robust, accurate, and reliable. Lastly, no model is complete without the proper tuning. In the section on hyperparameter tuning and optimization strategies, we delve into the fine art of tweaking model parameters to improve performance, navigating the balance between underfitting and overfitting, and understanding the impact of each adjustment. By the end of this chapter, you will have a strong foundation in AI model development, equipped with the knowledge and skills to build, scale, evaluate, and optimize your own AI models. Let's begin this exciting journey.

5.1 Implementing AI Models with TensorFlow

TensorFlow is a popular open-source library developed by Google for building and training machine learning and deep learning models. It provides a high-level API for defining and training models, along with utilities for running computations on GPUs.

Artificial intelligence (AI) has rapidly moved from a niche discipline to a central component of contemporary technology across various fields. It's akin to the silent maestro, orchestrating the symphony of our digital lives, from our web search results to our movie recommendations. One cornerstone of this AI revolution is the deep learning framework, and in the pantheon of such frameworks, TensorFlow undeniably holds a position of prominence. TensorFlow, developed by the Google Brain Team, is an open-source library used for numerical computation and the creation, training, and deployment of machine learning and deep learning models. It offers a flexible platform for defining and executing a wide range of algorithms, catering to both novices and experts in the AI domain.

Figure 5.1 The process to implement an AI model

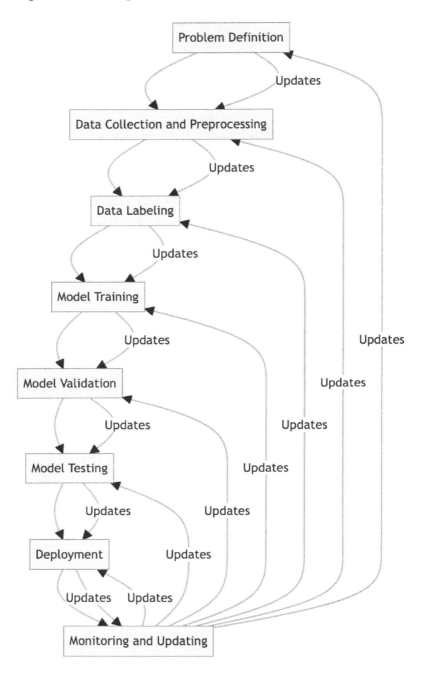

One of the key strengths of TensorFlow is its provision of a high-level Application Programming Interface (API). High-level APIs abstract away much of the complexity involved in building models, making it easier for users to design neural networks without worrying about the underlying mathematics or algorithm details. For example, to define a multi-layer perceptron (a type of neural network), users only need to specify the number of layers and their respective neuron counts, and TensorFlow takes care of the rest. This accessibility and ease of use enable a broad array of practitioners, researchers, and hobbyists to develop intricate AI models. To illustrate this, consider the example of creating a simple linear regression model with TensorFlow. First, we would define the placeholders for the features (X) and labels (y), followed by the weights (W) and bias (b) variables. Next, we would establish our prediction model and the cost function (mean squared error). Finally, we'd employ the Gradient Descent Optimizer, which TensorFlow conveniently provides, to optimize our model. Despite the complexity of these operations, TensorFlow's high-level API allows for clear, succinct code, making the development process considerably more manageable. Additionally, TensorFlow shines with its robust utilities for running computations on Graphics Processing Units (GPUs) and even across multiple machines and processors. This feature is particularly advantageous for large-scale, resource-intensive deep learning tasks. For instance, training a convolutional neural network on a vast image dataset can be computationally heavy and time-consuming when executed on a single CPU. However, TensorFlow's support for GPU-accelerated computing allows the same task to be completed in a fraction of the time.

The distributed computing feature of TensorFlow is another major asset for handling complex machine learning problems. It permits model training to be split over several machines, known as nodes, which can collectively process large datasets and complex models. This is especially useful in scenarios such as training a large transformer model for natural language processing tasks. TensorFlow stands as a pivotal tool in the world of AI, embodying a powerful synergy of simplicity and capability. Its high-level API facilitates the design and training of various machine learning and deep learning models, while its advanced features offer support for GPU computations and distributed computing. This unique blend positions TensorFlow as an instrumental component in any AI practitioner's toolkit, enabling the transformation of intricate algorithmic concepts into reality.

How to Implement AI models:

Implementing AI models using TensorFlow typically involves a series of systematic steps. The details might vary based on the specific type of model you're developing (e.g., regression, convolutional neural network, recurrent neural network, etc.), but the general process often follows this pattern:

Import Libraries:

Import TensorFlow and any other necessary libraries.

This step usually looks like: import tensorflow as tf.

When we talk about importing libraries, we're referring to the process of making certain code libraries available in our current Python environment. Libraries are collections of reusable code modules. By importing a library, we can use its predefined functions, methods, and classes without having to define them ourselves. This allows us to write more efficient and cleaner code.

TensorFlow, for example, is a comprehensive library that was developed by Google and is widely used for machine learning and deep learning tasks. It provides high-level APIs for defining and training models and running computations, which can be executed on a variety of hardware platforms, including CPUs, GPUs, and TPUs. TensorFlow also includes support for distributed computing, enabling you to train complex models on large datasets more quickly.

In Python, libraries are imported using the import statement followed by the name of the library. For example, to import TensorFlow, you would write:

```
import tensorflow as tf
```

The as keyword is used to create an alias for the library, which can save typing in the long run. In this case, tf is the commonly used alias for TensorFlow. Once you've imported TensorFlow like this, you can access its functions, methods, and classes using the tf prefix.

Here are some examples:

Creating a constant in TensorFlow: tf.constant(42)

Creating a variable in TensorFlow: tf.Variable([1, 2])

Constructing a neural network layer: layer = tf.keras.layers.Dense(10)

The specific libraries you need to import will depend on the task you're working on. For instance, for data manipulation and analysis, you might need to import pandas (import pandas as pd). For numerical computations, you might import NumPy (import numpy as np). If you're working with plots, you might import Matplotlib (import matplotlib.pyplot as plt). And, of course, when working with machine learning models in TensorFlow, you'd import TensorFlow itself.

Data Preprocessing:

Load and preprocess your data. This might involve normalization, handling missing values, or one-hot encoding for categorical variables. TensorFlow provides several utilities for data loading and preprocessing through its tf.data and tf.feature_column modules.

Data preprocessing is an essential step in machine learning. It involves transforming the raw data into a format that the machine learning algorithms can understand and work with effectively.

When we discuss data preprocessing, we're talking about a variety of tasks that might need to be performed depending on the specifics of the data and the problem we're trying to solve. Some of these tasks may include:

Loading data:

First, we need to load the data from its source, which could be a local file, a remote database, or an online source. TensorFlow provides utilities for loading data from a variety of sources through the tf.data module.

Handling missing values: Most real-world data is messy and can contain missing values. These missing values need to be handled because machine learning algorithms typically require complete data to work correctly. We can handle missing values in various ways, such as removing the rows or columns containing missing values or imputing missing values using a statistical method.

Normalization:

Machine learning algorithms can be sensitive to the scale of the features. Thus, it's often a good idea to normalize the data so that each feature has a similar scale. This typically involves scaling the values so that they have a mean of 0 and a standard deviation of 1.

Encoding categorical variables:

Machine learning algorithms usually work with numerical data. Therefore, if your data contains categorical variables (like 'color' or 'brand'), you need to convert these categories into numerical values. One common approach is one-hot encoding, which converts each category into a binary vector.

Splitting the data:

Finally, it's common to split the data into a training set and a test set. The training set is used to train the machine learning model, and the test set is used to evaluate its performance.

TensorFlow provides modules like tf.data and tf.feature_column for data loading and preprocessing:

The tf.data module provides functions for loading and preprocessing data. For example, tf.data.Dataset.from_tensor_slices function can be used to slice the input data into multiple manageable chunks or 'batches' which can be very useful when working with large datasets that cannot fit in memory.

The tf.feature_column module provides functions for representing and transforming different types of features.

For example, you can use tf.feature_column.numeric_column for numerical features or tf.feature_column.categorical_column_with_vocabulary_list for categorical features.

With these modules, you can streamline the data preprocessing pipeline, making it easier to handle complex data preprocessing tasks.

Define Model Architecture:

Specify the structure of your model. For instance, if you're creating a deep neural network, you'll define the number of hidden layers, the number of nodes in each layer, the activation functions, etc. TensorFlow's tf.keras API makes it straightforward to create models layer by layer.

Defining the model architecture is one of the crucial steps in implementing AI models with TensorFlow. The architecture of the model dictates how the input data is processed and transformed to produce the desired output. Depending on the problem you're trying to solve, you might choose a different type of model, such as a simple linear model, a deep neural network, a convclutional neural network for image processing, or a recurrent neural network for sequence data.

For instance, if you're creating a deep neural network, the architecture will define:

The number of hidden layers:

Deep neural networks have multiple layers between the input and output layer. Each layer is capable of learning different features from the input data. Deciding the number of layers in the network is problem-dependent and can significantly affect the model's performance.

The number of nodes in each layer:

Each layer in a neural network is made up of multiple nodes, or "neurons". Each node learns different aspects of the input data. Similar to the number of layers, the number of nodes in each layer can impact the performance of the model.

The activation functions:

Activation functions introduce non-linearity to the model, enabling it to learn more complex patterns. Common choices include the ReLU (Rectified Linear Unit), sigmoid, and tanh functions.

Other parameters:

Depending on the type of model, there might be other parameters to set. For example, for a convolutional neural network, you would also define the size and stride of the convolutional kernels.

TensorFlow's tf.keras API simplifies the process of defining the model architecture. The Sequential model API allows you to easily stack layers upon one another to create your model.

Here's an example of how you might define a simple neural network with two dense layers in TensorFlow:

```
from tensorflow.keras import Sequential
from tensorflow.keras.layers import Dense

model = Sequential()
model.add(Dense(32, activation='relu', input_shape=(10,)))
model.add(Dense(1, activation='sigmoid'))
```

In this example, we've created a model with one hidden layer of 32 nodes, using the ReLU activation function. The model's output layer has 1 node and uses the sigmoid activation function, making it suitable for a binary classification task. The input_shape argument in the first layer specifies the shape of the input data, in this case, a 10-dimensional vector.

Remember, the architecture you choose will greatly depend on the problem at hand, and often, finding the right architecture involves a lot of experimentation and fine-tuning.

Compile the Model:

Before training, you need to compile the model. This involves specifying the optimizer (such as SGD or Adam), the loss function (such as mean_squared_error for regression or crossentropy for classification), and any metrics you want to track during training (such as accuracy).

After defining your model's architecture, the next step is to compile your model. Compiling the model in TensorFlow configures the learning process and is an essential step before the model training.

Here's what happens when you compile your model:

Optimizer:

This is the algorithm that adjusts the weights of your network to minimize the loss function. The choice of optimizer can greatly influence the speed and quality of your model's learning process. There are several optimizers available in TensorFlow, with the most commonly used ones being Stochastic Gradient Descent (SGD), RMSprop, and Adam. Each of these optimizers has its strengths and weaknesses, and the choice of optimizer often depends on the nature of the problem at hand.

For instance, SGD is a simple and computationally efficient optimizer but may converge slowly or get stuck in suboptimal solutions. In contrast, Adam is more sophisticated, combining the best properties of other extensions of SGD to provide an optimization that can handle sparse gradients and is relatively robust to the choice of hyperparameters.

Loss Function:

This is the function that measures how well your model is doing on the training data. It's what the optimizer tries to minimize. The choice of the loss function depends on the task. For instance, for regression tasks, we usually use Mean Squared Error (MSE). For binary classification, we often use binary cross-entropy, and for multi-class classification, we typically use categorical cross-entropy.

Metrics:

These are functions used to judge the performance of your model. Unlike the loss function, these do not need to be differentiable, and they do not directly affect the training process. Instead, they provide interpretability and are used to monitor the training and testing steps. For instance, 'accuracy' is often used for classification problems. It simply calculates the percentage of correct predictions made by the model. Other examples include Precision, Recall, and AUC-ROC.

Here's how you can compile a model in TensorFlow:

```
model.compile(optimizer='adam',
        loss='binary_crossentropy',
        metrics=['accuracy'])
```

In this example, we're using the Adam optimizer, binary cross-entropy as the loss function (making this model suitable for a binary classification task), and we're tracking accuracy as our performance metric. Now the model is ready to be trained on data.

Train the Model:

You can now train your model using your preprocessed data. You'll specify the number of epochs (full passes through the dataset) and the batch size (number of samples to process at once).

Once the model is compiled, the next step is to train it on the data. The process of training the model involves feeding the model our training data and letting it learn the patterns in this data over a specified number of iterations. Each iteration over the complete dataset is referred to as an 'epoch'.

Here's how you perform model training in TensorFlow:

Epochs:

An epoch is a single pass through the entire training dataset. The number of epochs is a hyperparameter that defines the number times that the learning algorithm will work through the entire training dataset. Training a model for too many epochs can lead to overfitting, while training for too few can mean the model may have more to learn about the data. The right number of epochs is usually found through trial and error and is usually in the range of 10-100, although it can be more or less depending on the specific problem and the amount of data you have.

Batch size:

The batch size is a hyperparameter that defines the number of samples to work through before updating the internal model parameters. For example, if you have 1000 training samples and you set your batch size to 500, then each epoch will consist of 2 updates to the model's weights. Large batch sizes can result in faster progress in training, but may not converge as fast. Smaller batch sizes train slower, but can converge faster. It's definitely a case of trial and error and really depends on the specific problem and model architecture you're working with.

Here's how you train a model with TensorFlow:

history = model.fit(X_train, y_train, epochs=10, batch_size=32, validation_data=(X_val, y_val))

In this example, X_train and y_train are the feature and target data for training. We've set the number of epochs to 10 and the batch size to 32. We're also using a validation set (X_val, y_val), against which the model's performance is evaluated after each epoch.

During the training, TensorFlow updates the model's weights to minimize the loss. After the training, the model will have learned a representation from the input data that can be used to make predictions on unseen data. The fit function returns a 'history' object which contains the loss values and metric values at each epoch, which can be helpful to visualize the training progress.

Evaluate the Model:

After training, it's important to evaluate the model's performance on unseen data. You would typically use a separate test set for this, and you might measure metrics such as accuracy, precision, recall, or F1 score.

Following the training phase, evaluating the model's performance is crucial. This step aims to test the model's ability to generalize to new, unseen data. It allows you to see how well your model has learned the underlying patterns in your training data and how well it can apply this knowledge to data it wasn't trained on. This is where your test set comes into play.

The first thing you need to do is have your model predict outputs for your test data. In TensorFlow, you use the .predict() method:

```
predictions = model.predict(X_test)
```

In this example, X_test represents your features in the test data. The predictions variable will contain the model's predicted outputs.

To evaluate the model, TensorFlow allows you to use the .evaluate() method:

```
test_loss, test_accuracy = model.evaluate(X_test, y_test)
```

Here, X_test and y_test are your test data and the corresponding true labels, respectively. model.evaluate() returns the loss value & metrics values for the model in test mode.

Depending on the problem at hand, you might use different metrics for evaluation. For binary classification problems, you might use metrics like precision, recall, F1-score, Area Under the Receiver Operating Characteristics curve (AUROC), etc. For regression problems, Mean Squared Error (MSE), Root Mean Squared Error (RMSE), Mean Absolute Error (MAE), R-Squared, etc., might be your metrics of choice.

The TensorFlow Keras API has several built-in metrics that can be used, and it's also possible to define and use your custom metrics if needed.

It's important to note that high performance on the training set but low performance on the test set could be an indication of overfitting, a phenomenon where the model learns the training data too well and loses its ability to generalize. Various techniques like regularization, dropout, or gathering more data can be used to mitigate overfitting.

Tune the Model:

Based on your evaluation, you might decide to adjust the model's parameters for better performance. This could involve changing the model architecture, the learning rate, or other hyperparameters. TensorFlow's Keras Tuner is a handy tool for this step.

Model tuning is the stage of the Machine Learning workflow where you fine-tune the hyperparameters of your model to improve its performance. Hyperparameters are the configuration variables of the model, i.e., parameters that are not learned from the data. They are set before the learning process begins. They include, but are not limited to, the learning rate, batch size, number of layers in the model, number of units in each layer, regularization parameters, etc.

Often, the initial run of training a model doesn't yield the best possible results. The hyperparameters chosen might not be optimal. Hyperparameter tuning is the process of finding the best set of hyperparameters for your model.

TensorFlow provides a tool called the Keras Tuner for hyperparameter tuning. Keras Tuner offers several methods to adjust model parameters, such as Random Search, Hyperband, and Bayesian Optimization.

Let's say, for instance, you are unsure about the best number of units in a Dense layer of your model, or the best learning rate for the Adam optimizer. Here's how you could tune these parameters using Keras Tuner:

```
from kerastuner import HyperModel, RandomSearch


class MyHyperModel(HyperModel):
    def build(self, hp):
        model = tf.keras.models.Sequential()
        model.add(tf.keras.layers.Dense(
            units=hp.Int('units', min_value=32, max_value=512, step=32),
            activation='relu')
```

```
    )
    model.add(tf.keras.layers.Dense(10, activation='softmax'))
    model.compile(
        optimizer=tf.keras.optimizers.Adam(
            hp.Choice('learning_rate', values=[1e-2, 1e-3, 1e-4])),
        loss='categorical_crossentropy',
        metrics=['accuracy'])
    return model


hypermodel = MyHyperModel()


tuner = RandomSearch(
    hypermodel,
    objective='val_accuracy',
    max_trials=10,
    executions_per_trial=3,
    directory='random_search',
    project_name='helloworld')


tuner.search_space_summary()


tuner.search(X_train, y_train, epochs=10, validation_data=(X_test, y_test))


best_hps = tuner.get_best_hyperparameters()[0]
```

In the code snippet above, hp.Int('units', min_value=32, max_value=512, step=32) is used to define an integer hyperparameter with possible values ranging from 32 to 512 in steps of 32. hp.Choice('learning_rate', values=[1e-2, 1e-3, 1e-4]) is used to define a categorical hyperparameter with possible values 0.01, 0.001, and 0.0001.

After the tuning process is complete, the optimal hyperparameters can be fetched using tuner.get_best_hyperparameters()[0].

By using such techniques, you can optimize your model's hyperparameters for your specific problem to achieve better performance. But remember, it's also crucial to monitor for signs of overfitting during this process. If your model performs exceptionally well on your training data but poorly on your validation/test data, it may be overfitting, and you'll need to take steps to address this, such as collecting more data, simplifying your model, or applying regularization techniques.

Predict New Instances:

Once you're satisfied with your model, you can use it to make predictions on new, unseen data.

Predicting new instances is the final step where you use your trained and fine-tuned model to make predictions or infer on new, unseen data. This is the primary aim of most machine learning models - to learn from the existing data and predict outcomes for new inputs.

To use your TensorFlow model for predictions, you would typically use the predict() method. Let's say we have new data stored in a variable named new_data:

predictions = model.predict(new_data)

The predict() function returns an array of predictions for each instance in the new_data.

However, before you make predictions, the new data must be preprocessed in the exact same way as your training data. This might involve steps like normalization, handling missing values, or one-hot encoding for categorical variables. Any transformations or preprocessing done on the training data must be remembered and applied to new data as well.

Also, keep in mind that the output of model.predict() will depend on your model and the problem at hand:

For a regression model, the output is the predicted numeric value.

For a binary classification model, the output is a probability that the instance belongs to the positive class. You may want to apply a threshold to these probabilities to get a binary prediction.

For a multi-class classification model, the output is a probability distribution over all classes. The predicted class is typically taken to be the one with the highest probability.

This is the stage where all the effort in data gathering, preprocessing, model design, and training pays off. The model is now capable of making predictions on new data, helping you to make data-driven decisions.

Save and Load Models:

TensorFlow provides functionalities to save and load models. This means you can re-use your trained models in the future without having to retrain them.

Once your model is trained and fine-tuned, you don't have to go through the entire process each time you want to make predictions on new data. TensorFlow provides convenient methods to save your model's architecture and trained weights, and later load them when needed. This is particularly useful for deep learning models, which often take a long time to train.

To save a model, you would use the save() method of your model. Here is an example:

```
# Save the model
model.save('my_model.h5')  # creates a HDF5 file 'my_model.h5'
```

The save() method stores everything about the model:

The architecture of the model, allowing to re-create the model.

The weights of the model.

The training configuration (loss, optimizer).

The state of the optimizer, allowing to resume training exactly where you left off.

Later on, when you want to load the model, you can use the load_model() function from tensorflow.keras.models:

```
from tensorflow.keras.models import load_model

# Load the model
loaded_model = load_model('my_model.h5')
```

Now loaded_model is exactly the same as the model you saved. You can use this model to make predictions on new data, or even continue training it.

It's also possible to save only the architecture of the model or only the weights, depending on your needs. This is useful in situations where you might want to train the same model architecture with different datasets or if you want to use the pre-trained weights of a model for transfer learning.

This capability of TensorFlow to save and load models makes the library even more versatile and suitable for real-world applications. It ensures that the computational expense incurred during model training can be a one-time cost, and the benefits can be reaped over time, across multiple tasks and datasets.

Remember, while these steps provide a broad overview, implementing an AI model involves many nuanced decisions and tasks that depend on your specific problem and dataset. Furthermore, these steps are often not strictly linear; for instance, you might find yourself going back to tweak your preprocessing after evaluating your model's performance.

5.2 Implementing AI Models with PyTorch

Implementing AI Models with PyTorch entails a shift in focus from TensorFlow, with the spotlight moving onto PyTorch - another favorite among machine learning and deep learning practitioners. PyTorch, developed by Facebook's AI Research lab, is known for its intuitive interface and ease of use, particularly when it comes to the development and debugging of models, thanks to its dynamic computational graph.

In contrast to TensorFlow's static computational graph (which requires defining the entire graph before running the session), PyTorch's dynamic computational graph allows for adjustments to be made to the graph at runtime. This makes it easier to manipulate and change the graph on-the-fly, which can be particularly beneficial in research settings where model architectures might need to be tweaked frequently and experiments are iterative.

Efficient memory usage is another advantage that PyTorch brings to the table, offering significant savings when it comes to memory-intensive tasks such as training large deep learning models.

In this section of the book, readers can expect to learn how to implement AI models using PyTorch. The processes might include steps similar to those in TensorFlow, such as data preprocessing, defining model architecture, compiling the model, and training it. However, the methods and syntax will likely differ due to the differences in the libraries.

It would be crucial in this section to highlight the circumstances and use-cases where one library might be more advantageous over the other. While PyTorch is lauded for its flexibility and efficiency in research and development, TensorFlow might be preferable for deployment in production settings due to its comprehensive ecosystem and support for various platforms.

By providing a comparative perspective on TensorFlow and PyTorch, this section will equip readers with an understanding of both libraries, enabling them to make informed decisions about which one to use based on their specific requirements and use-cases.

Import Libraries:

Import PyTorch and any other necessary libraries. Typically, this looks like:

The first step in any PyTorch project is to import the necessary libraries.

```
import torch
import torchvision
```

Let's break down what these libraries do:

torch:

This is the main PyTorch library. It provides data structures for multi-dimensional tensors and defines mathematical operations over these tensors. Additionally, it provides many utilities for efficient serializing of Tensors and arbitrary types, and other useful utilities.

torchvision:

This is a companion package to PyTorch that consists of popular datasets, model architectures, and common image transformations for computer vision. It simplifies the process of loading data from common image and video formats, and it includes several predefined models (like ResNet and VGG) that you can use out-of-the-box.

By importing these libraries, we gain access to the functionality they provide, enabling us to use PyTorch's tensor computations, like those found in NumPy but with GPU acceleration, along with a variety of high-level functions specifically designed for machine learning.

It's worth noting that depending on the specifics of your project, you may also need to import other libraries or modules. For instance, you might need numpy for numerical operations, matplotlib for plotting, or pandas for data manipulation.

Data Preprocessing:

Load and preprocess your data. This could involve normalization, data augmentation, or handling missing values. PyTorch provides several utilities for data loading and preprocessing through its torchvision.transforms module.

In any machine learning project, data preprocessing is a critical step. It involves preparing the initial raw data into a format that can be readily and accurately analyzed. In PyTorch, this process often involves several key steps:

Data Loading:

PyTorch provides the torch.utils.data.DataLoader class to load your data in a convenient format. If you're working with image data, you can also leverage the datasets in torchvision.datasets for standard datasets like MNIST, CIFAR10, and ImageNet.

For custom datasets, you will need to implement a subclass of torch.utils.data. Dataset, defining the __len__ and __getitem__ methods to handle accessing the dataset elements.

Normalization:

It's often a good practice to normalize your input data, i.e., change the values to ensure that they fall within a standard range, typically between 0 and 1, or so that they have a mean of 0 and a standard deviation of 1. This is important for most machine learning algorithms to perform optimally.

PyTorch's torchvision.transforms.Normalize method allows you to normalize a tensor image with mean and standard deviation. This transform does not support different-sized images.

Data Augmentation:

Data augmentation is a technique used to artificially expand the size of a training dataset by creating modified versions of images in the dataset. This can help improve model performance and ability to generalize.

Common data augmentation techniques include rotation, scaling, translation, flipping, and more. In PyTorch, you can use methods from torchvision.transforms, like RandomHorizontalFlip, RandomCrop, etc., to perform data augmentation.

Handling Missing Values:

If your dataset has missing values, these will need to be addressed before training your model. Depending on the situation, you might choose to ignore those samples, fill in the missing values with a specific value (like the mean or median of the feature), or use a more complex method like a regression model or k-nearest neighbors.

These steps help ensure that your data is in a format and state that your machine learning model can accept and perform well on. It's also worth noting that the specifics of these steps can vary depending on the type of data you're working with (e.g., images vs. text vs. structured data), and the specific problem you're trying to solve.

Define Model Architecture:

Specify the structure of your model. You'll define the type of layers (such as linear, convolutional, recurrent), the activation functions, and other parameters like the number of hidden units. PyTorch uses a subclass of torch.nn.Module to define these architectures.

Creating a model architecture in PyTorch involves several steps. The model architecture defines the structure of the neural network including the type of layers, activation functions, and other parameters like the number of hidden units.

Defining the Model Class: The first step in defining a model architecture in PyTorch is to create a new class for the model. This class should inherit from the torch.nn.Module base class which provides many helpful methods and attributes.

For example:

```python
import torch.nn as nn

class MyModel(nn.Module):
    def __init__(self):
        super(MyModel, self).__init__()
```

Adding Layers: The next step is to add layers to the model. This is done in the __init__ method of the model class. PyTorch provides a wide variety of layer types that can be used including linear (nn.Linear), convolutional (nn.Conv2d), and recurrent (nn.LSTM, nn.GRU) layers.

For example, to add a linear layer with 10 input features and 1 output feature, you would do:

```python
self.linear = nn.Linear(10, 1)
```

Defining Forward Pass:

In the forward method of your model class, you will define how the input data flows through the layers. You will also specify the activation functions for each layer. Common activation functions include ReLU (nn.ReLU), sigmoid (torch.sigmoid), and softmax (nn.Softmax).

For example, to implement a forward pass with our linear layer and a ReLU activation function:

```python
def forward(self, x):
    x = self.linear(x)
    x = nn.ReLU()(x)
    return x
```

The above code illustrates a simple linear regression model. For a more complex model like a convolutional neural network, more layers and other components would need to be added.

Remember that the architecture of your model will depend on the specific task at hand. It's also worth noting that designing a model architecture is an iterative process. You might need to try different architectures and configurations to find the best one for your specific task.

Define Loss Function and Optimizer:

Define a loss function that will be minimized during training. Common loss functions are provided in the torch.nn module, such as torch.nn.CrossEntropyLoss() for classification tasks, and torch.nn.MSELoss() for regression tasks. Also, define an optimizer, which updates the model's parameters based on the gradients computed during backpropagation. PyTorch provides various optimization algorithms under torch.optim module, such as SGD, RMSprop, and Adam.

In any machine learning task, we need a way to measure how well our model is performing. This is where the loss function comes in. The loss function quantifies how far off our predictions are from the true values. During training, the goal is to minimize this loss.

PyTorch provides a variety of loss functions in the torch.nn module that you can use depending on your specific task. For instance, for a classification task, you might use torch.nn.CrossEntropyLoss(), which is suitable for multi-class classification problems. On the other hand, for a regression task, you might use torch.nn.MSELoss(), which computes the mean squared error between the predicted and actual values, making it suitable for tasks where you're predicting a continuous value.

Here's an example of how you might define a loss function in PyTorch:

```
criterion = nn.CrossEntropyLoss()
```

In this line of code, criterion is a variable that holds a reference to the instance of the CrossEntropyLoss class.

In addition to the loss function, you also need to define an optimizer when training your model. The optimizer's job is to update the model's parameters in a way that reduces the loss. The updates are based on the gradients computed during backpropagation, which is a process that computes the gradient of the loss function with respect to the model's parameters.

PyTorch provides several optimization algorithms under the torch.optim module. For example, you can use Stochastic Gradient Descent (SGD), RMSprop, or Adam, each of which has different ways of adjusting the weights with the goal of decreasing the loss.

Here's how you might define an optimizer in PyTorch:

```
optimizer = torch.optim.Adam(model.parameters(), lr=0.001)
```

In this code, torch.optim.Adam is the optimizer (in this case, Adam), model.parameters() tells the optimizer what parameters to update, and lr=0.001 sets the learning rate, which controls how big the updates are.

Both the choice of loss function and optimizer can have a big impact on how well your model learns from the data. You might need to experiment with different combinations and settings to find what works best for your specific task.

Train the Model:

Training the model involves feeding it input data and having it make predictions, comparing the predictions to the correct output (labels), calculating the loss, and finally updating the model's weights using the optimizer. This process is often done in a loop, where each complete pass over the data is called an epoch.

Training an AI model is the stage where it learns patterns from the input data. In PyTorch, training a model usually involves the following steps

Feedforward:

You input your data into the model. This is typically done in batches, rather than all at once, especially for large datasets. The data is processed through each layer of the model until a prediction is produced. This is the forward pass.

Compute Loss:

The model's predictions are compared to the true values using a loss function. This function computes the difference between the model's predictions and the actual values to give a measure of how well the model is performing. A smaller loss indicates better performance.

Backpropagation:

This is where the magic of deep learning happens. Backpropagation is an algorithm for efficiently computing the gradient (rate of change) of the loss function with respect to each model parameter. In simpler terms, it figures out which parameters in the model contributed to the model's loss.

Update Weights:

The last step is updating the model parameters (weights and biases) using the gradients computed in the backpropagation step. This is done via the optimization algorithm you chose (like SGD or Adam). This update step is what allows the model to learn from the data iteratively and improve its predictions.

This process is typically repeated for a certain number of epochs. An epoch is one complete pass through the entire training dataset. The number of epochs is a hyperparameter that you can tune.

Here's an example of what a basic training loop might look like in PyTorch:

```python
# number of epochs
epochs = 10

# loop over the dataset multiple times
for epoch in range(epochs):

    running_loss = 0.0
    for i, data in enumerate(trainloader, 0):
        # get the inputs; data is a list of [inputs, labels]
        inputs, labels = data

        # zero the parameter gradients
        optimizer.zero_grad()

        # forward + backward + optimize
        outputs = model(inputs)
        loss = criterion(outputs, labels)
        loss.backward()
        optimizer.step()

        # print statistics
        running_loss += loss.item()

    print(f'Epoch: {epoch+1}, loss: {running_loss/len(trainloader)}')

print('Finished Training')
```

In this example, trainloader is an instance of a data loader that provides batches of data. The optimizer.zero_grad() call is used to clear the gradients from the last step (gradients are accumulated by default). The loss.backward() line computes the gradient of the loss with respect to the parameters (backpropagation), and optimizer.step() updates the parameters.

Evaluate the Model:

After training, evaluate the model's performance on unseen data. PyTorch provides various ways to calculate performance metrics that can help in evaluating the model's performance.

After training, it's important to evaluate the model's performance on unseen data. This is typically done using a separate validation or test dataset that the model hasn't seen during training. The purpose of this step is to assess how well the model generalizes to new data, which is crucial for determining its real-world utility.

Evaluation involves using the trained model to make predictions on the test dataset and then comparing these predictions to the actual labels. The comparison is done using appropriate performance metrics. The choice of performance metrics depends on the problem and the model. For instance, accuracy, precision, recall, F1 score, and area under the ROC curve are commonly used metrics for classification problems. For regression problems, mean squared error, root mean squared error, mean absolute error, and R^2 score are commonly used.

Here is a simple example of how to evaluate a model in PyTorch:

```
correct = 0
total = 0
```

```
# since we're not training, we don't need to calculate the gradients for our out-
```

puts

```
with torch.no_grad():
    for data in testloader:
        images, labels = data
        # calculate outputs by running images through the network
        outputs = model(images)
        # the class with the highest energy is what we choose as prediction
        _, predicted = torch.max(outputs.data, 1)
        total += labels.size(0)
        correct += (predicted == labels).sum().item()

print('Accuracy of the network on the test images: %d %%' % (
    100 * correct / total))
```

In this example, testloader is a PyTorch DataLoader that provides batches of test data, model is the trained model, and images and labels are the input data and corresponding true labels. The model's outputs are computed with model(images), and the predicted labels are determined with torch.max(outputs.data, 1)[1], which returns the index with the highest value along dimension 1 (across the columns). Finally, the number of correct predictions is summed up and divided by the total number of predictions to calculate the accuracy.

Remember that evaluation should be done in a context that doesn't calculate gradients, hence the use of the torch.no_grad() context manager. This is because we don't need to update the weights of the network during testing, and excluding unnecessary computations can speed up the code.

Save and Load Models:

PyTorch provides methods to save and load models, which is very useful when you have large models or you want to pause your training and resume later.

Save/Load Model State_dict:

This is the more recommended approach as it allows for more flexibility. A state_dict is simply a Python dictionary that maps each layer in the model to its trainable parameters (weights and biases).

Saving a model:

torch.save(model.state_dict(), PATH)

Loading a model:

model = ModelClass() # replace ModelClass with the class of your model

model.load_state_dict(torch.load(PATH))

Here, you first need to initialize an object of the same class as your model, then you load the parameters into this object. This approach requires you to have the model's class definition available at runtime.

Another important thing to note is that the model's parameters are stored on the same device on which the model was trained. So, if you trained your model on a GPU and are loading it on a machine without a GPU, you need to map the parameters to the CPU using the map_location argument in torch.load():

model.load_state_dict(torch.load(PATH, map_location=torch.device('cpu')))

Overall, saving and loading models allows for a lot of flexibility and is an essential part of working with PyTorch models.

Predict New Instances:

Use your trained model to make predictions on new, unseen data.

Once your PyTorch model is trained and you're satisfied with its performance on your validation dataset, you can use it to make predictions on new, unseen data. This is usually the ultimate goal of most machine learning pipelines. The following steps outline how to use your model for predictions:

Data Preprocessing:

New data needs to be preprocessed in the same way your training and validation data were prepared. This might involve normalization, reshaping, or encoding depending on what preprocessing steps were applied initially. This ensures that the new data is in the correct format and has the same feature distribution as the training data.

Model Evaluation Mode:

PyTorch models have two modes: training and evaluation. You need to switch the model to evaluation mode using model.eval(). This is important as some layers like dropout or batch normalization behave differently during training and testing.

No Gradient Computation:

During inference, we don't need to compute gradients. Disabling gradient computation can save memory and make the process faster. In PyTorch, this can be done using torch.no_grad().

Prediction:

To make a prediction, you pass your new data to the model as you would in training. However, instead of calculating the loss and updating the weights, you can directly obtain the output. The output will typically be the raw prediction values or class probabilities in the case of classification tasks.

Here's a Python code snippet showing these steps:

```
# Switch to evaluation mode
model.eval()

# Preprocess the new data
new_data = preprocess(new_data)  # replace with your preprocessing function
```

```
# Disable gradient computation
with torch.no_grad():
    inputs = new_data.to(device)  # replace `device` with your device (cpu or cuda)
    outputs = model(inputs)


# If the task was a classification task, apply softmax to obtain probabilities
probabilities = torch.nn.functional.softmax(outputs, dim=1)


# Get the predicted class
_, predicted_class = torch.max(probabilities, dim=1)
```

In this code, new_data is the new, unseen data on which you want to make predictions, and model is your trained PyTorch model. device refers to the device on which the model is, which could be a CPU or a CUDA device for a GPU.

Keep in mind, the exact steps may vary depending on the specifics of your project and model.

Tune the Model:

You may need to adjust the model's hyperparameters based on the evaluation results for better performance. This could involve changing the learning rate, batch size, number of layers in the model, etc.

Model tuning, often referred to as hyperparameter tuning, is the process of adjusting the settings of your model to optimize its performance. In machine learning and deep learning, even small changes in hyperparameters can have a significant impact on a model's accuracy, precision, recall, and other performance metrics.

Here are the steps you might follow when tuning your PyTorch model:

Identify Hyperparameters:

The first step is to identify which hyperparameters you will adjust. These may include learning rate, batch size, number of layers or units per layer in a neural network, weight initialization scheme, activation function, dropout rate, type of optimizer, etc.

Define a Search Strategy:

You need to decide how you will search through the space of possible hyperparameter combinations. You may want to do a grid search, which systematically tests every combination of hyperparameters. Alternatively, you might choose a random search, which randomly selects combinations to test. More sophisticated methods like Bayesian optimization are also possible but may be more complex to implement.

Cross-validation:

You should split your training data into a smaller training set and a validation set. You train the model on the smaller training set with a certain set of hyperparameters, then evaluate its performance on the validation set. The goal is to find hyperparameters that minimize the validation error.

Iterate:

Repeat the training and evaluation process for each combination of hyperparameters in your search. Keep track of the performance for each set of hyperparameters.

Select Best Model:

At the end of this process, choose the model with the hyperparameters that performed best on the validation set.

For instance, PyTorch doesn't provide a built-in tool for hyperparameter tuning. However, you can use Python libraries such as Optuna or Ray Tune which offer sophisticated hyperparameter tuning functionalities and integrate well with PyTorch.

Here is a simple example of tuning learning rate and batch size using Optuna:

```python
import optuna

def objective(trial):
    # Define hyperparameters to optimize
    lr = trial.suggest_loguniform('lr', 1e-5, 1e-1)
    batch_size = trial.suggest_categorical('batch_size', [32, 64, 128, 256])

    # Create a dataloader with the batch size
    dataloader = DataLoader(dataset, batch_size=batch_size)

    # Create a model, loss function and optimizer
    model = create_model()  # replace with your model creation function
    loss_func = nn.CrossEntropyLoss()
    optimizer = torch.optim.SGD(model.parameters(), lr=lr)

    # Train the model and return the validation error
    train(model, optimizer, loss_func, dataloader)
    val_error = validate(model, val_dataloader)  # replace with your validation function

    return val_error

# Create a study object and optimize the objective
study = optuna.create_study(direction='minimize')
study.optimize(objective, n_trials=100)
```

In this code, objective is a function that takes a trial object, trains a model with hyperparameters suggested by the trial, and returns the validation error. The create_study function creates a new study, and the optimize function runs the optimization. In this case, the learning rate and batch size that minimize the validation error are sought. Note that you need to replace create_model, train, and validate with your actual functions.

Keep in mind that hyperparameter tuning can be time-consuming, especially with large datasets or complex models. Therefore, it's often a good idea to start with a smaller subset of your data or a simpler model to identify promising hyperparameters before tuning the full model on all your data.

These steps provide a high-level view of implementing AI models with PyTorch. Each project might have specific needs or constraints, but these steps should cover the majority of typical model implementation tasks.

5.3 Handling Large-Scale Training and Distributed Computing

Large-scale training and distributed computing have become crucial as the scale of data continues to expand and machine learning models become increasingly complex. This expansion in scale and complexity can drastically increase the computational requirements for training a model, often beyond the capacity of a single machine or local computing resources. The ability to handle large-scale training and effectively leverage distributed computing resources has thus become a fundamental skill in the modern machine learning toolbox.

The Challenge of Large-Scale Training

Training a machine learning model involves iteratively adjusting its parameters based on a dataset until it can accurately predict the output for a given input. As the size of the dataset grows, so does the amount of computation required to train the model. This increase in computation can lead to extended training times and increased memory requirements. Similarly, as models become more complex, with millions or even billions of parameters, the computational load increases.

Strategies for Large-Scale Training

There are several strategies for handling large-scale training, which can be broadly classified into two categories: hardware solutions and software solutions. Hardware solutions involve using more powerful computing resources, such as high-performance CPUs, GPUs, and TPUs (Tensor Processing Units), as well as distributed computing infrastructure. Software solutions involve techniques to optimize computation, such as batch processing, parallel processing, and various forms of gradient descent optimization.

Batch Processing:

This technique involves splitting the training dataset into smaller subsets, or batches. The model's parameters are then updated after each batch. This method can significantly reduce the memory requirements and can lead to faster convergence of the model.

Batch processing is a vital computational technique used in training machine learning models, particularly in the context of neural networks and deep learning. The primary reason for adopting batch processing is the sheer scale of data and the computational burden it imposes.

To understand batch processing, we first need to revisit how training in machine learning occurs. Training involves feeding data to the model and adjusting the model's parameters to minimize the loss function. In essence, the loss function measures the discrepancy between the model's predictions and the actual values.

When you have a large dataset, it's not feasible to feed all data into the model at once due to memory constraints - this is where the concept of a 'batch' comes in. The entire dataset is divided into several subsets, known as batches. Each batch is fed into the model one at a time. After each batch is processed, the loss is calculated and used to update the model parameters. This process is then repeated for the next batch and so forth until all batches (the entire dataset) have been used for training - this constitutes one epoch. The entire process is then repeated for several epochs until the model's performance stops improving or begins to worsen.

For instance, consider you have a dataset of 10,000 samples and you choose a batch size of 100. This means that in one epoch, you would have 100 iterations (10,000 / 100), and the model parameters would be updated 100 times.

Batch processing has several advantages:

Memory Efficiency:

Since only one batch of data is loaded into memory at a time, batch processing is memory-efficient and enables you to train on large datasets that wouldn't fit into memory if loaded all at once.

Faster Convergence:

In theory, using the entire dataset to calculate each update to the model parameters (known as batch gradient descent) would lead to the steepest gradient and fastest convergence. However, in practice, the noise introduced by using a subset of the data (mini-batch gradient descent) often provides a form of regularization that leads to faster convergence in deep learning models.

Parallel Processing:

Batch processing can take advantage of vectorized operations and parallel processing capabilities of modern GPUs, further accelerating the training process.

It's worth noting that the choice of batch size can significantly affect the model's performance and the training speed. It's often a hyperparameter that is tuned during the model development process.

Parallel Processing:

In parallel processing, different parts of the computation are performed simultaneously on different cores of a CPU, different CPUs, or different machines. This strategy can greatly reduce the total computation time.

Parallel processing is a computing technique that leverages multiple computational resources concurrently to execute tasks faster. In the context of training machine learning models, parallel processing can help significantly reduce training times, particularly for large-scale models and datasets.

Let's break down the concept of parallel processing further:

Understanding Parallelism:

A machine learning model's training involves executing many mathematical operations. In a traditional (serial) computing setting, these operations are performed one after another, even if they are independent. This sequential execution can be a bottleneck when dealing with large-scale tasks. Parallel processing, however, executes multiple independent operations simultaneously, thus speeding up the computation. The concept of parallelism has revolutionized the way machine learning models are trained, particularly in dealing with large-scale tasks. To fully comprehend its impact, we must first delve into the traditional, sequential way of executing computations in machine learning, also known as serial computing. Machine learning models, at their core, are mathematical structures. They involve a plethora of mathematical operations that range from simple arithmetic to complex calculus. During the training of a machine learning model, these operations are carried out repeatedly in a process called an epoch. Each epoch represents a single pass through the entire dataset, where the model learns to refine its predictions. When the training involves a small dataset, performing these operations sequentially or serially - one after the other - poses no issue. However, imagine training a deep learning model on a dataset of millions of images. The sheer scale of the operations needed, even in a single epoch, is staggering. In a serial computing setting, the model has to wait for one operation to be completed before the next one starts. This sequential execution can become a significant bottleneck, causing the training process to be laboriously long.

This is where the concept of parallelism comes into play. Parallel processing, a cornerstone of high-performance computing, is designed to execute multiple independent operations simultaneously. In the context of machine learning, instead of waiting for one operation to finish before starting the next, parallel processing runs multiple operations at the same time. It leverages the fact that many of the operations during model training are independent of each other, meaning the outcome of one operation does not affect the outcome of the other.

For instance, consider the process of updating the weights of a neural network using gradient descent. In each layer of the network, these updates are independent - the update of one weight does not depend on the update of another. In a serial setting, these updates are performed one-by-one, but with parallelism, they can be carried out simultaneously, leading to substantial time savings. Therefore, parallel processing provides an efficient solution to the computational challenges posed by large-scale machine learning tasks. It transforms the previously linear, time-consuming sequence of operations into a concurrent process, significantly speeding up the computation and making the training of complex models on large datasets feasible.

In essence, the concept of parallelism has played a pivotal role in propelling the field of machine learning forward. It has not only made it possible to perform computationally intensive tasks but also significantly reduced the time required to train models, thereby accelerating the pace of development and discovery in the field.

Levels of Parallelism:

Parallelism in machine learning can occur at several levels:

Parallelism, a powerful concept in machine learning, holds the key to efficiently training complex models on massive datasets. At its heart, parallelism in machine learning exploits the power of concurrent computation to speed up the training process. It operates on several levels: data parallelism, model parallelism, and task parallelism. Understanding these levels helps us harness the full potential of parallel computing in machine learning. Data parallelism is the first level of parallelism. In this approach, the training dataset is divided into smaller subsets, each handled by a separate computational resource, such as a CPU core or a GPU. The machine learning model is duplicated across these resources, and each copy learns independently from its allocated data subset. This simultaneous learning accelerates the training process. Imagine a scenario where you have four GPUs at your disposal. With data parallelism, you could effectively reduce the training time to approximately one-fourth by dividing your dataset into four parts and training the model on each GPU simultaneously. Data parallelism is particularly popular in training deep learning models, where large-scale data and computationally intense models are the norms. Next, we have model parallelism. As the name suggests, different parts of the model itself are assigned to different computational resources. For instance, in a multi-layered neural network, different layers might be allocated to different GPUs. Each GPU then computes its part of the forward and backward passes - the two key steps in neural network training. After each pass, results are synchronized across GPUs, ensuring the model learns consistently. Model parallelism is handy when dealing with models too large to fit into the memory of a single computational resource.

Finally, task parallelism focuses on running different tasks of the same program in parallel. Take, for example, a machine learning pipeline, where data needs to be fetched, preprocessed, and used for training. With task parallelism, these tasks could run simultaneously on different cores or processors, reducing the overall time to complete the pipeline. Instead of waiting for data fetching to complete before starting preprocessing, task parallelism allows these steps to be performed concurrently, thus enhancing efficiency. Parallelism, with its various levels, is a potent weapon in a machine learning practitioner's arsenal. It reduces training time and computational load, making it possible to handle more extensive and more complex tasks. As machine learning models continue to grow in size and computational demand, understanding and implementing these different levels of parallelism become increasingly critical in the pursuit of more robust and advanced AI systems. Hardware for Parallel Processing: Parallel processing is possible because of the specific hardware capabilities of modern CPUs and GPUs. CPUs (Central Processing Units) usually have multiple cores that can execute tasks independently. GPUs (Graphics Processing Units), originally designed for rendering graphics, have hundreds or thousands of smaller cores that are well-suited for the matrix and vector operations common in machine learning tasks.

In the realm of machine learning, the efficacy of parallel processing owes its credit largely to the capabilities of modern hardware, specifically Central Processing Units (CPUs) and Graphics Processing Units (GPUs). These technological advancements have revolutionized the field, enabling us to train more complex models on larger datasets in less time. CPUs, the brains of any computer, have evolved over the years to become multi-core processors. Each core in a CPU can execute tasks independently, lending itself to parallelism. This means that if we have a CPU with multiple cores, we can run different tasks or processes simultaneously. For example, if a CPU has four cores, it can theoretically run four different tasks at the same time. This ability has a profound impact on machine learning where large amounts of data need to be processed, and complex mathematical calculations are performed.

However, the rise of GPUs has taken parallel processing to a whole new level. GPUs were initially designed to render graphics in video games, a task that requires simultaneous computation of millions of pixels. To fulfill this demand, GPUs were equipped with hundreds or even thousands of smaller cores, a massive leap from the limited number of cores in a CPU. These GPU cores are well-suited for the matrix and vector operations that are commonplace in machine learning tasks. For example, in deep learning, a subtype of machine learning, calculations usually involve operations on high-dimensional matrices. These operations are highly parallelizable, and a GPU, with its multitude of cores, can perform many operations simultaneously, thus greatly accelerating the computations. The application of GPUs in machine learning has been transformative. Training deep learning models, for instance, which was once considered an arduously long process, has been significantly expedited thanks to GPUs. Today, the widespread use of GPUs in machine learning extends beyond deep learning to other areas such as reinforcement learning and natural language processing. In conclusion, the landscape of machine learning has been dramatically reshaped by the development of multi-core CPUs and, more importantly, GPUs. These hardware advancements have unlocked the full potential of parallel processing, enabling us to develop more sophisticated AI models and opening up new possibilities for future innovations.

Parallel processing in the context of batch processing means that each batch's computations can be done independently, allowing for the computations of multiple batches to be performed simultaneously. This can lead to a significant reduction in training time. However, it's worth noting that managing parallel computations involves some overhead (like coordinating tasks and synchronizing results), and the optimal number of tasks to run in parallel depends on several factors, including the model architecture, batch size, and specific hardware used.

So, with parallel processing, not only can you process larger datasets more efficiently using batch processing, but you can also speed up the training process by distributing the computation across multiple cores or machines. This is especially valuable in deep learning and other machine learning tasks that require intensive computations.

GPU Acceleration:

Graphics Processing Units (GPUs) are particularly well-suited to the types of computations required for machine learning, namely large-scale matrix operations. Training a model on a GPU can be significantly faster than training it on a CPU.

Graphics Processing Units (GPUs) have emerged as a game changer in the field of machine learning and deep learning, thanks to their high computational capability which dramatically accelerates model training time. This increase in speed is due to the architectural differences between CPUs (Central Processing Units) and GPUs. CPUs, the traditional core of a computer, are designed for general-purpose computing. They are exceptionally good at executing a series of dependent instructions quickly, making them ideal for tasks that require complex logic and decision-making. However, when it comes to handling the large-scale matrix and vector operations that are at the heart of machine learning algorithms, CPUs are often outperformed by GPUs. GPUs were originally developed for rendering graphics in video games, a task that requires simultaneous processing of large blocks of data to adjust the pixels on the screen. To handle this, GPUs were designed with hundreds, or even thousands, of cores capable of handling multiple threads simultaneously. This inherent parallelism, where many calculations are executed concurrently, makes GPUs especially efficient for the types of operations found in machine learning workloads. Machine learning, particularly deep learning, involves a lot of linear algebra operations (like multiplications and additions of matrices or vectors). These operations can be performed in parallel, meaning they can be broken down into smaller operations that are computed simultaneously. Since a GPU has many more cores than a CPU, it can execute many more operations at the same time, leading to faster computation times and hence, faster model training. However, it's not just about the number of cores. GPUs also have a high bandwidth memory which allows for faster data transfer, another factor that accelerates computation in machine learning tasks. In essence, while CPUs are great for tasks that require decision making and control, GPUs excel in data parallel tasks prevalent in machine learning. Leveraging GPU acceleration not only expedites model training, but it also allows for larger, more complex models to be trained, paving the way for continued innovation in the field of artificial intelligence.

Distributed Computing:

Distributed computing involves training a model on multiple machines, each of which computes a part of the total computation. This can be done in a data-parallel manner, where each machine trains on a different subset of the data, or in a model-parallel manner, where each machine computes a different part of the model.

Distributed computing is a method of performing computational tasks by utilizing multiple machines or nodes that work together to complete a larger computation. In the context of training machine learning models, distributed computing is often employed to handle large datasets or complex models that require significant computational resources. When training a model using distributed computing, the computation is divided among multiple machines. There are two primary approaches to distributing the workload: data-parallel and model-parallel.

In data-parallel distributed computing, each machine receives a different subset of the data. For example, if you have a dataset of images, one machine might train on images 1-1,000, another on images 1,001-2,000, and so on. Each machine performs the same computations on its subset of the data, such as forward and backward passes through the model. The results are then combined, typically through a process called gradient averaging, to update the model's parameters and synchronize the training across all machines. This approach is effective when the model's architecture is relatively simple, and the dataset can be easily divided.

In contrast, model-parallel distributed computing involves dividing the model itself among multiple machines. Each machine is responsible for computing a specific part of the model. For example, in a deep neural network, one machine may compute the convolutional layers, while another handles the recurrent layers. The inputs and outputs of each machine are passed between them to complete the forward and backward passes. This approach is particularly useful when dealing with complex models that cannot fit into the memory of a single machine or when specific parts of the model require different computational resources.

Distributed computing offers several advantages. It allows for faster training by parallelizing the computations across multiple machines, enabling a higher throughput of data processing. It also enables the use of larger datasets and more complex models that would be impractical or infeasible to handle on a single machine.

However, distributed computing also introduces challenges. Communication between machines can be a bottleneck, especially when dealing with large amounts of data or complex models. Synchronization of the training process and handling potential failures or network issues requires careful design and implementation. Overall, distributed computing plays a crucial role in scaling up machine learning tasks, enabling faster training, handling large datasets, and tackling complex models by utilizing the collective computational power of multiple machines.

Cloud-Based Solutions

Cloud computing platforms like Google Cloud, Amazon Web Services (AWS), and Microsoft Azure offer on-demand access to powerful computing resources, including CPUs, GPUs, and distributed computing infrastructure. These platforms allow for easy scaling of resources as needed, providing a flexible solution for large-scale model training. They also provide managed machine learning platforms, like Google Cloud ML Engine, Amazon SageMaker, and Azure Machine Learning, which simplify the process of setting up and running large-scale training jobs.

Example: Distributed Training with TensorFlow

Consider training a deep learning model with TensorFlow on a large dataset. If the dataset is too large to fit in the memory of a single machine, or if the model is too complex to be trained on a single machine in a reasonable amount of time, distributed training can be used. TensorFlow provides a distributed training API which allows the training job to be spread across multiple machines.

To use TensorFlow's distributed training API, you would start by defining your model and training procedure just as you would for a non-distributed training job. Then, you would create a tf.distribute.Strategy object, which defines the distribution strategy to use. For example, to train the model on multiple GPUs on a single machine, you could use tf.distribute.MirroredStrategy. To train on multiple machines, each with multiple GPUs, you could use tf.distribute.experimental.MultiWorkerMirroredStrategy.

Once you've created your tf.distribute.Strategy object, you can use it to wrap your optimizer and model definition. The strategy object takes care of distributing the training job across the available resources and aggregating the results.

Handling large-scale training and distributed computing is a complex but essential task in modern machine learning. Understanding the various strategies and tools available for this task can greatly improve the efficiency and effectiveness of model training.

5.4 Model Evaluation and Validation Techniques

Model evaluation and validation are crucial steps in the development of AI models. They enable us to assess the performance and generalization capabilities of our models. In this essay, we will delve into the realm of model evaluation and validation techniques, exploring various metrics, concepts, and advanced techniques used in this domain.

Metrics for Model Performance Assessment:

When evaluating AI models, several metrics serve as performance indicators. Accuracy, precision, recall, and the F1 score are widely used to gauge model effectiveness. Accuracy measures the proportion of correctly predicted instances, while precision quantifies the proportion of true positives out of all positive predictions. Recall, also known as sensitivity, measures the proportion of true positives predicted correctly. The F1 score combines precision and recall into a single metric, providing a balanced assessment of model performance.

Example 1:

Suppose we have an image classification model trained to distinguish between cats and dogs. Accuracy can determine the percentage of correctly classified images, precision can quantify how many of the predicted cat images are actually cats, recall can indicate how many actual cat images were correctly identified, and the F1 score offers a comprehensive evaluation of both precision and recall.

Techniques for Model Validation:

Cross-validation and train-test splits are commonly used techniques for model validation. Cross-validation divides the dataset into multiple subsets, or "folds," and iteratively trains and evaluates the model on different combinations of these folds. This technique provides a robust estimation of model performance by reducing bias introduced by a single train-test split.

Train-test splits involve dividing the dataset into two subsets: one for training the model and another for testing its performance. This approach helps evaluate how well the model generalizes to unseen data. It is important to maintain a proper balance between the sizes of the training and test sets to avoid underfitting or overfitting.

Example 2:

In a text classification task, cross-validation can be employed to assess the model's performance by dividing the dataset into, say, five folds. The model is trained and evaluated five times, with each fold serving as a test set once. This ensures a more reliable evaluation of the model's ability to generalize to different data subsets.

Advanced Techniques for Model Evaluation:

Advanced techniques such as ROC curves, confusion matrices, and precision-recall curves provide deeper insights into model performance. ROC (Receiver Operating Characteristic) curves visualize the trade-off between true positive rate (sensitivity) and false positive rate. They help determine an optimal threshold for binary classification models.

Confusion matrices display the performance of a classification model by showcasing the number of true positives, true negatives, false positives, and false negatives. This information enables a comprehensive understanding of the model's accuracy and misclassification patterns.

Precision-recall curves graphically represent the relationship between precision and recall at different probability thresholds. They provide valuable information about the trade-offs between precision and recall and aid in selecting an appropriate threshold for model deployment.

Example 3:

Consider a fraud detection model where detecting fraudulent transactions is of utmost importance. ROC curves can illustrate the model's performance by showing the relationship between the true positive rate (sensitivity) and the false positive rate. By analyzing the curve, we can identify the threshold that balances the need for correctly identifying fraud (high recall) while minimizing false alarms (high precision).

Model evaluation and validation techniques play a critical role in assessing the performance and generalization capabilities of AI models. By utilizing metrics like accuracy, precision, recall, and the F1 score, along with techniques like cross-validation and train-test splits, developers can gain valuable insights into their models' effectiveness. Additionally, advanced techniques such as ROC curves, confusion matrices, and precision-recall curves offer a deeper understanding of model performance, aiding in decision-making processes. Employing these techniques ensures the development of robust and reliable AI models for various applications.

5.5 Hyperparameter Tuning and Optimization Strategies

Hyperparameter tuning and optimization strategies play a crucial role in fine-tuning AI models to achieve their optimal performance. In this section, we will explore the concept of hyperparameters, their significance in model development, and various techniques for tuning and optimizing them.

Understanding Hyperparameters:

Hyperparameters are configuration settings that determine the behavior and performance of AI models. Unlike model parameters, which are learned during the training process, hyperparameters are set before training begins and influence how the model learns. Examples of hyperparameters include learning rate, batch size, regularization strength, and the number of layers or units in a neural network.

The Importance of Hyperparameter Tuning:

Hyperparameters significantly impact a model's performance and generalization capabilities. Choosing appropriate values for hyperparameters can enhance a model's ability to learn complex patterns, prevent overfitting or underfitting, and expedite convergence during training. However, there is no one-size-fits-all set of hyperparameters that work well for every model or dataset. Therefore, hyperparameter tuning is essential to find the optimal configuration for a specific task.

Hyperparameter Tuning Techniques:

Grid Search:

Grid search is a systematic technique that explores a predefined grid of hyper-parameter values. It exhaustively evaluates the model's performance for each combination of hyperparameters to identify the best configuration. Although grid search is simple to implement, it can be computationally expensive when dealing with a large number of hyperparameters or a wide range of possible values.

Grid Search Technique:

Grid search is a systematic technique that builds a grid of hyperparameter values to be explored. It exhaustively evaluates the model's performance by training and testing it for each combination of hyperparameters within the grid. The performance metric, such as accuracy or loss, is then recorded for each configuration. Finally, the combination that yields the best performance is selected as the optimal hyperparameter configuration.

Implementation and Considerations:

To implement grid search, one must define a grid by specifying the hyperparameters and their corresponding values. For example, if we have two hyperparameters, learning rate and batch size, and we want to test three values for each, we would have a grid of 3x3 configurations. Each configuration is then evaluated using cross-validation or train-test splits to obtain a performance metric.

Advantages of Grid Search:

One of the main advantages of grid search is its simplicity. It is straightforward to implement and does not require extensive computational knowledge. Grid search also provides a comprehensive exploration of the hyperparameter space, ensuring that no configuration is overlooked. It is especially useful when the search space is relatively small or when specific combinations are suspected to yield better results based on prior knowledge.

Limitations and Computational Complexity:

Grid search has some limitations, primarily due to its computational complexity. As the number of hyperparameters and their values increase, the search space expands exponentially. This can lead to a combinatorial explosion of configurations, resulting in significant computational requirements. Grid search becomes impractical when dealing with a large number of hyperparameters or a wide range of possible values.

Example:

For instance, in a convolutional neural network for image classification, grid search could explore different combinations of learning rates (0.001, 0.01, 0.1) and batch sizes (16, 32, 64). By evaluating nine configurations, we can identify the hyperparameter combination that yields the best accuracy.

Random Search:

Random search selects hyperparameter values randomly from predefined distributions or ranges. It samples a set of configurations and evaluates their performance. This technique is often more efficient than grid search, as it does not exhaustively search the entire hyperparameter space. Random search can lead to the discovery of good hyperparameter configurations, particularly when the search space is large or complex.

Random Search Technique:

In random search, the hyperparameters are defined with a range or distribution from which values are randomly selected. A fixed number of configurations are sampled from this range, and the model's performance is evaluated for each configuration. This randomness allows for a broader exploration of the hyperparameter space, potentially uncovering configurations that might not be considered in a systematic manner.

Advantages of Random Search:

Efficiency:

Random search is often more efficient than grid search, particularly when dealing with a large or complex hyperparameter space. By randomly sampling configurations, random search can potentially find good hyperparameter combinations with fewer evaluations compared to exhaustively searching the entire space.

Flexibility:

Random search offers greater flexibility in selecting hyperparameters. It allows for a diverse range of values and distributions, enabling exploration beyond preconceived notions or assumptions about the optimal hyperparameter values. This flexibility makes random search suitable for situations where prior knowledge is limited or when the relationship between hyperparameters and model performance is unclear.

Parallelization:

Random search lends itself well to parallelization. Multiple configurations can be evaluated concurrently, utilizing available computational resources effectively. This parallelization capability further enhances the efficiency of random search, enabling the evaluation of a larger number of configurations in a shorter time.

Example:

Suppose we are tuning hyperparameters for a deep learning model used in natural language processing. The learning rate hyperparameter could be sampled randomly from a uniform distribution between 0.001 and 0.1, while the number of hidden units in the recurrent layer could be randomly selected from a discrete set of values. By sampling a set of configurations and evaluating their performance, random search can identify hyperparameter combinations that lead to improved model performance.

Bayesian Optimization:

Bayesian optimization employs probabilistic models to estimate the performance of different hyperparameter configurations. It sequentially selects new configurations to evaluate based on the information gained from previous evaluations. By modeling the performance landscape, Bayesian optimization focuses on promising regions of the hyperparameter space, leading to faster convergence. This technique is particularly effective when the evaluation of each configuration is time-consuming or computationally expensive.

Probabilistic Modeling for Hyperparameter Tuning:

Bayesian optimization employs probabilistic models to capture the performance landscape of AI models. These models provide an estimation of how well a specific hyperparameter configuration is expected to perform without actually evaluating it. By utilizing these models, Bayesian optimization intelligently selects new configurations to evaluate based on the information gained from previous evaluations.

Sequential Selection of Configurations:

Bayesian optimization operates in a sequential manner, iteratively evaluating and updating the probabilistic model. The initial evaluations are typically performed using a small set of randomly selected configurations. Based on the results, the model is updated, and a new configuration is selected for evaluation. This process continues until a termination condition, such as a maximum number of evaluations or a convergence criterion, is met.

Focusing on Promising Regions:

One key aspect of Bayesian optimization is its ability to focus on promising regions of the hyperparameter space. The probabilistic model estimates the performance and uncertainty associated with each configuration. By incorporating this uncertainty, Bayesian optimization can identify regions that are likely to contain configurations with high performance. This enables the method to efficiently explore the hyperparameter space, bypassing unpromising regions and converging more quickly towards optimal configurations.

Advantages of Bayesian Optimization:

Efficient Exploration:

Bayesian optimization significantly reduces the number of hyperparameter evaluations compared to exhaustive search techniques like grid search. By actively seeking out promising regions, it avoids wasting evaluations on unpromising configurations, leading to faster convergence.

Handling Time-consuming Evaluations:

In scenarios where evaluating each configuration is computationally expensive or time-consuming (e.g., training deep neural networks on large datasets), Bayesian optimization proves particularly advantageous. By intelligently selecting configurations to evaluate, it optimizes the allocation of computational resources, making efficient use of available time and reducing the overall evaluation cost.

Adaptive and Robust:

Bayesian optimization adapts to the performance landscape by updating the probabilistic model with each evaluation. It can handle noisy or uncertain evaluations, making it robust in real-world scenarios where performance measurements may have inherent variability or noise.

Example:

Suppose we are tuning hyperparameters for a reinforcement learning algorithm. Bayesian optimization starts with a small set of randomly selected hyperparameter configurations and evaluates their performance. Based on these initial evaluations, the probabilistic model is updated, and a new configuration is selected for evaluation. Bayesian optimization gradually discovers configurations that lead to better performance, focusing on regions that show high promise based on the probabilistic model's estimates.

Optimization Strategies:

In addition to hyperparameter tuning techniques, several optimization strategies can improve model performance:

Regularization:

Regularization techniques, such as L1 and L2 regularization, help prevent overfitting by introducing penalty terms into the model's loss function. These penalties discourage the model from relying too heavily on certain features or parameters, promoting generalization to unseen data.

Learning Rate Schedules:

Adjusting the learning rate over the course of training can accelerate convergence and prevent overshooting or getting stuck in suboptimal solutions. Learning rate schedules, such as step decay, exponential decay, or adaptive learning rates, dynamically modify the learning rate based on predefined rules or the model's performance.

Adaptive Optimization Algorithms:

Traditional optimization algorithms like stochastic gradient descent (SGD) can be enhanced with adaptive techniques such as Adam, RMSprop, or Adagrad. These algorithms dynamically adjust the learning rate for each parameter, often based on the historical gradients. They improve convergence speed and robustness by adapting to different regions of the loss landscape.

Hyperparameter tuning and optimization strategies are essential for maximizing the performance of AI models. Through techniques like grid search, random search, and Bayesian optimization, developers can identify the optimal configuration of hyperparameters for a specific task. Additionally, employing regularization, learning rate schedules, and adaptive optimization algorithms can further enhance model performance and generalization. The careful selection and optimization of hyperparameters empower AI models to achieve their full potential and deliver superior results in various domains.

Chapter 6

Integration and Deployment

Overview:

6.1 Choosing the Right Deployment Approach

6.2 Designing APIs and Interfaces for Integration

6.3 Containerization and Scalability Considerations

6.4 Testing and Quality Assurance of Deployed Models

6.5 Monitoring, Logging, and Error Handling

Introduction:

Creating an effective AI model is only part of the story. In the grand scheme of things, a model's ultimate purpose is to integrate and deploy into real-world systems, where it can deliver genuine value. In this chapter, we will guide you through the crucial phases of AI model integration and deployment. Choosing the right deployment approach is our starting point. Here, we consider various factors like the specific use case, infrastructure constraints, and performance requirements that ultimately inform our choice of deployment strategy.

Designing APIs and interfaces for integration is the next crucial step. These APIs act as the conduit through which different software components communicate with the AI model. We will look at principles and best practices for designing these critical interfaces. In modern software development, containerization has emerged as a key technique for deploying AI models. We will discuss how this works and why it's beneficial. Additionally, we will explore scalability considerations, understanding how to design and deploy models that can effectively scale to meet demand.

The importance of testing and quality assurance cannot be overstated. Before a model is deployed, it must undergo rigorous testing to ensure that it performs as expected. We will delve into the techniques and methodologies used to validate the performance of AI models. Finally, we discuss the crucial tasks of monitoring, logging, and error handling. These processes ensure that we can keep track of our model's performance in real-time, rapidly identify and resolve issues, and maintain high availability and reliability.

6.1 Choosing the Right Deployment Approach

In AI model deployment, choosing the right approach is an important decision that affects how the model will operate in a production environment. The choice of deployment strategy often depends on several factors:

Application's Specific Requirements:

Different applications may have different needs. For example, a model that is used for real-time recommendations on a high-traffic website might need a deployment strategy that prioritizes low latency and high availability. On the other hand, a model used for analyzing historical data might be run less frequently and have different needs.

AI models are developed to meet varying needs and objectives across numerous applications, ranging from real-time personalization to large-scale data analysis. Understanding the specific requirements of the application is paramount in selecting the right deployment strategy.

Consider an AI model developed for real-time recommendations on a high-traffic e-commerce website. This model would need to respond rapidly to user interactions and dynamically provide personalized recommendations. Such an application necessitates a deployment strategy that can accommodate high request volumes, deliver responses within a short timeframe, and stay robust during peak traffic periods. This scenario calls for a strategy that emphasizes low latency and high availability, possibly utilizing a powerful cloud-based server or an optimized on-premise infrastructure.

Contrastingly, an AI model designed for analyzing historical data may present a different set of requirements. This type of model could be used to mine insights from past sales records, social media data, or customer service logs. Unlike the real-time recommendation system, this model may not need to operate continuously or process instantaneous requests. Instead, it might be run intermittently, possibly in response to specific organizational queries or at regular intervals, such as monthly or quarterly. In such cases, a high-cost, continuously running server may not be necessary. Depending on the data size and processing time, even a well-equipped local machine could suffice.

The requirements of an AI application significantly influence its deployment approach. Real-time, high-traffic applications often demand high-availability, low-latency solutions, possibly using cloud or high-performance on-premise servers. Conversely, intermittent or batch-processing tasks may permit more cost-effective, lower-performance options. Understanding these needs is the first step in devising a suitable, efficient, and cost-effective deployment strategy for AI models.

Scale of the Model:

Larger, more complex models may require more computational resources and thus may necessitate a deployment approach that can provide such resources. Small models, in contrast, can be deployed on lighter and cheaper infrastructures.

The scale of an AI model plays a significant role in determining its deployment strategy. In the realm of AI and machine learning, models can vary enormously in complexity and size, influencing not only their performance but also their computational demands. A large, intricate model like a deep neural network with millions of parameters would require substantial computational resources for operation. Conversely, a simpler, smaller model such as a logistic regression or decision tree could operate effectively with significantly fewer resources. Take a large-scale model designed to carry out complex tasks, such as a convolutional neural network used for high-resolution image recognition. This model, with its numerous layers and millions of parameters, necessitates powerful computational capabilities for efficient operation. Running such a model on a limited infrastructure could lead to slow response times, or worse, a complete failure to function. Hence, for deploying this kind of model, a robust infrastructure with powerful CPUs, ample memory, and possibly GPU acceleration would be required. This could entail a high-performance on-premise server or a cloud-based solution from providers like Google Cloud, AWS, or Azure. On the other end of the spectrum, consider a lightweight model like a decision tree used for a simple classification task. With its comparatively fewer parameters and less complex computations, this model can function effectively on less powerful infrastructures. Deployment could occur on an on-premise server with moderate specifications or even an edge device like a smartphone or IoT device, depending on the model's requirements. The choice between these extremes involves careful consideration of the model's scale and the available computational resources. Larger models necessitate a more robust infrastructure to function efficiently, which can often involve higher costs and greater energy consumption. Smaller models, conversely, offer more flexibility, enabling deployment on less powerful and potentially more cost-effective infrastructures. By accurately understanding the relationship between model scale and computational demands, businesses can make informed decisions on their AI deployment strategies, optimizing for both performance and cost.

Frequency of Model Updates:

If the model needs to be updated frequently (e.g., because the underlying data changes rapidly), a deployment strategy that allows for quick and seamless model updates would be ideal.

Cost:

Deployment can involve costs related to infrastructure, maintenance, and computational resources. Therefore, budget constraints must be considered when choosing a deployment strategy.

The cost factor plays an integral role in determining an appropriate strategy for deploying AI models. These costs extend beyond the initial development of the model to include ongoing expenses associated with infrastructure, maintenance, computational resources, and potential upgrades. In the era of AI and machine learning, where models can range from small and simple to large and complex, the cost implications of these models can vary dramatically and must be duly considered in the deployment strategy.

The first significant cost factor to consider is the infrastructure. Depending on the complexity and size of the AI model, you might need robust computational resources to effectively run it. These resources could include high-performance servers, cloud-based platforms, or even edge devices for lightweight models. High-performance servers and cloud platforms, while offering significant computational power and scalability, come with recurring expenses. These expenses can include rental costs for cloud platforms or energy consumption and depreciation costs for on-premise servers. Conversely, deploying on edge devices like smartphones or IoT devices may involve lower costs but may not be suitable for larger models. Maintenance cost is another critical aspect. Deploying an AI model is not a one-time process; instead, it is a continuous one that requires regular model updates, troubleshooting, and system upgrades. The model needs to adapt to evolving data trends and requirements, which might necessitate re-training or fine-tuning. This continuous process of maintaining and updating the model can be resource-intensive and hence can contribute to the overall cost.

Finally, the cost of computational resources, including processing power, memory, and storage, directly impacts the deployment strategy. Running large-scale AI models requires significant computational power and memory, leading to increased costs. On the other hand, smaller, less complex models can operate efficiently with fewer computational resources, leading to cost savings.

Balancing these cost factors is a strategic decision that organizations must make when planning their AI deployment. It involves a careful examination of the organization's budget constraints, the model's requirements, and the anticipated return on investment from the model. By understanding these cost dynamics, organizations can choose a deployment approach that aligns with their financial resources and AI needs, ensuring cost-effectiveness while also achieving the desired AI performance.

Latency Requirements:

Some applications require making predictions in real-time, which necessitates low-latency deployment strategies. In other cases, where immediate responses are not required, latency might be less of a concern. Latency, the time delay experienced in a system, holds a pivotal place when determining the deployment strategy for AI models. The latency requirement of an application can substantially influence the design, deployment, and success of AI models in real-world situations. This is particularly critical in applications that require real-time predictions and immediate responses, emphasizing the importance of low-latency deployment strategies.

The urgency of real-time applications can be seen in various domains. In autonomous driving systems, for example, the AI model must process and respond to real-time data within fractions of a second to ensure safe and effective operation. Any delay in decision-making can potentially lead to dangerous situations. Similarly, in high-frequency trading systems, investment decisions based on real-time market data need to be made instantly to capitalize on fleeting opportunities. Any latency in such situations could translate into substantial financial losses.

Conversely, some applications do not necessitate instantaneous responses. For instance, an AI model deployed for data analysis or business intelligence might not require real-time predictions. Here, latency can be relatively higher as the model might be analyzing historical data to provide insights for strategic decision-making rather than instantaneous operational decisions.

Choosing an AI deployment strategy in the context of latency requirements involves considering the specific use-case, the complexity of the model, and the necessary infrastructure. High-performance servers or powerful cloud-based platforms might be used for applications requiring low-latency responses. Simultaneously, lighter infrastructure could suffice for less urgent applications. Further, certain techniques like model pruning, quantization, or using more straightforward models can also help reduce latency.

Understanding the latency requirements of an application is fundamental when deploying an AI model. The choice of deployment strategy should aim for an optimal balance between providing the required speed of response and managing costs, complexity, and other operational considerations. By taking latency requirements into account, organizations can enhance the utility, efficiency, and effectiveness of their AI models.

Taking these factors into account, there are several deployment options available:

On-Premise Servers:

This involves deploying the model on servers that are physically located at the organization's site. This approach gives the organization complete control over the infrastructure but also means that they are responsible for all maintenance and updates.

n-Premise Servers:

As technology continues to evolve, organizations are met with various choices regarding how and where to deploy their machine learning models. One such option is the utilization of on-premise servers. The term 'on-premise' refers to a software deployment method where the application or service is run and managed on computers situated within the physical confines of the organization itself.

On-premise servers come with their unique set of advantages and disadvantages. On the positive side, they offer an increased level of control to the organization. Given that the servers are physically located on the organization's premises, it provides them the autonomy to tailor their system configuration to their specific needs. This flexibility extends to the customization of security protocols, which can be of paramount importance for organizations handling sensitive data.

Furthermore, the lack of reliance on external network connectivity means that the system can maintain operational even during periods of internet downtime, providing consistent model performance. Also, in-house servers can sometimes offer improved latency times due to the proximity of the servers to the end-users.

On the flip side, opting for on-premise servers places the responsibility of maintenance squarely on the organization's shoulders. This includes dealing with potential hardware failures, carrying out regular updates, and ensuring the security of the system. The cost associated with these responsibilities can be significant, not just in terms of finance but also in terms of time and human resources.

Additionally, unlike cloud-based services that can offer virtually limitless scalability, the capacity of on-premise servers is bound by the physical hardware present. This means that in situations of unexpected traffic spikes or expansion, the organization may find itself unprepared.

While on-premise servers offer a high level of control and potentially improved latency, organizations choosing this route must be prepared to handle all associated maintenance, updates, and costs. They must also consider the scalability limitations and plan their resource allocation accordingly. As with any strategic decision, organizations must weigh these factors against their specific needs and circumstances when deciding whether an on-premise deployment approach is suitable for their machine learning models.

Cloud-Based Platforms:

As organizations seek solutions to handle the deployment of machine learning models, one approach that has seen significant growth and adoption is the use of cloud-based platforms. Providers such as Amazon Web Services (AWS), Google Cloud Platform (GCP), and Microsoft Azure offer a variety of services tailored to support the deployment, scaling, and management of machine learning models.

Cloud-based platforms are a form of off-premise hosting where the computational resources are provided over the internet. This setup can considerably simplify the maintenance aspect of model deployment. Unlike on-premise servers where the responsibility of system maintenance lies with the organization, cloud providers take over the maintenance tasks, ensuring that the servers are regularly updated and that the system remains secure.

Another significant advantage of cloud-based platforms is scalability. The cloud offers virtually limitless resources, allowing an organization to easily adjust its resource allocation in response to its needs. This flexibility can be particularly useful when dealing with large machine learning models or fluctuating workloads.

Additionally, cloud platforms often come with a range of tools and services designed to assist in model management, monitoring, and optimization. These platforms also have robust support for distributed computing, making it easier to handle large-scale data processing and model training tasks.

However, while cloud-based platforms come with these advantages, they also come with ongoing costs. Unlike on-premise servers where the organization makes a one-time investment in the hardware, cloud services usually follow a pay-as-you-go model. This means that the organization pays for the computational resources it uses, which can add up over time.

Another consideration is data security and privacy. When using a cloud service, sensitive data is stored and processed outside the organization's direct control, which may not be suitable for certain applications or may require additional measures to ensure data protection.

In conclusion, cloud-based platforms can offer simplified maintenance, high scalability, and a host of helpful tools for machine learning model deployment. However, organizations must be aware of the associated ongoing costs and need to carefully manage data security and privacy when using these platforms. As always, the selection of the right deployment approach should take into account the specific needs, resources, and constraints of the organization.

Edge Devices:

In some cases, models might be deployed directly onto edge devices (like smartphones or IoT devices). This can reduce latency and allow for offline functionality but also places constraints on the size and complexity of the model.

As the landscape of machine learning evolves, the deployment of models is increasingly extending beyond traditional server-based environments. One such trend is the deployment on edge devices, which includes smartphones, Internet of Things (IoT) devices, and other embedded systems.

Edge deployment of machine learning models involves running these models directly on the end-user device. This strategy comes with certain unique advantages. One of the most prominent is reduced latency. Because the inference computation is performed directly on the device, the need for data to travel to a central server is eliminated, resulting in faster response times. This can be critical for applications that require real-time predictions, such as autonomous vehicles, augmented reality applications, and certain healthcare devices. Another significant advantage is the ability to function offline. Since the models reside on the device, they can operate independently of internet connectivity. This can be particularly beneficial for applications that need to function in remote areas or situations where consistent internet connectivity is not guaranteed.

Edge deployment also offers benefits in terms of data privacy. As data is processed on the device, less sensitive information is transferred over the network, reducing the risk of data breaches.

However, while deploying machine learning models on edge devices comes with these benefits, it also brings about its own set of challenges. Given the limited computational resources and memory of edge devices compared to traditional servers or cloud platforms, there are constraints on the size and complexity of the models that can be deployed. Large deep learning models may not be feasible, necessitating the use of smaller, more efficient models or techniques like model pruning or quantization to reduce the model's size without a significant drop in performance.

Additionally, the variety of edge devices, each with its unique hardware and software configurations, can add to the complexity of model deployment. Developers need to ensure that models are optimized to run efficiently across different types of devices, which may require platform-specific adaptations.

In conclusion, while edge deployment offers the benefits of reduced latency, offline functionality, and increased privacy, it also brings challenges related to limited computational resources and device variability. The decision to deploy on edge devices should thus consider these factors and the specific requirements of the application.

Hybrid Approaches:

In some cases, a combination of the above strategies might be used. For example, a model might be initially trained in the cloud and then deployed on an edge device for inference.

As the field of machine learning continues to evolve, developers are exploring new strategies that can optimally leverage the available resources. One such strategy is the use of hybrid approaches in the deployment of machine learning models, wherein the advantages of multiple deployment strategies are combined to achieve the most efficient, cost-effective, and application-appropriate solution. The hybrid deployment approach can take various forms, depending on the requirements of the machine learning application. For instance, a common hybrid method is to use cloud-based platforms for training the model and then deploy the trained model on edge devices for inference. In this approach, the model takes advantage of the substantial computational resources and scalable storage options offered by the cloud for the training process, which often requires high processing power and large amounts of data. Cloud platforms such as Amazon Web Services (AWS), Google Cloud, and Microsoft Azure offer specialized machine learning services and hardware accelerators like GPUs and TPUs, making them suitable environments for intensive model training.

Once the model is trained, it can be deployed onto edge devices for inference.

As discussed earlier, performing inference at the edge can significantly reduce latency and allow for real-time predictions. It can also provide offline functionality, data privacy, and reduce the amount of data transmitted over the network, which can be beneficial in terms of both cost and privacy. However, it's worth noting that the hybrid approach also comes with its complexities. For instance, the model trained in the cloud needs to be optimized and possibly compressed to fit onto the edge device without compromising its performance significantly. It also needs to be compatible with the hardware and software configurations of the device. Furthermore, managing the model's lifecycle, including version control, updates, and monitoring, can become more complex in a hybrid environment. In conclusion, while a hybrid deployment approach can bring together the strengths of cloud and edge deployments, it requires careful management and optimization to ensure that the transition from the cloud to the edge is smooth and that the model performs optimally in both environments. The choice of a hybrid approach should, therefore, be driven by the specific requirements and constraints of the application, including factors like latency requirements, data privacy, computational resources, and cost considerations. Each of these deployment options has its pros and cons, and the best choice often depends on the specific use case and requirements. This section would discuss these factors in more detail, helping the reader make an informed decision for their particular situation.

6.2 Designing APIs and Interfaces for Integration

Creating a robust and user-friendly interface between machine learning models and applications or end-users is a key aspect of effective model deployment. This involves the design and implementation of Application Programming Interfaces (APIs) and user interfaces. APIs serve as the communication conduit between the machine learning model and the software applications that utilize it. Designing an API for a machine learning model involves defining clear rules of interaction that allows the application to feed data to the model, obtain the model's predictions, and potentially even request additional information, such as the confidence associated with each prediction.

There are several important considerations when designing such APIs. Firstly, it is necessary to clearly define the endpoints. In the context of APIs, an end-

AI Model Design:A Comprehensive Guide to Development, Integration, and Deployment

point refers to a specific URL where an API can be accessed by a software application. For example, you might have one endpoint for obtaining predictions and another for submitting new data to the model.

Secondly, you need to determine the data formats for inputs and outputs. For instance, will the API accept data in JSON format, or does it need to be in a specific proprietary format? Similarly, in what format will the model's predictions be returned? This decision heavily influences how easily the API can be integrated into existing systems and applications.

Another crucial aspect is versioning. If you plan to update or refine your model over time, your API needs to be designed with versioning in mind. This ensures that applications using the API continue to function correctly even as the model evolves.

Last but not least, security measures should be in place to prevent unauthorized access and to ensure data privacy. APIs are gateways to your models and could potentially be exploited if not adequately protected.

On the other hand, designing the user interface involves creating a visual platform where users can interact with the machine learning model or the application embedding it. A well-designed user interface can hide the underlying complexities of the model, yet present the outputs in a clear, intuitive, and actionable manner. The user interface could also include mechanisms for users to provide feedback on the model's predictions, which could serve as valuable input for future model refinement. The design of APIs and interfaces plays a crucial role in the integration of machine learning models into larger systems or applications. While this process involves various considerations, when done correctly, it can significantly enhance the effectiveness and usability of the deployed models.

Designing APIs and user interfaces for integration is a multi-step process that involves planning, designing, implementing, testing, and maintaining the API and user interface. Here are the steps in detail:

Identify the Needs:

Understand the user's needs and the application requirements. This helps define what functions the API needs to provide and how the user interface should be designed. This step involves interacting with stakeholders and end-users, and understanding the existing software system, if any.

At this stage, we are considering the needs of two types of users. Firstly, there are the end-users who will interact with the user interface. Secondly, there are other developers or systems who will interact with the API. When considering the needs of the end-users, you need to understand their goals and how they will be using the application. This understanding can be built through user interviews, surveys, or studying user behavior. For example, if you are designing a machine learning application, you might ask questions like: How do users want to input data? What output are they interested in? How can the output be presented in the most useful and intuitive way? The existing software system also plays a significant role. This includes other software that will interact with the API or UI, existing codebases, and tech stacks. Understanding these can highlight constraints and opportunities in the design and implementation of the API or UI. When considering the needs of the developers or systems who will interact with the API, it is important to understand their technical requirements. What kind of data will they be sending and receiving? What is the expected load on the system? How can the API be designed to ensure efficient and reliable communication?

Interacting with stakeholders is an important part of this step. Stakeholders can include product managers, other developers, data scientists, business analysts, and anyone else who has an interest in the application. Stakeholder requirements can provide valuable insights into the functional and non-functional requirements of the system.

Identifying the needs involves understanding user requirements, system requirements, and stakeholder requirements, and using this understanding to define the API and UI's functionality and behavior.

Plan the API:

Decide the endpoints the API will have, the HTTP methods each endpoint will respond to, and the data each endpoint will receive and send. This step involves designing the URL structure, determining the required inputs and outputs, and deciding how the API will handle different HTTP methods like GET, POST, PUT, DELETE etc.

The planning process starts with designing the endpoints of the API. Endpoints are the touchpoints of interaction; they are the routes or URLs where your API can be accessed by clients. For instance, in a machine learning application, you might have an endpoint like '/predict' that takes input data and returns a prediction.

When designing the URL structure for your endpoints, a good practice is to use a clear and intuitive naming system. The URLs should effectively describe the resources they represent. For example, if you have an API that provides access to user information in a system, an appropriate URL might be '/users' for accessing all users, and '/users/{id}' for accessing a specific user.

Once the endpoints have been decided, the next step is to determine the HTTP methods each endpoint will respond to. HTTP methods define the type of request a client can make to your API. The common HTTP methods include GET (retrieve data), POST (send data), PUT (update data), and DELETE (remove data).

For each endpoint, you'll need to decide what data it will receive and what it will send back. The data received by an endpoint is usually sent as part of the request body in POST and PUT requests. The data sent by an endpoint is the response to the client's request. In a machine learning application, for instance, a '/predict' endpoint might receive input data and send back a prediction.

Planning the API is a collaborative process that involves the API designers, developers, and possibly the end-users or other stakeholders. This step is key to ensuring that the API is well-structured, intuitive, and capable of efficiently meeting the application requirements. It provides a roadmap that guides the subsequent development and integration stages of the API.

Design the User Interface:

Based on the user requirements and application needs, design a user interface that is intuitive, easy to use, and aligns with the application's overall design. The interface should clearly represent the model's outputs and provide a way for users to interact with it.

User Interface (UI) design is a multidisciplinary process that involves understanding user behavior, aesthetic appeal, and the technical feasibility of implementing designs. It's about creating an interface that's easy to use, efficient, and enjoyable, and helps users achieve their goals with the application. In the context of AI, the user interface could be a dashboard that displays model predictions, an input field that accepts user queries, or even a chatbot that interacts with users.

To start with, you need to have a good understanding of who your users are and what they need. This can be achieved through user research, surveys, and by studying user personas and scenarios. Each user might have a different goal when using the application, and the UI should cater to these various needs. Once you understand your users' needs and behavior, you can start designing the interface. This involves deciding on the layout of the interface, choosing the right components (buttons, forms, tables, etc.), picking appropriate colors and fonts, and making sure the design aligns with the overall aesthetic and brand identity of the application. The user interface should clearly represent the model's outputs in a way that's easy for users to understand. For example, if the AI model is a recommendation system, the interface might display a list of recommended items along with their relevant details. If the AI model is used for data analysis, the interface could use charts and graphs to visualize the results. User interaction is another crucial aspect of UI design. The interface should provide a clear and efficient way for users to interact with the AI model, whether that's by inputting data, adjusting parameters, or initiating model training or predictions.

Finally, it's essential to iterate on the design based on user feedback and usability testing. The UI design process doesn't end when the interface is built – it's a continuous process of testing, learning, and improving to ensure the interface remains effective and user-friendly as the application evolves.

Implement the API:

With the design in place, the next step is to implement the API using an appropriate programming language and framework. The implementation should follow the design closely and include all planned endpoints, methods, and data handling processes.

After the planning phase where the API's structure, endpoints, and data handling processes have been meticulously planned and designed, you then transition into the actual coding phase. The choice of programming language for implementation would generally depend on factors such as the development team's proficiency, the existing tech stack, and the specific requirements of the API. Languages like Python, Node.js (JavaScript), Ruby, and Java are frequently used for API development. Typically, a web framework that complements the chosen language is used to expedite the process. These frameworks provide a structure for the application and often include libraries and tools that make it easier to build the API. For example, if Python is the chosen language, frameworks such as Flask or Django might be used. In the implementation phase, developers write code to create the API endpoints that were designed in the planning phase. Each endpoint corresponds to a specific URL where the API can receive requests and send responses. These endpoints are configured to handle specific HTTP methods (GET, POST, PUT, DELETE, etc.), according to what was decided in the design phase.

Developers also implement the necessary logic to process incoming requests, carry out appropriate actions (like fetching data from a database, or making predictions with a machine learning model), and structure the response data. This also involves handling potential errors and providing meaningful feedback to the user.

Additionally, the implementation phase should also consider security and performance. Techniques such as rate limiting (to prevent abuse of the API), input validation (to protect against malicious data), and caching (to improve response times) can be implemented.

Once the API is implemented, it should be thoroughly tested to ensure it works as intended, follows the design, handles errors gracefully, and meets all the requirements outlined in the initial stages. Developers can use automated testing tools and frameworks to verify the correctness, completeness, security, and performance of the API.

Implement the User Interface:

After the design is ready, develop the user interface using suitable front-end technologies. This includes writing the HTML, CSS, and JavaScript code, and ensuring the interface communicates effectively with the API.

HTML is the standard language for creating the structure and content of web pages, including text, images, and interactive forms. CSS is used for styling these web elements, including layout, colors, fonts, and transitions. JavaScript adds interactivity to the web pages, handling actions like clicks, scrolls, and updates to the content. In the context of integrating a machine learning model with an application, the user interface might include elements for users to input data, buttons to trigger predictions, and displays to show the model's outputs. JavaScript would be used to handle these interactions, making requests to the back-end API when needed and updating the display based on the responses received. The user interface implementation phase should ensure that the interface communicates effectively with the back-end API. This involves sending requests to the correct API endpoints, providing the required data in the correct format, and handling the API responses appropriately. This is usually done using JavaScript's Fetch API or libraries like Axios. For more complex applications, front-end frameworks like React, Angular, or Vue.js may be used. These frameworks provide structures and patterns for building larger applications, and can help manage the complexity of the user interface code. Importantly, the implemented user interface should closely follow the original designs and meet all the usability and accessibility requirements. The interface should be thoroughly tested on various devices and screen sizes to ensure a good user experience. Ultimately, the goal of implementing the user interface is to provide users with an easy, intuitive, and efficient way to interact with the machine learning model, enabling them to input data, trigger model predictions, and understand the outputs.

Test the API and User Interface:

Conduct thorough testing to ensure that the API and user interface function as expected. This involves unit testing, integration testing, system testing, and user acceptance testing.

Unit Testing:

In the context of an API, unit testing typically involves testing individual endpoints to ensure they behave as expected given a certain input. For the UI, this might involve testing individual components (like buttons, forms, or displays) to make sure they work correctly.

Integration Testing:

Once individual components or units have been tested, the next step is to test them together. In the context of an API, this might mean testing how different endpoints interact. For a UI, this could mean testing how different components work together, such as a form that submits data to an API and a display that shows the response.

System Testing:

System testing involves testing the entire system as a whole. This includes not only the API and UI, but also any other components of the system, such as databases or third-party services. This type of testing is designed to catch any issues that might arise when all parts of the system interact.

User Acceptance Testing (UAT):

This is the final phase of testing, where actual users test the system. The aim is to confirm that the system is ready for release and works as expected in real-world scenarios. Feedback from UAT can lead to further improvements in the system.

It's important to note that testing should be done in various environments (like development, staging, and production) and on different devices and browsers (for UI) to ensure consistency and compatibility. Automated testing tools can be used to streamline the process and continuous integration/continuous deployment (CI/CD) practices can be implemented to automatically run tests before deploying new versions of the system.

By following these testing steps, developers can catch and fix any issues early in the development process, and ensure that both the API and the user interface function correctly, provide a good user experience, and meet all necessary requirements.

Deploy and Maintain:

After successful testing, deploy the API and user interface. After deployment, regular maintenance is required to handle bug fixes, updates, and improvements. This might involve adding new endpoints to the API, updating the user interface, or improving the security features. Deployment is the process of making the API and user interface available for use, typically on a server that can be accessed by the end users. This could be on an on-premise server, a cloud-based server, or even on edge devices, depending on the specific requirements of the project. Deployment also often involves setting up any necessary databases or other backend services that the API and UI rely on. Deployment can be a complex process that requires careful planning to ensure minimal disruption of services. It's also essential to consider security aspects during deployment, making sure that sensitive data is protected and that the server is secured against potential attacks. Once the API and user interface are deployed, the process doesn't stop there. Regular maintenance is crucial to keep the system running smoothly and securely.

Maintenance involves various activities, including:

Monitoring, updating, troubleshooting, security updates, and user support - these are the vital pillars in the process of maintaining an API and user interface post-deployment.

Constant monitoring is necessary to ensure that the system operates at its optimal capacity. It involves keeping a watchful eye on server performance indicators such as CPU and memory usage, response times of the API, and error rates. It serves as a first line of defense in identifying any potential problems before they escalate, ensuring that users experience minimal disruptions. As the technological landscape continually evolves, the updating process becomes critical. Whether it's to incorporate new features, improve the existing system performance, or keep pace with technological advancements, updates may encompass adding new endpoints to the API, refreshing the user interface design or functionality, or modernizing backend services. Despite the best efforts in design and testing, the real-world operation might reveal issues previously unseen. Troubleshooting and bug fixes become an ongoing task in the maintenance phase. It involves not only rectifying these issues but also adjusting the system to prevent their recurrence. With the increasing sophistication of cyber threats, continuous security updates are essential to safeguard the system and its data. From patching identified vulnerabilities to updating encryption protocols and modifying data handling processes, security remains an ever-evolving challenge. Lastly, user support is pivotal in the maintenance phase. From resolving user-specific issues, answering queries, to providing detailed documentation, support teams ensure the smooth operation for users, thereby enhancing their overall experience. Each of these components plays a vital role in ensuring the deployed API and user interface continue to serve their intended purpose efficiently and effectively, providing a seamless experience for users while staying secure and up-to-date in an ever-evolving technological landscape.

Through the process of deployment and maintenance, the designed API and interface can serve its intended users effectively, securely, and efficiently over time.

Document:

Proper documentation of the API is essential for it to be used effectively by other developers. The documentation should include details on endpoints, request format, response format, error messages, and any other details needed to use the API. User interface should also have a user manual, if necessary.

Proper documentation forms a cornerstone of a well-structured API and user interface. It serves as an invaluable resource for developers and users alike, guiding them in effectively utilizing the system. For an API, the documentation should meticulously detail the endpoints, outline the request and response formats, describe potential error messages, and provide any other necessary instructions that would aid its usage. This information becomes the roadmap, offering a comprehensive understanding of how the API functions, and ensures that developers can integrate it seamlessly into their applications. Similarly, for a user interface, a well-crafted user manual or a help guide can significantly enhance user experience. While the aim should always be to design an intuitive interface that a user can navigate without assistance, providing a detailed guide can help users understand the functionality in depth and make the most out of the system. In essence, thorough documentation serves as a communication tool between the system's creators and its users, enabling efficient use of the system, aiding problem-solving, and ultimately ensuring the system can function at its full potential. It is not just a formality, but a crucial element that supports the overall success of the API and user interface.

Remember, designing effective APIs and user interfaces requires careful planning, continuous testing, and regular updates based on user feedback and evolving needs.

6.3 Containerization and Scalability Considerations

In the context of deploying machine learning models and applications, the term "Containerization" refers to the practice of encapsulating or packaging up software code and all its dependencies so that it can run uniformly and consistently on any infrastructure. This is typically achieved using container platforms like Docker. Containers are lightweight, standalone, and executable software packages that include everything needed to run a piece of software, including the code, a runtime, libraries, environment variables, and config files. Scalability, on the other hand, refers to the ability of a system, network, or process to handle a growing amount of work, or its potential to be enlarged to accommodate that growth. In the context of machine learning applications, scalability considerations might include how to handle increasing data volume or how to maintain performance as the number of users increases.

When deploying machine learning models, both containerization and scalability are crucial considerations:

Containerization and scalability are integral aspects of deploying machine learning models, facilitating consistency across environments and allowing the application to adapt to varying demands respectively. Containerization involves the encapsulation of the machine learning model, alongside its dependencies, within a container. This assures the reliable execution of the model, irrespective of the environment, be it a developer's local machine, a testing environment, or a production server. This approach greatly streamlines the deployment process and prevents complications that could arise due to differences in dependencies or environment setup. Tools such as Docker serve as a linchpin in the creation of these containers.

On the other hand, scalability is the system's ability to handle a growing amount of work or expand in response to an increased demand. This becomes particularly crucial when deploying machine learning models that may have to deal with large volumes of data or serve a multitude of users with predictions. Therefore, planning and strategizing for scalability is of utmost importance. Potential strategies may include segmenting data into smaller, more manageable batches, dividing computations across several servers (known as horizontal scaling), or boosting the resources of a single server (referred to as vertical scaling). Moreover, numerous cloud providers offer auto-scaling features that dynamically adjust resources in alignment with the demand, further reinforcing scalability. The interplay between containerization and scalability forms the cornerstone of a robust and adaptable system that can not only provide consistent performance across various environments but also readily scale in response to increasing demands.

The integration of these considerations helps in achieving a system that is not only robust and consistent but also able to handle increased load and provide reliable service over time.

6.4 Testing and Quality Assurance of Deployed Models

Chapter 6.4, "Testing and Quality Assurance of Deployed Models," dives into the methods and processes utilized to ensure that a machine learning model works correctly and as expected after being deployed. Quality assurance encompasses several practices and techniques aimed at preventing defects and mistakes in the machine learning models and avoiding problems when delivering solutions or services to the end-users.

Model testing is a critical component of this process, which includes steps such as unit testing (testing individual parts of the model), integration testing (testing the model as a whole), and validation testing (testing the model against the validation set). Model testing also involves performance testing where the model is evaluated under varying loads, and stress testing, where the model's robustness is tested under extreme loads.Quality assurance of deployed models is not only about making sure that the model is technically sound but also involves validating that the model meets the business needs and provides meaningful value. This often includes processes for ongoing model monitoring and retraining to ensure the model continues to perform well as new data comes in.

Besides these, an important aspect of quality assurance is handling edge cases and ensuring the model doesn't behave erratically or fail under such scenarios. It also includes checking the model against ethical, legal, and fairness considerations, especially in sensitive applications.

Therefore, testing and quality assurance is a vital part of the model's life cycle to ensure the reliability, accuracy, and robustness of the model, thereby helping in building trustworthy and effective machine learning solutions.

6.5 Monitoring, Logging, and Error Handling

Section 6.5, "Monitoring, Logging, and Error Handling," is about the essential practices of supervising deployed machine learning models to ensure they are performing as expected and dealing effectively with any errors or issues that may arise.

Monitoring involves continuously observing the model's performance in a live setting. This can include tracking various metrics like model accuracy, prediction time, system latency, and more. Monitoring allows for the detection of any drop in performance or other anomalies in real-time, which may indicate that the model needs to be retrained or that there's an issue with the data or infrastructure. It can also help ensure the model's resources are being used effectively and can provide valuable insights into how the model is being used. Logging refers to the practice of recording events that occur while the model is running. Logs can provide valuable data for troubleshooting, for understanding how the model is behaving, and for auditing purposes. Logs may include information about the input data, the model's predictions, any errors that occur, system metrics, and more. Error handling is about how the system responds when something goes wrong. This might involve defining fallback strategies for when the model fails, ensuring the system fails gracefully, and providing clear error messages. Error handling can also include setting up alerts or triggers for certain events or conditions, so issues can be detected and addressed promptly.

In the context of deployed machine learning models, effective monitoring, logging, and error handling are essential for maintaining a reliable, robust system, and for quickly detecting and resolving issues. They also contribute to creating a system that is transparent, auditable, and trustworthy.

Chapter 7

Continuous Learning and Improvement

Overview:

7.1 Online Learning Techniques and Strategies

7.2 Incorporating Feedback Loops for Model Improvement

7.3 Adaptive Learning and Personalization

7.4 Incremental Model Updates and Version Control

7.5 Balancing Stability and Innovation in Model Evolution

Introduction:

Section 7.1 "Online Learning Techniques and Strategies" discusses methods to continually adapt and improve models based on new data that becomes available after deployment. Online learning techniques allow models to learn from new examples in real-time or near real-time, which is particularly useful for applications where the data distribution can change over time.

7.1 Online Learning Techniques and Strategies

In an ever-evolving world, data distributions and trends can change rapidly. Therefore, models that were once highly effective may lose their performance over time as they become outdated. Here, the concept of "Online Learning Techniques and Strategies," as discussed in Section 7.1, comes into play. Online learning is a method of machine learning where the model learns incrementally from a data stream, updating its parameters as new data arrives. This is in contrast to batch learning techniques, where the model is trained once using a large, fixed dataset and is not updated unless retrained. Online learning can adapt to new patterns in data as they emerge, making it particularly useful for scenarios where the underlying data distribution may evolve over time. This might include applications like financial markets, web analytics, sensor data, or other domains where new data is continuously being generated. Online learning techniques include methods like Stochastic Gradient Descent, where the model parameters are updated after seeing each new training example, rather than after the entire batch of data. This allows the model to adapt quickly to new information. Furthermore, online learning strategies might also involve deciding when and how to update the model. For instance, you could update the model with every new piece of data, or you could wait until you've accumulated a certain amount of new data before updating. Similarly, you might choose to give more weight to recent data if you believe it to be more relevant. The adoption of online learning techniques and strategies can help ensure that your machine learning model remains effective and relevant as new data becomes available after its initial deployment.

7.2 Incorporating Feedback Loops for Model Improvement

Section 7.2 "Incorporating Feedback Loops for Model Improvement" delves into strategies for using feedback from model predictions to update the model. This feedback could come from users (e.g., whether a recommended item was useful or not) or from new data (e.g., the actual outcome of a prediction).

Feedback loops play a crucial role in enhancing the performance of machine learning models post-deployment. A feedback loop, in the context of machine learning, is a process where the model's predictions are collected and evaluated for accuracy, and then this information is fed back into the model as a learning signal.

Feedback can come from different sources. In some cases, it might come directly from users. For instance, a recommendation system might ask users to rate its recommendations, providing direct feedback on the model's performance. In other cases, feedback might be obtained indirectly. For instance, a spam detection model might receive feedback based on whether users mark an email as spam or not. Once gathered, this feedback can be used to update the model. If the model is making incorrect predictions, the feedback loop allows it to learn from these mistakes. This process enables the model to continually improve and adapt to new data or changing conditions, ensuring its performance remains high over time. Incorporating feedback loops effectively requires careful planning. It's necessary to define how feedback will be collected, how it will be processed, and how it will be used to update the model. Moreover, it's important to consider potential delays in feedback, and how they might impact the model update process.

Thus, feedback loops serve as a potent tool for continual learning and improvement, keeping the models relevant, and their performance optimal in the long run.

7.3 Adaptive Learning and Personalization

Adaptive learning is an approach where machine learning models evolve based on the new data they process. This ability to adapt is critical in environments where data distributions change over time, which is quite common in real-world scenarios. It helps in maintaining the relevance of the models and their predictions, thereby enhancing their usefulness.

Personalization, on the other hand, involves tailoring the outputs of a machine learning model to the specific characteristics or needs of individual users. The concept of personalization has gained significant attention, especially in the realms of recommendation systems, targeted advertising, and user experience enhancement.

For example, recommendation systems utilized by e-commerce or streaming platforms personalize content suggestions based on individual user behavior, preferences, and history. Similarly, marketing models could segment users based on their previous interactions, demographic information, or other identifiable patterns, allowing for personalized marketing campaigns.

A significant aspect of this section could be strategies for implementing adaptive learning and personalization, considering factors such as user privacy, data collection, and ensuring the model's ability to adapt quickly and accurately to changing user behaviors. The challenge lies in maintaining a balance between personalization (for better user experience) and user privacy, ensuring ethical and responsible use of data. Moreover, real-world examples and case studies could be discussed to provide a practical perspective on implementing adaptive learning and personalization strategies.

7.4 Incremental Model Updates and Version Control

Incremental model updates refer to the technique where a model is fine-tuned or retrained with new data, rather than being trained from scratch. This process allows the model to assimilate new patterns from recent data while preserving the learned knowledge from previous training sessions. It's a method that is particularly beneficial when dealing with large-scale data or in scenarios where the model needs to adapt to ever-changing data distributions in real-time or near real-time. However, model updates need to be managed efficiently to prevent potential disruptions in the deployed services. That's where the concept of version control comes into play. Version control in the context of machine learning models involves tracking and managing different versions of models, much like software versioning. It ensures that multiple versions of a model can exist concurrently, allowing for smooth rollbacks if a newly deployed version encounters issues. Moreover, it's also important to consider how to handle live traffic during model updates. Techniques such as Canary Deployment or Blue-Green Deployment could be discussed in this section. Canary Deployment involves directing a small proportion of live traffic to the new model and gradually increasing it if no issues are detected. On the other hand, Blue-Green Deployment means having two production environments (blue and green) where one serves live traffic while the other is used for updates and testing. Once the new version is ready and tested, the roles of the environments are switched. In essence, this section is expected to present strategies and practices to ensure that model updates, versioning, and live traffic handling are done in a controlled and reliable manner, mitigating potential risks associated with model evolution.

7.5 Balancing Stability and Innovation in Model Evolution

Lastly, section 7.5 "Balancing Stability and Innovation in Model Evolution" likely discusses the trade-off between maintaining a stable, well-functioning model and updating the model to incorporate new features, techniques, or data. This could involve methods for robust testing, rollback strategies, or multi-armed bandit strategies for A/B testing of models.

Maintaining stability involves careful management of the deployed models to ensure that they continue to perform at the expected level. This is particularly important for mission-critical applications where failures or sudden drops in performance can have significant consequences. Various strategies can be employed to ensure stability, including robust testing procedures, careful monitoring of model performance, and the use of rollback strategies to revert to a previous version of a model if issues arise with a new version.

At the same time, innovation in model evolution is also crucial. Over time, new data may become available, new feature engineering techniques may be developed, or more advanced model architectures may be invented. Incorporating these innovations can lead to substantial improvements in model performance. However, each change also introduces potential risks, as it may inadvertently introduce bugs or degrade model performance. One way to balance stability and innovation is through the use of A/B testing or multi-armed bandit strategies. In A/B testing, a new model (or version of a model) is deployed alongside the existing model, and a portion of the traffic is directed to each. By comparing the performance of the new and existing models on real-world traffic, it's possible to evaluate whether the new model provides a significant improvement without fully committing to the change. Similarly, multi-armed bandit strategies can be used to balance exploration (trying out new models or techniques) and exploitation (sticking with the best-known approach) in a more dynamic and potentially more efficient way. This section likely presents strategies and best practices for balancing the need for stability and innovation in the process of model evolution, aiming to guide practitioners in managing the continuous learning and improvement of their machine learning systems.

Chapter 8

Ethical and Responsible AI Design

Overview:

8.1 Ensuring Fairness, Transparency, and Explainability

8.2 Addressing Bias and Discrimination in AI Models

8.3 Privacy and Security Considerations

8.4 Compliance with Regulatory Frameworks

8.5 Establishing Ethical Guidelines for AI Model Design

Introduction:

As AI models increasingly permeate our lives, the ethical and responsible design of these models has become a subject of paramount importance. This chapter delves into the key principles and considerations necessary to create AI systems that are not only effective but also ethical and responsible. We begin by addressing the concepts of fairness, transparency, and explainability in AI models. As AI is being entrusted with ever more significant decisions, it's critical that these systems are fair in their predictions and transparent in their operations, with explainability allowing users to understand how these predictions are made.

Next, we discuss how to address biases and discrimination in AI models. The data used to train models can often carry unconscious biases, which can lead to discriminatory outcomes. We explore strategies to identify and mitigate such biases to ensure equitable results. Privacy and security considerations form the next part of our discussion. With models often handling sensitive data, it's crucial to build systems that respect user privacy and ensure data security. We will discuss the key principles and best practices in this area. We also tackle the issue of compliance with regulatory frameworks. As AI is a rapidly evolving field, so too are the laws and regulations surrounding it. We'll explore how to design and operate AI systems that not only comply with these regulations but also anticipate future legal landscapes.

Finally, we emphasize the importance of establishing ethical guidelines for AI model design. These guidelines can provide a roadmap to navigate the various ethical dilemmas that can arise during the AI model design and deployment process.

8.1 Ensuring Fairness, Transparency, and Explainability

Fairness in AI essentially means that the AI system should not create or propagate unfair bias or discrimination. It should treat all individuals and groups equitably. This is particularly important in fields like finance, hiring, and law enforcement, where AI decisions can have significant impacts on individuals' lives. Fairness also includes ensuring that the benefits of AI are accessible and beneficial to all, not just a select few. Transparency is about making the AI's decision-making process clear and understandable to people. It involves describing the AI system in a manner that users can understand, which often requires avoiding technical jargon. It's about answering questions like: What data is the AI system using? How is it processing that data? On what basis is it making decisions? Transparent AI systems allow users to understand why certain actions are being taken and help to build trust in the system. Explainability is closely related to transparency. It goes a step further to ensure that the reasoning behind each specific AI decision can be understood by humans. This is challenging with complex models like deep neural networks, which are often described as "black boxes" because their internal workings are difficult to interpret. Explainable AI aims to make these black boxes as clear as glass boxes, with methods being developed to explain AI reasoning in a human-understandable way. These three concepts – fairness, transparency, and explainability – are the cornerstones of ethical AI design. By focusing on them, we can create AI systems that not only make accurate predictions but also respect human values and rights. They are crucial for the responsible development and deployment of AI, as they encourage user trust, promote inclusivity, and ensure that AI technologies are a force for good.

Moving forward from the bedrock of fairness, transparency, and explainability, these ethical considerations become instrumental in shaping the AI of the future. As we integrate AI into more areas of our lives, it's imperative that these technologies uphold the highest ethical standards to garner public trust and ensure their beneficial use. Trust in AI is more than just about its technical reliability; it's also about how well the AI aligns with our societal values and expectations. This involves guaranteeing that AI systems do not perpetuate harmful biases or discrimination and ensuring that they are designed and used in ways that respect our fundamental rights and freedoms. Moreover, the focus on inclusivity is essential to prevent the creation of a digital divide, where only certain groups reap the benefits of AI technologies while others are left behind. Inclusivity ensures that AI technologies are accessible to all and that they cater to the diverse needs of all users, regardless of their age, gender, ethnicity, disability, or socio-economic status. Finally, by ensuring that AI technologies are a force for good, we are looking beyond their immediate utility and considering their broader impact on society. This means using AI to tackle pressing societal challenges, from climate change to healthcare, and ensuring that these technologies contribute positively to human well-being and societal progress. Ultimately, ensuring fairness, transparency, and explainability in AI systems is more than just a technical challenge. It's also a social, moral, and political endeavor. By adhering to these principles, we can guide AI development in a direction that not only respects our human values and rights but also leverages the transformative potential of AI to create a more fair, inclusive, and sustainable future.

8.2 Addressing Bias and Discrimination in AI Models

Addressing Bias and Discrimination in AI Models is a fundamental challenge that hinges on the nuanced understanding of machine learning paradigms and data patterns. AI models are a reflection of the data on which they are trained; hence, any inherent bias present in the training data can lead to skewed outcomes, magnifying social inequalities, and perpetuating discrimination. For example, facial recognition systems trained predominantly on light-skinned male faces have been reported to exhibit higher error rates when identifying women and individuals with darker skin tones. To tackle this issue, it is vital first to identify potential biases. This can be achieved through rigorous exploratory data analysis, application of statistical tests, or employing bias detection tools. IBM's AI Fairness 360, an open-source toolkit, provides a set of metrics to check for biases in datasets and machine learning models.

Once identified, managing bias necessitates thorough data cleaning and pre-processing methods. Techniques like up-sampling underrepresented classes or down-sampling overrepresented ones can help balance biased data. In situations where certain features (like race or gender) directly introduce bias, these can be omitted or their impact can be minimized using techniques like fairness constraints or adversarial debiasing. The final step involves mitigating the effect of these biases. This can be done by employing fairness-enhancing algorithms during model training, or by applying post-hoc fairness corrections after the model's predictions are made.

Efforts to mitigate bias and prevent discrimination should not be viewed as a one-off task but rather as an ongoing process. The key is to establish a continuous learning loop where AI models are frequently re-evaluated and refined to ensure fairness. By incorporating such steps into their workflow, practitioners can design more robust and ethically sound AI systems.

8.3 Privacy and Security Considerations

Privacy and Security Considerations is a critical facet of AI systems that frequently manage extensive datasets, often encompassing sensitive personal information. This highlights the need for robust mechanisms to safeguard this data against both inadvertent leaks and malicious exploitation, particularly in the era of stringent regulatory controls like GDPR and CCPA.

Preserving privacy in AI systems often involves a delicate balance between data utility and individual anonymity. Traditional methods of data anonymization, such as removing direct identifiers, are no longer considered sufficient due to the risks of re-identification. Instead, advanced techniques like differential privacy offer promising avenues. Differential privacy provides a mathematical guarantee of privacy by adding carefully calibrated noise to the data or query results, thus masking individual data points while maintaining overall data utility. For example, Apple uses differential privacy to collect user data without being able to identify individual users. In terms of security, AI models are not only used to enhance security systems but are also themselves targets of cyber-attacks. Adversarial attacks, where slight manipulations in the input can lead to drastically incorrect outputs, pose significant threats to AI systems. Defending against such attacks involves complex techniques such as adversarial training, where the model is trained on both original and adversarial examples, or defensive distillation, where the model is trained to generalize from softened output distributions. Additionally, the secure sharing of AI models across different parties without revealing sensitive information is another crucial aspect of AI security. Homomorphic encryption and secure multi-party computation are advanced cryptographic techniques that enable computations on encrypted data, offering possibilities for secure AI model training and deployment. Privacy and security considerations in AI are a complex interplay of regulatory compliance, technological innovation, and ethical responsibility, and are integral to the trustworthiness and sustainability of AI systems.

8.4 Compliance with Regulatory Frameworks

The realm of AI is subject to an ever-evolving landscape of regulatory frameworks, underscoring the importance for AI practitioners to stay informed and ensure compliance, thereby avoiding legal, ethical, and reputational ramifications. This portion of our discussion will delve into prominent regulatory frameworks and elucidate strategies for designing AI models compliant with them.

At a global scale, various jurisdictions have adopted distinct approaches towards AI regulation. The European Union has been at the forefront, proposing comprehensive regulations like the General Data Protection Regulation (GDPR) and more recently, the Artificial Intelligence Act, aimed at establishing legal requirements for AI systems. These regulations encompass concepts like 'right to explanation', where individuals can seek rationale behind automated decisions, and stricter controls for 'high-risk' AI applications such as biometric identification. For example, an AI-based recruitment tool must be designed to provide justification for its hiring recommendations, enabling transparency and accountability. In contrast, the United States has espoused sector-specific regulations, such as the Health Insurance Portability and Accountability Act (HIPAA) for AI applications in healthcare, which stipulates stringent safeguards for handling Protected Health Information (PHI). An AI model used for predicting disease progression, for instance, must be designed to de-identify PHI and employ rigorous data encryption techniques to comply with HIPAA.

Further complexity arises with emerging regulatory concepts like AI Ethics Guidelines, Responsible AI Licenses, and Algorithmic Accountability. These underscore the need for proactive and holistic compliance strategies, such as Privacy by Design and Security by Design, where compliance requirements are ingrained into the AI design process from the outset, rather than being an afterthought. A predictive policing AI model, for example, must incorporate bias mitigation strategies at the design stage itself, to ensure adherence to principles of fairness and non-discrimination. Navigating the dynamic terrain of AI regulation necessitates a sound understanding of the law, strategic foresight, and an ethic of care. This allows the construction of AI models that are not only legally compliant but also trusted by users and society at large.

8.5 Establishing Ethical Guidelines for AI Model Design

Establishing ethical guidelines for AI model design is not just about following best practices; it is about consciously embedding ethical considerations into the fabric of the AI model's lifecycle. This segment elaborates on how to formulate these guidelines and enforce their compliance, thereby fostering an environment of responsible AI usage. One of the initial steps in creating an ethical AI model is incorporating principles such as fairness, accountability, transparency, and explainability (FATE) during the design phase. For instance, an AI model used for loan approval should be designed to avoid favoring or disadvantaging certain demographics (fairness). Furthermore, clear lines of accountability should be established to respond to any unexpected outputs or consequences.

Transparency involves ensuring the decision-making processes of the AI model are easily understood and explainable to stakeholders, which is especially crucial in areas such as healthcare or judiciary where the implications of decisions are far-reaching. For instance, an AI model used to diagnose diseases should provide clear rationales for its predictions, making it more comprehensible for doctors and patients. Enforcing these guidelines requires a robust governance structure and culture of ethical awareness. Regular audits, both internal and external, can assess AI models against these ethical guidelines. These audits could leverage Explainable AI (XAI) techniques to decipher complex AI decision-making processes. For example, a feature importance audit on a predictive policing AI model can help uncover if the model is unintentionally relying heavily on sensitive attributes like race or ethnicity, enabling early detection and mitigation of bias. Lastly, fostering an organizational culture that values ethics in AI is vital. This can be achieved through regular training, encouraging open discussions on ethical dilemmas, and rewarding ethical decision-making. By embedding ethical considerations in all aspects of AI model design, organizations not only mitigate reputational and regulatory risks but also build trust with their users, thereby enhancing the societal acceptance of AI.

Chapter 9

Collaboration and Teamwork

Overview:

9.1 Building Cross-Disciplinary AI Teams

9.2 Effective Communication and Collaboration Strategies

9.3 Version Control and Collaboration Tools

9.4 Balancing Individual Expertise with Team Contributions

9.5 Promoting a Culture of Continuous Learning and Innovation

Introduction:

The final chapter of the book, Chapter 9, is titled "Collaboration and Teamwork." This chapter delves into the importance of building effective and efficient teams in the field of AI and offers strategies for ensuring successful collaboration and communication within such teams.

9.1 Building Cross-Disciplinary AI Teams

In Section 9.1, "Building Cross-Disciplinary AI Teams," the author likely underscores the significance of having a diverse team with different areas of expertise in order to address the broad spectrum of challenges posed by AI development. This might involve combining skills from areas like data science, software engineering, user experience design, and domain-specific knowledge.

To handle the intricacies of AI development, it's pivotal to build a team with expertise in data science, the bedrock upon which machine learning models are built. Data scientists bring the ability to extract insights from data and frame them into actionable models, an invaluable asset in AI development.

However, AI development is not only about creating mathematical models. Software engineering skills are crucial for building reliable, scalable, and efficient applications to use these models. Software engineers ensure that the developed models are well-integrated into the system, creating an end-to-end application that seamlessly incorporates the AI model.

In addition, given the human-centered nature of many AI applications, the inclusion of user experience (UX) design skills is also essential. UX designers can help to ensure that the applications are easy to use and provide value to the end-user, which can significantly increase the adoption and success of the AI system.

Domain-specific knowledge is another critical component to consider when building an AI team. This knowledge varies depending on the area where the AI application will be deployed, for example, healthcare, finance, or retail. Having team members who understand the domain's specific challenges, needs, and regulatory environment can inform the design of the AI system, ensuring it addresses relevant problems and aligns with industry-specific considerations.

Hence, a well-rounded, cross-disciplinary AI team that amalgamates these different skill sets can ensure a more comprehensive and effective approach to AI development, driving the success of AI projects.

How to build a Cross-displinaary AI team:

Building a cross-disciplinary AI team is a critical process that involves a series of systematic steps. These steps encompass understanding the project requirements, identifying necessary roles, hiring the right talents, and fostering effective collaboration.

Understand the Project Requirements:

The first step in building a cross-disciplinary AI team is to thoroughly understand the requirements of the AI project. Consider the scope, the desired outcomes, the technology stack, and the necessary skills to carry out the project.

The process of building a cross-disciplinary AI team commences with gaining a thorough comprehension of the project's requirements. This understanding forms the foundation for all subsequent steps in team assembly. The imperative factors to consider at this stage include the scope of the project, the anticipated outcomes, the technological resources at disposal, and the essential skills needed to facilitate the project. In essence, a comprehensive evaluation of these parameters helps delineate the framework within which the AI project operates, thereby setting the stage for identifying the specific roles and expertise needed in the team. Identify Necessary Roles: With a clear understanding of the project requirements, the next step is to identify the roles needed. Typical roles in an AI project include data scientists, machine learning engineers, data engineers, software developers, project managers, UX/UI designers, and domain experts. Having established a firm grasp of the project requirements, the ensuing step revolves around identifying the requisite roles that will form the team structure. An AI project typically necessitates a diverse ensemble of professionals, each bringing a unique set of skills to the table. These roles commonly encompass data scientists, who bring the statistical and analytical prowess; machine learning engineers, who develop the algorithms; data engineers, who ensure seamless data flow and management; software developers, who build the supportive software infrastructure; project managers, who oversee the project's progression and ensure adherence to timelines and objectives; UX/UI designers, who ensure the end product is user-friendly and intuitive; and domain experts, who provide the necessary industry-specific insights. This diverse array of roles underscores the interdisciplinary nature of AI projects, thereby emphasizing the need for collaborative teamwork.

Hiring the Right Talent:

Once the roles have been defined, the process of hiring can begin. Look for individuals who not only possess the technical skills required for their roles but also demonstrate an ability to collaborate, adapt, and learn. Cognitive diversity is also important - teams composed of individuals who think differently tend to be more innovative and resilient.

Once the roles essential to the project are delineated, the subsequent phase entails acquiring the right talent to fill these positions. This hiring process should focus on sourcing individuals who go beyond merely fulfilling the technical prerequisites of their roles. They should also exhibit an aptitude for collaboration, as teamwork is crucial in such an interdisciplinary setting. The capacity for adaptation and eagerness to learn should also be high on the list of desired traits, considering the rapidly evolving landscape of AI technology. An additional facet to consider is cognitive diversity. Teams that embody a mix of different thinking patterns are generally more innovative, as they approach problem-solving from various angles. Moreover, such teams are more resilient, given their capacity to adapt and find solutions in the face of challenges. Hence, the right talent for an AI team blends technical expertise with an aptitude for continuous learning and a disposition towards collaboration.

Role Allocation:

After hiring, assign roles based on each individual's strength. It's important to recognize that each team member brings unique perspectives and skills to the table. Ensure each member's role aligns with their expertise and interest.

Upon successful completion of the hiring process, the subsequent step is role allocation. This crucial stage should revolve around designating responsibilities in accordance with each team member's proficiencies. Acknowledging that each member boasts a unique skill set and perspective is key to capitalizing on individual strengths. Consequently, it becomes essential to align each member's role with their specific expertise and areas of interest. By doing so, not only can one maximize the potential of each team member, but also foster a more engaged and motivated team. This careful alignment of roles within the cross-disciplinary AI team will empower it to effectively handle the complexities and challenges of AI projects.

Foster Collaboration:

Promote a collaborative culture where team members feel comfortable sharing ideas and giving feedback. Use collaborative tools to facilitate communication, and hold regular team meetings to discuss progress, obstacles, and future plans.

Nurturing a collaborative environment within your team is a pivotal step in establishing a robust, cross-disciplinary AI team. Encourage a culture that embraces the exchange of ideas and values constructive feedback. This inclusive environment should make team members feel comfortable voicing their opinions and suggestions. Utilize collaboration tools, such as shared documents, messaging platforms, and project management software, to streamline communication and coordination within the team. Regular team meetings, where progress updates are shared, challenges are discussed, and future plans are devised, are integral to maintaining alignment and fostering a sense of shared purpose. By doing so, a spirit of collaboration and teamwork is cultivated, driving the team towards successful project execution. Continuous Learning and Development: Encourage team members to continually develop their skills and knowledge. This could be through internal training, attending conferences, or giving team members time to learn new skills independently. Cultivating an environment of continuous learning and development is fundamental for the progression of a cross-disciplinary AI team. Encourage each team member to continuously enhance their skills and expand their knowledge. This could be accomplished through various means such as facilitating internal training sessions, providing opportunities to attend relevant conferences or workshops, or allocating time for team members to independently explore and learn new skills. Such an environment not only equips the team to stay abreast of the rapidly evolving field of AI, but it also fuels innovation, increases job satisfaction, and promotes a culture of growth and development within the team.

Performance Evaluation and Feedback:

Regularly evaluate the team's performance and provide constructive feedback. This not only helps to maintain high performance but also ensures that any issues are quickly identified and addressed. Implementing a process for regular performance evaluation and feedback is critical in maintaining a high-performing cross-disciplinary AI team. This practice involves assessing the team's performance in line with project objectives and providing constructive, candid feedback to each member. Regular evaluations not only help maintain optimum performance levels by reinforcing successful practices but also provide an opportunity to promptly identify and rectify any issues or inefficiencies. Further, they foster an environment of open communication and continuous improvement, where team members feel valued and motivated to contribute their best towards the team's goals. Encourage Innovation: Foster a culture that encourages innovative thinking. Even if an idea does not lead to a successful outcome, the process of exploring new ideas can often lead to valuable insights. Cultivating an atmosphere that inspires innovative thinking is a crucial step in building an effective cross-disciplinary AI team. Encourage team members to think outside the box and propose new ideas, fostering a safe environment where all thoughts are considered valuable. Even if a proposed idea does not immediately lead to a successful outcome, the exploration process can often bring about fresh perspectives and valuable insights. This culture of innovation fuels creative problem-solving, agility, and a growth mindset, thereby driving the team's collective intellectual potential and capacity for breakthroughs. These steps, while not exhaustive, provide a systematic approach to building a cross-disciplinary AI team, ensuring a rich mixture of skills and perspectives to drive successful AI projects.

9.2 Effective Communication and Collaboration Strategies

Section 9.2, "Effective Communication and Collaboration Strategies," is probably devoted to the crucial aspects of successful teamwork - communication and collaboration. The author might provide strategies for facilitating clear and effective communication, managing conflicts, and fostering a collaborative environment.

The author might discuss various communication strategies, such as ensuring regular team meetings, promoting open dialogue, and encouraging feedback. This might involve the practice of active listening where team members attentively listen and respond to each other's ideas, fostering mutual understanding and respect. This section could also address conflict resolution strategies. As AI projects often involve complex decision-making and may cause disagreements, effective conflict management strategies are critical to maintain a harmonious and productive team environment. In addition, the author might discuss ways to foster a collaborative environment where every team member feels valued and involved. This might include building trust among team members, promoting diversity and inclusivity, and creating a safe space where team members are not afraid to express their ideas or concerns. Furthermore, the use of collaborative tools might also be discussed in this context. Tools like shared document platforms, project management tools, and communication apps can help streamline workflows, facilitate efficient communication, and enable real-time collaboration, particularly in distributed teams.

The goal of the strategies discussed in this section would be to maximize the collective intelligence of the team, driving innovation, and ultimately leading to more effective and successful AI projects.

Let's discuss three strategies for effective communication and collaboration in the context of AI project teams.

Foster Open Dialogue and Encourage Feedback:

Open dialogue is vital for effective communication within a team. Encourage all team members to share their thoughts, ideas, and concerns freely without fear of judgment or retribution. Regular team meetings can provide a forum for open discussion. But also remember to foster an environment where ad hoc discussions are welcomed. Equally important is encouraging feedback. Constructive feedback can lead to improvements and innovations, while also promoting learning and growth within the team. Effective communication is the bedrock of any successful team, especially when navigating the complexities of AI projects. One particularly potent method of cultivating effective communication within a team is to foster open dialogue and encourage feedback. Open dialogue in a team setting is instrumental for the exchange of ideas, knowledge, and problem-solving strategies. Encouraging all team members to voice their thoughts, ideas, and concerns can significantly enrich the project with a plethora of perspectives and solutions. It empowers every team member to contribute to the project, fostering a sense of ownership and commitment towards the team's collective goals. For instance, let's consider a team working on developing a machine learning model for a predictive analytics task. Suppose a certain team member has an innovative idea to improve the model's accuracy by incorporating a new feature engineering technique they learned recently. In an environment that encourages open dialogue, they would feel confident in sharing this idea with the rest of the team. This could potentially lead to the improvement of the model's performance, thereby contributing to the success of the project. However, it's not just formal settings such as team meetings where such dialogue should be promoted. An atmosphere where spontaneous or ad hoc discussions are welcomed can also foster creativity and problem-solving, as team members feel free to exchange thoughts or brainstorm solutions at any time.

Alongside promoting open dialogue, encouraging feedback is equally crucial. Constructive feedback serves as a catalyst for growth, learning, and innovation. It helps identify areas for improvement and prompts the team to explore new approaches or strategies. Returning to our example, if the proposed feature engineering technique doesn't yield the expected improvement, constructive feedback could guide the team in understanding the shortcomings and devising an alternate strategy.

The synergy between fostering open dialogue and encouraging feedback sets the stage for a continuous learning environment. Here, every member feels valued and is driven to improve not only their work but also the overall project outcome. By emphasizing these elements, AI project teams can significantly enhance their communication effectiveness, paving the way for successful project completion and an enriched team experience.

Leverage Collaborative Tools:

In today's digital world, there is a plethora of collaborative tools that can facilitate effective communication and collaboration. These tools range from project management tools (like JIRA or Trello) to communication platforms (like Slack or Microsoft Teams), shared document platforms (like Google Docs or Confluence), and version control systems (like Git). These tools help keep everyone on the same page, streamline workflows, and facilitate real-time communication and collaboration, particularly crucial for distributed teams.

In the modern era, marked by significant advancements in technology, the traditional boundaries of workplaces have expanded far beyond physical office spaces. Digital collaborative tools have become integral to facilitating effective communication and collaboration among team members, whether they share a physical workspace or work remotely from different corners of the world.

Collaborative tools come in various forms, each serving a unique purpose in enhancing the team's efficiency and communication. Let's consider project management tools such as JIRA or Trello, to begin with. These tools allow teams to organize their tasks, set deadlines, and track progress efficiently. They provide a clear visual representation of the project's status, enabling every team member to see the big picture and understand their role within it.

For example, imagine a team building an AI model to predict stock prices. The team could use a tool like JIRA to assign tasks for data gathering, feature selection, model development, testing, and deployment. Each member can see the overall progress, who's responsible for each task, and when the tasks are due, leading to better project coordination and management. Moreover, effective communication platforms such as Slack or Microsoft Teams have transformed the way teams interact. They support real-time conversations, facilitating quick problem-solving and decision-making. Channels or threads can be created for different topics, keeping discussions organized and relevant. Continuing with our previous example, a data engineer encountering a problem while processing a dataset could quickly post a message in a dedicated Slack channel. Other team members could then promptly respond with advice or suggestions, significantly reducing downtime and promoting a collaborative problem-solving approach.

Shared document platforms like Google Docs or Confluence, on the other hand, enable teams to collectively work on documents, keep shared notes, and maintain documentation. These platforms promote transparency and knowledge sharing among team members. For instance, the team could maintain a shared Google Doc to keep notes from their brainstorming sessions or to write documentation for their AI model. Lastly, version control systems such as Git are critical when working on shared codebases. They allow multiple team members to work on the same code simultaneously without overriding each other's changes. In the context of AI, where code forms a substantial part of the project, version control is indispensable. Collectively, these collaborative tools not only facilitate seamless communication and collaboration but also foster a sense of community among team members. They ensure that everyone stays informed and connected, irrespective of their geographical location, enabling teams to function effectively and harmoniously in pursuit of their collective goals.

Promote Active Listening:

Active listening is a fundamental communication skill that promotes understanding and fosters mutual respect. It involves fully focusing on the speaker, avoiding interruptions, and responding thoughtfully. By promoting active listening, you can ensure that all team members feel heard and valued, which in turn can boost team morale and productivity. Active listening is more than just hearing the words spoken by another person. It is a comprehensive communication strategy that involves paying full attention, exhibiting thoughtful body language, avoiding interruptions, and providing meaningful responses. Encouraging active listening within a team is crucial for promoting mutual understanding, respect, and ultimately fostering a healthy work environment. Imagine a team brainstorming ideas for an AI project. Each member brings to the table unique perspectives, experiences, and skills. To harvest the collective potential, each voice should be heard, and each idea should be considered. It is here that active listening plays a pivotal role. Active listening starts with attention. Team members need to offer their undivided attention to the speaker, avoiding distractions and focusing solely on understanding the speaker's point of view. This is particularly crucial in a technical field like AI, where complex concepts and strategies are frequently discussed. For instance, when a data scientist explains a new algorithm they have developed, their colleagues must listen attentively to understand the algorithm's functionality and potential application. Non-verbal cues are another crucial aspect of active listening. This includes maintaining eye contact, nodding to show understanding, and exhibiting open body language. These signals communicate respect and genuine interest in what the speaker is saying. For instance, when a project manager outlines the project timeline, team members can show their engagement through their body language, making the manager feel valued and encouraging open communication. Avoiding interruptions is equally important. By allowing the speaker to finish their thoughts before asking questions or providing feedback, you foster an environment where everyone feels comfortable expressing their ideas. This approach is beneficial during problem-solving discussions, where understanding the full context of an issue is crucial before proposing solutions. Lastly, active listening involves responding thoughtfully to the speaker. This could be through reflective responses, summarizing the speaker's points, or asking relevant questions. For instance, after a machine learning engineer describes a challenge they're facing, a colleague might respond by summarizing the issue and asking clarifying questions. By promoting active listening, every team member feels heard and valued, fostering a sense of unity and mutual respect. This improved communication can lead to more effective collaboration, boosting the team's overall morale and productivity. Consequently, the entire team is more likely to be successful in their collective objectives, leading to superior outcomes in their AI projects.

By implementing these strategies, AI project teams can enhance their communication, foster a collaborative environment, and thus increase their overall effectiveness and productivity.

9.3 Version Control and Collaboration Tools

The next section, 9.3 "Version Control and Collaboration Tools," might focus on the technical aspects of collaboration in AI, discussing how tools like Git for version control, and platforms like GitHub or GitLab, can be used to collaborate on code. Other tools, like project management software or documentation platforms, might also be discussed.

Version control systems, such as Git, are fundamental tools for software and AI development teams. They allow multiple people to work on the same codebase simultaneously without overwriting each other's changes. Additionally, they provide a history of changes, enabling developers to track the evolution of a project and facilitating troubleshooting by allowing them to pinpoint when a particular issue first emerged.

Platforms like GitHub or GitLab provide a shared space for hosting code repositories, making them accessible to all team members, wherever they might be. They offer additional features useful for collaboration, such as issue tracking, pull requests for code review, and integrations with other tools, like continuous integration/continuous deployment (CI/CD) systems. Furthermore, in the realm of AI projects, version control is not limited to code. Models, training data, and configurations may also need to be versioned. Tools like DVC (Data Version Control) are built specifically for this purpose, enabling AI teams to keep track of different versions of data sets and machine learning models, which is crucial for reproducibility and iterative development. Beyond code and model versioning, project management tools (like Jira, Trello) and documentation platforms (like Confluence or Google Docs) are equally vital for efficient teamwork. Project management tools help in organizing, tracking, and prioritizing work, while documentation platforms provide a centralized location for knowledge sharing and collaboration. Utilizing these tools effectively can streamline workflows and enhance team productivity. In essence, "Version Control and Collaboration Tools" in the context of AI projects refers to the diverse set of software tools that assist teams in effectively working together on complex tasks, managing code and model versions, tracking project progress, and maintaining knowledge continuity.

9.4 Balancing Individual Expertise with Team Contributions

Section 9.4, "Balancing Individual Expertise with Team Contributions," likely discusses the importance of valuing each team member's unique skills and knowledge, while also emphasizing the need for collaboration and collective decision-making. The author might offer advice on how to balance the benefits of individual expertise with the synergistic potential of teamwork.

In AI projects, individuals often have areas of specific expertise, such as data preprocessing, model architecture design, or deployment and scaling. Each of these specialties is critical to the success of the project, and recognizing and utilizing individual expertise is key. This could mean deferring to an individual's judgment in their area of expertise, or dividing tasks based on individual strengths. However, the overall success of an AI project is usually not the result of isolated efforts, but rather the collective work of the entire team. Therefore, fostering a culture of collaboration and collective decision-making is equally important. This could involve regular team meetings to discuss the project's progress, brainstorming sessions to solve problems, or joint decision-making on key aspects of the project. In other words, "Balancing Individual Expertise with Team Contributions" involves recognizing and leveraging each team member's unique skills and knowledge, while ensuring that the entire team is working together towards a common goal. This balance is crucial in creating a team that is more than the sum of its parts, where the diverse set of skills and perspectives of individual members is harmonized into an effective and cohesive unit.

For example, a data engineer might be the expert in creating efficient data pipelines, while a machine learning engineer might have the most knowledge about designing and training models. While each of these individuals should take the lead in their area of expertise, it's essential that they collaborate closely. The data engineer needs to understand the requirements of the machine learning model, and the machine learning engineer needs to understand the constraints and possibilities of the data pipeline. Regular communication and joint problem-solving can ensure that these individual contributions come together seamlessly to produce a well-functioning AI system.

9.5 Promoting a Culture of Continuous Learning and Innovation

The final section, 9.5 "Promoting a Culture of Continuous Learning and Innovation," could cover the importance of fostering an environment that encourages learning and innovation. Given the rapidly evolving nature of AI, the author likely emphasizes the need for teams to continually update their knowledge and skills and to be open to new ideas and approaches.

In the final section, "Promoting a Culture of Continuous Learning and Innovation," the author probably underscores the importance of a work environment that not only values existing knowledge but also the perpetual pursuit of learning and innovation. Given the speed at which the field of artificial intelligence evolves, being equipped with the latest knowledge and skillset is crucial for a team to remain effective and competitive. The author might discuss the importance of continuous professional development, which can involve training programs, workshops, online courses, and attending conferences and seminars. However, fostering a culture of continuous learning is not just about professional development. It's also about creating an environment where curiosity is encouraged, and questions and exploration are valued. This can be done by promoting open dialogue, where team members feel safe to share their ideas, ask questions, and even make mistakes, as these are often the first steps towards innovation. Innovation, on the other hand, is about more than just coming up with new ideas. It's about being willing to change established processes and take risks in the pursuit of improvement and efficiency. The author might discuss strategies for promoting innovation, such as allocating time for team members to work on their own projects or ideas, encouraging diverse thinking, and creating a safe space for risk-taking. For instance, a company could introduce "innovation days," where team members are encouraged to spend time exploring new ideas or technologies. This not only promotes continuous learning but can also lead to novel solutions that can improve the team's work. Another strategy could be holding regular brainstorming sessions where team members are encouraged to think outside the box and propose new ways of doing things. By promoting a culture of continuous learning and innovation, teams can ensure they remain on the cutting edge of AI development.

Chapter 10
Future Trends and Challenges

Overview:

10.1 Emerging AI Technologies and Trends

10.2 Ethical and Legal Challenges in AI Model Design

10.3 Impact of AI on Society and Workforce

10.4 The Role of AI Model Designers in Shaping the Future

10.5 Final Thoughts

Introduction:

Chapter 10, "Emerging AI Technologies and Trends," aims to provide a look into the future of Artificial Intelligence. We will explore the technologies currently at the bleeding edge of the field, and consider the trends that could define the landscape of AI in the coming years. In the section on "Ethical and Legal Challenges in AI Model Design," we discuss the complex ethical conundrums and legal issues that are emerging as AI becomes more deeply embedded in society. These challenges necessitate a multidisciplinary approach, combining insights from computer science, law, philosophy, and more. The "Impact of AI on Society and Workforce" segment reviews the transformative effects of AI. From reshaping the labor market to influencing social dynamics, we delve into the ways AI will redefine the societal structure and how we can prepare for these changes. We then move on to discuss "The Role of AI Model Designers in Shaping the Future." This section underscores the crucial responsibility of AI designers and developers in steering the direction of AI technology, ensuring it is used to the benefit of all of humanity.

10.1 Emerging AI Technologies and Trends

In the chapter on "Emerging AI Technologies and Trends", we delve into the pioneering advancements reshaping the contours of AI. This progression is represented by the seismic shift towards explainable AI, a burgeoning field focused on creating transparent models that deliver interpretable and easily understood outcomes. For instance, techniques like LIME (Local Interpretable Model-Agnostic Explanations) and SHAP (SHapley Additive exPlanations) are increasingly being employed to shed light on the typically opaque decision-making processes of complex AI models. Simultaneously, the intersection of quantum computing and AI marks another notable trend. Quantum machine learning, for instance, is an emerging field that leverages the principles of quantum mechanics to improve computational speed and create sophisticated models, capable of solving problems currently considered intractable by classical computers.

Furthermore, we see the application of AI broadening, with its tendrils extending into various sectors. In healthcare, AI is transforming disease prediction and diagnosis, drug discovery, and personalized medicine, leading to improved patient outcomes. An example of this would be Google's DeepMind's protein-folding AI, AlphaFold, which has revolutionized bioinformatics by accurately predicting protein structures. In climate science, AI is helping to refine climate models, predict climate change patterns, and optimize renewable energy sources. In the creative realm, AI is inspiring new modes of artistic expression, like OpenAI's MuseNet, which composes original songs in a wide array of genres and styles.

These trends not only signify the far-reaching potential of AI but also underscore the dynamic and rapidly evolving nature of this field.

10.2 Ethical and Legal Challenges in AI Model Design

"Ethical and Legal Challenges in AI Model Design" casts a critical lens on the multifaceted complexities involved in crafting AI with due regard for ethical norms and legal directives. As the role of AI augments in the fabric of our daily existence, so too does the need to navigate intricate issues such as privacy, bias, accountability, and transparency. Privacy remains at the vanguard of these ethical debates, given the vast swathes of personal data that AI systems often require for functioning. Cases like the Cambridge Analytica scandal, where data of millions of Facebook users was misused for political advertising, underscore the urgent need for robust privacy safeguards. AI systems must be designed with privacy-preserving technologies such as differential privacy and federated learning, ensuring data utility while protecting individual identities. Bias in AI, often a mirror of societal biases, raises serious ethical concerns too. High-profile instances like Amazon's recruitment AI, which was found to be biased against women, highlight this issue. It's essential to incorporate robust techniques to identify and mitigate bias in AI models, promoting fairness and equity.

Accountability and transparency in AI are intertwined concepts that deal with understanding AI decisions and attributing responsibility for these decisions. AI, particularly deep learning models, are often criticized as being "black boxes" due to their inscrutable decision-making processes. Explainable AI (XAI) is an emerging trend addressing this opacity, aiming to make AI decisions interpretable to humans. Moreover, clear accountability frameworks need to be established, ensuring that adverse AI-induced outcomes can be attributed to identifiable entities. From a legal perspective, AI is challenging traditional legal norms, leading to a constantly evolving regulatory landscape. For instance, the EU's General Data Protection Regulation (GDPR) has provisions directly affecting AI, like the "right to explanation", where individuals can ask for explanations on automated decisions. AI model designers must remain agile, staying abreast of these regulatory changes and ensuring that their models are designed in compliance with these laws.

The journey to ethical and legally compliant AI is a complex endeavor, necessitating a multidisciplinary approach that incorporates ethical considerations right from the model design stage and a robust understanding of the dynamic legal landscape.

10.3 Impact of AI on Society and Workforce

"Impact of AI on Society and Workforce" (10.3) delves into the profound societal transformations instigated by the widespread application of AI technologies. These changes, affecting all spheres of human activity, illuminate the dual nature of AI as both a tool of empowerment and a potential source of disruption.

A major focus area is the AI-driven shift in the labor market. AI's capacity to automate routine tasks has led to a fear of job displacement. High-profile examples, such as the use of autonomous vehicles in transportation or AI chatbots in customer service, underscore this concern. However, while certain roles may become obsolete, AI is also anticipated to create new job categories, needing skills in AI model design, ethics, regulation, and more. Moreover, AI can augment human capabilities, making employees more productive in their roles. As Erik Brynjolfsson and Andrew McAfee argue in "The Second Machine Age," while technology can replace certain jobs, it also creates opportunities for roles that leverage uniquely human skills like creativity and emotional intelligence. The social implications of AI are equally significant. Personalized recommendations on streaming platforms, AI-driven matchmaking on dating apps, or AI-powered predictive policing are all instances of how AI shapes our societal interactions. While these applications can enhance convenience and efficiency, they also raise concerns about privacy and the potential for manipulation.

Moreover, the security implications of AI are profound. Cybersecurity, for instance, is now a cat-and-mouse game between AI-driven security systems and AI-powered malicious actors. The advent of deepfakes, AI-generated realistic images or videos, poses new challenges for information authenticity and trust. Finally, the broad societal implications of AI usage encompass both the opportunities it offers and the risks it poses. AI's potential to address grand challenges, like climate change or disease diagnosis, is immense. However, unchecked use of AI, without adequate consideration of ethics and regulation, can lead to societal harm, such as discriminatory outcomes or privacy infringements. As such, understanding and shaping the societal impact of AI is a responsibility that extends beyond AI model designers to involve all stakeholders in society.

10.4 The Role of AI Model Designers in Shaping the Future

"The Role of AI Model Designers in Shaping the Future" (10.4) highlights the consequential role played by AI model designers in directing the trajectory of AI development and its myriad applications. As the principal architects and stewards of this revolutionary technology, AI model designers bear a profound responsibility to ensure that AI is designed and employed in ways that are ethically sound, fair, and ultimately beneficial to society. AI model designers are, in essence, the cartographers of a new technological landscape, shaping the terrain of artificial intelligence as it continues to evolve. Their role transcends mere technical expertise. They're not just creating algorithms or designing neural networks; they're framing the AI-driven future and ensuring that its values align with those of society.

For instance, when an AI model designer is building a predictive policing model, it's their responsibility to ensure that the model does not reinforce societal biases, thereby exacerbating systemic injustices. Similarly, if they're developing a facial recognition system, they must ensure it respects user privacy and is transparent in its use. Moreover, AI model designers have a key role in democratizing AI technology. For instance, by creating user-friendly tools and platforms that enable non-specialists to utilize AI, they can broaden access to AI's benefits. This inclusive approach is exemplified by the proliferation of 'drag-and-drop' machine learning platforms, such as Google's AutoML or Microsoft's Azure Machine Learning, which lower the barriers to AI utilization. Furthermore, AI model designers also play a pivotal role in the discourse surrounding AI regulation. With their deep technical expertise, they can inform the design of regulatory frameworks that are robust yet flexible, ensuring AI's safe use without stifling innovation.

In essence, AI model designers are not just shaping AI; they're shaping society. They are the custodians of an extraordinary power, and with it comes an extraordinary responsibility to wield it in a manner that respects our collective values and enhances our collective wellbeing.

10.5 Final Thoughts

As we gaze into the future, the landscape of AI is bound to evolve, unearthing new technologies, trends, ethical challenges, and impacting society and the workforce in unforeseen ways. Amid this flux, the role of AI model designers will become even more critical.

As AI model designers, you are the architects of the future. As you shape AI models, you will also be shaping the contours of society, influencing decisions, and impacting lives. Thus, approach this journey with curiosity, humility, and a deep sense of responsibility. Continue to learn, adapt, collaborate, innovate, and above all, strive to design AI models that drive positive change.

Remember, in your hands lie the power to create AI models that can solve some of the most complex challenges that we face today. Use this power wisely, ethically, and empathetically. Embrace the exciting journey that is AI model design, and may your journey contribute to a better, more equitable, and prosperous world.

Conclusion

As we journey through the terrain of AI model design, we recognize its transformative power, as well as the challenges and responsibilities it carries. Through this book, we have delved into the intricate process of designing AI models, from understanding the problem, defining objectives, managing data, choosing algorithms, developing, integrating, and deploying models, to ensuring ethical considerations and fostering effective collaboration. As the concluding chapter of our exploration, we reflect on the key takeaways and insights gleaned throughout the journey.

Firstly, the power of AI models in problem-solving is immense, stretching across diverse domains, driving innovation, efficiency, and transformative impact. The intricate marriage of data, algorithms, and computational power lends AI its capacity to understand complex patterns and make accurate predictions. Yet, wielding this power calls for a deep understanding of the components of AI model design and the application of a thoughtful process, such as Design Thinking, to ensure effective and ethical outcomes.

Secondly, defining clear objectives, aligning with stakeholders, and managing data responsibly are fundamental to successful AI model design. From the selection of suitable algorithms and models to the careful implementation and evaluation, the process is a delicate dance of precision, creativity, and technical prowess. Integrating and deploying models further require a keen eye for scalability, quality assurance, and error handling.

Thirdly, AI model design is not a static process, but a dynamic journey that calls for continuous learning, adaptation, and improvement. This constant evolution involves not only the AI models but also the individuals and teams working on them. It is here that the power of collaboration and effective teamwork comes into play, contributing significantly to the successful design and deployment of AI models.

Lastly, AI model design is deeply intertwined with ethical responsibility. Ensuring fairness, transparency, addressing bias, and adhering to regulatory frameworks are non-negotiable aspects of the process. As we stand at the crossroads of technology and ethics, the role of AI model designers in shaping an equitable future cannot be overstated.

Appendix

Glossary of Key Terms

1. Artificial Intelligence (AI): A branch of computer science that aims to create systems capable of performing tasks that require human intelligence, such as visual perception, speech recognition, decision-making, and language translation.

2. Machine Learning (ML): A subset of AI that involves the development of algorithms that allow computers to learn from and make decisions or predictions based on data.

3. Deep Learning (DL): A subset of machine learning that uses neural networks with many layers (hence 'deep') to analyze various factors and variables in large volumes of data.

4. Data Preprocessing: The process of cleaning and transforming raw data before it's used in machine learning models, which can include dealing with missing or inconsistent data, normalization, and outlier detection.

5. Neural Network: A type of machine learning model that is designed to mimic the way a human brain works, consisting of interconnected nodes (or 'neurons') organized into layers.

6. Supervised Learning: A type of machine learning where the model is trained on a labeled dataset, i.e., a dataset where the target outcome is known.

7. Unsupervised Learning: A type of machine learning where the model is trained on an unlabeled dataset, i.e., a dataset where the target outcome is unknown.

8. Reinforcement Learning: A type of machine learning where an agent learns to make decisions by performing actions and receiving rewards or penalties.

9. Transfer Learning: A machine learning method where a pre-trained model is used as a starting point for a similar problem.

10. Hyperparameter Tuning: The process of choosing a set of optimal hyperparameters for a learning algorithm.

11. Overfitting: A modeling error that occurs when a function is too closely fit to a limited set of data points and may fail to generalize well to new data.

12. Underfitting: A modeling error that occurs when a function is too simple to capture the underlying structure of the data adequately.

13. Bias: In machine learning, bias can refer to the assumptions made by a model that lead it to ignore certain aspects of the data. It can also refer to the systematic unfairness towards certain groups due to the data or the way the model is trained.

14. Ethics in AI: The study of the moral issues that arise as a result of the design, development, deployment, and use of AI technologies.

15. Version Control: A system that records changes to a file or set of files over time so that specific versions can be recalled later.

16. Containerization: A lightweight form of virtualization that allows for applications to be bundled and run in isolated user spaces known as containers.

17. Scalability: The ability of a system, network, or process to handle a growing amount of work or its potential to expand to accommodate that growth.

18. Regression: A type of supervised learning approach commonly used for prediction of continuous outcomes.

19. Classification: A type of supervised learning approach used for predicting categorical outcomes.

20. Clustering: A type of unsupervised learning used to group similar instances on the basis of features.

21. Dimensionality Reduction: Techniques used to reduce the number of feature variables in a dataset, each representing a dimension in feature space.

22. Feature Selection: The process of selecting a subset of relevant features for use in model construction.

23. Feature Engineering: The process of creating new features or modifying existing ones to improve model performance.

24. Cross-Validation: A resampling procedure used to evaluate machine learning models on a limited data sample.

25. Convolutional Neural Network (CNN): A type of neural network typically used for image processing, which includes convolutional layers that filter inputs for useful information.

26. Recurrent Neural Network (RNN): A type of neural network where connections between nodes form a directed graph along a temporal sequence, useful for dealing with sequential data.

27. Generative Adversarial Network (GAN): A class of machine learning systems where two neural networks contest with each other to capture the data

distribution.

28. Natural Language Processing (NLP): A subfield of AI that focuses on enabling computers to understand and process human language.

29. Chatbots: An AI-based software designed to interact with humans in their natural languages.

30. Robotics Process Automation (RPA): The use of AI and machine learning to automate high-volume, repetitive tasks.

31. Ensemble Methods: Techniques that create multiple models and then combine them to produce improved results.

32. Data Augmentation: Techniques used to increase the amount of data by adding slightly modified copies of already existing data.

33. AutoML: Automated machine learning, a process of automating the end-to-end process of machine learning.

34. Edge Computing: A distributed computing paradigm which brings computation and data storage closer to the location where it is needed, to improve response times and save bandwidth.

35. Federated Learning: A machine learning approach that trains an algorithm across multiple decentralized devices holding local data samples, without exchanging them.

36. Explainable AI (XAI): An area in AI which aims to make AI decisions understandable and transparent to human users.

37. Differential Privacy: A system for publicly sharing information about a dataset by describing the patterns of groups within the dataset while withholding information about individuals in the dataset.

38. Data Mining: The process of discovering patterns in large data sets involving methods at the intersection of machine learning, statistics, and database systems.

39. Data Imputation: The process of replacing missing data with substituted values.

40. Model Deployment: The process of making your model available in production environment where it can provide predictions on unseen data.

Sample Code Snippets

This section includes example code snippets. These examples can be presented in popular programming languages used in AI, like Python or R.

Python Code Snippet for a Simple Linear Regression Model using scikit-learn

```python
from sklearn.linear_model import LinearRegression
from sklearn.model_selection import train_test_split
import pandas as pd

# Load dataset
data = pd.read_csv('data.csv')

# Split dataset into features (X) and target (y)
X = data.drop('target', axis=1)
y = data['target']

# Split dataset into training set and test set
X_train, X_test, y_train, y_test = train_test_split(X, y, test_size=0.2)

# Create a Linear Regression model object
regression = LinearRegression()

# Train the model using the training sets
regression.fit(X_train, y_train)

# Make predictions using the testing set
y_pred = regression.predict(X_test)
```

Project: Building a Handwritten Digit Classifier Using TensorFlow and the MNIST Dataset

Project Overview

In this project, we will be building a Convolutional Neural Network (CNN) to classify handwritten digits. We will use the MNIST dataset, a standard dataset in machine learning, containing 60,000 training images and 10,000 test images of handwritten digits.

Step 1: Load the Data

First, we will load the MNIST dataset, which is conveniently provided in TensorFlow's dataset API.

```
import tensorflow as tf

# Load MNIST dataset
mnist = tf.keras.datasets.mnist
(train_images, train_labels), (test_images, test_labels) = mnist.load_
data()
```

Step 2: Preprocess the Data

Next, we preprocess the data by scaling our dataset. This step ensures that our model trains faster.

```
# Normalize the image data
train_images = train_images / 255.0
test_images = test_images / 255.0
```

Step 3: Build the Model

We will now build our model. We will use a simple architecture with two convolutional layers, followed by two dense layers.

```
model = tf.keras.models.Sequential([
  tf.keras.layers.Flatten(input_shape=(28, 28)),
  tf.keras.layers.Dense(128, activation='relu'),
  tf.keras.layers.Dropout(0.2),
  tf.keras.layers.Dense(10)
])
```

Step 4: Compile the Model

Before training the model, we need to choose a loss function, an optimizer, and metrics to monitor.

```
model.compile(optimizer='adam',
        loss=tf.keras.losses.SparseCategoricalCrossentropy(from_logits=True),
        metrics=['accuracy'])
```

Step 5: Train the Model

We are now ready to train our model.

```
model.fit(train_images, train_labels, epochs=5)
```

Step 6: Evaluate the Model

Finally, we evaluate the performance of our model on the test dataset.

```
test_loss, test_acc = model.evaluate(test_images, test_labels, verbose=2)
```

```
print('\nTest accuracy:', test_acc)
```

In this project, you have built a simple yet effective model to classify handwritten digits. Congratulations! Remember, in a real-world scenario, you might need to further tweak the model architecture, the parameters, or preprocess the data to improve the model's performance.

Bibliography

- Russell, S. J., & Norvig, P. (2020). Artificial Intelligence: A Modern Approach. 4th Edition. Pearson.

- Provost, F., & Fawcett, T. (2013). Data Science for Business: What You Need to Know about Data Mining and Data-Analytic Thinking. O'Reilly Media, Inc.

- Hastie, T., Tibshirani, R., & Friedman, J. (2009). The Elements of Statistical Learning: Data Mining, Inference, and Prediction. Springer Series in Statistics. 2nd Edition. Springer.

- Domingos, P. (2015). The Master Algorithm: How the Quest for the Ultimate Learning Machine Will Remake Our World. Basic Books.

- Bostrom, N. (2016). Superintelligence: Paths, Dangers, Strategies. Oxford University Press.

- Kelleher, J. D., Mac Namee, B., & D'Arcy, A. (2020). Fundamentals of Machine Learning for Predictive Data Analytics: Algorithms, Worked Examples, and Case Studies. MIT Press.

- Brownlee, J. (2020). Machine Learning Mastery With Python: Understand Your Data, Create Accurate Models and Work Projects End-To-End. Machine Learning Mastery.

- Muller, A. C., & Guido, S. (2017). Introduction to Machine Learning with Python: A Guide for Data Scientists. O'Reilly Media, Inc.

- Devlin, J., Chang, M.W., Lee, K., and Toutanova, K. (2019). BERT: Pre-training of Deep Bidirectional Transformers for Language Understanding. In Proceedings of the 2019 Conference of the North American Chapter of the Association for Computational Linguistics.

- Radford, A., Wu, J., Child, R., Luan, D., Amodei, D., and Sutskever, I. (2019). Language Models are Unsupervised Multitask Learners. OpenAI Blog.

- "Practical Bayesian Optimization of Machine Learning Algorithms" by Jasper Snoek, Hugo Larochelle, and Ryan P. Adams. Published in Advances in Neural Information Processing Systems 25, 2012.

- "Random Search for Hyper-Parameter Optimization" by James Bergstra and Yoshua Bengio. Published in Journal of Machine Learning Research, 2012.

- "Hyperparameter Optimization: A Review" by Jan Hendrik Metzen. Published in Frontiers in Machine Learning and AI, 2019.

- "A Tutorial on Bayesian Optimization of Expensive Cost Functions, with Application to Active User Modeling and Hierarchical Reinforcement Learning" by Eric Brochu, Vlad M. Cora, and Nando de Freitas. Published in arXiv preprint arXiv:1012.2599, 2010.

- "Algorithms for Hyper-Parameter Optimization" by James Bergstra, Rémi Bardenet, Yoshua Bengio, and Balázs Kégl. Published in Advances in Neural Information Processing Systems 24, 2011.

- "Reinforcement Learning: An Introduction" by Richard S. Sutton and Andrew G. Barto (MIT Press, 2018)

- "Deep Reinforcement Learning" by Pieter Abbeel and John Schulman (Morgan & Claypool Publishers, 2019)

- "Reinforcement Learning and Optimal Control" by Dimitri P. Bertsekas (Athena Scientific, 2019)

- "Reinforcement Learning: State-of-the-Art" edited by Marco Wiering and Martijn van Otterlo (Springer, 2012)

- "Hands-On Machine Learning with Scikit-Learn, Keras, and TensorFlow" by Aurélien Géron. Publisher: O'Reilly Media, Year: 2019.

- "Designing Data-Intensive Applications: The Big Ideas Behind Reliable, Scalable, and Maintainable Systems" by Martin Kleppmann, Published by O'Reilly Media, 2017.

- "Building Machine Learning Powered Applications: Going from Idea to Product" by Emmanuel Ameisen, Published by O'Reilly Media, 2020.

- "Python for Data Analysis: Data Wrangling with Pandas, NumPy, and IPython" by Wes McKinney, Published by O'Reilly Media, 2017.

- "Deep Learning" by Ian Goodfellow, Yoshua Bengio, and Aaron Courville. Publisher: The MIT Press, Year: 2016.

- "Online Learning and Online Convex Optimization" by Shai Shalev-Shwartz, 2012, Cambridge University Press.

- "The Feedback Loop: Using Data to Boost Student Learning" by Jane E. Pollock, 2018, Solution Tree Press.

- "Personalized Digital Advertising: How Data and Technology Are Transforming How We Market" by Diaz Nesamoney, 2015, FT Press.

- "Continuous Delivery: Reliable Software Releases through Build, Test, and Deployment Automation" by Jez Humble and David Farley, 2010, Addison-Wesley Professional.

- "Ethics of Artificial Intelligence and Robotics" by Vincent C. Müller, published by Stanford University Press in 2020.

- "Artificial Unintelligence: How Computers Misunderstand the World" by Meredith Broussard, published by MIT Press in 2018.

- "The Ethical Algorithm: The Science of Socially Aware Algorithm Design" by Michael Kearns and Aaron Roth, published by Oxford University Press in 2019.

- "Team Geek: A Software Developer's Guide to Working Well with Others" by Brian W. Fitzpatrick and Ben Collins-Sussman, Published by O'Reilly Media, 2012.

- "Accelerate: The Science of Lean Software and DevOps: Building and Scaling High Performing Technology Organizations" by Niccle Forsgren, Jez Humble, and Gene Kim, Published by IT Revolution Press, 2018.

- "Learning Agile: Understanding Scrum, XP, Lean, and Kanban" by Andrew Stellman and Jennifer Greene, Published by O'Reilly Media, 2014.

- "Peopleware: Productive Projects and Teams" by Tom DeMarco and Timothy Lister, Published by Dorset House, 1987.

- "Scrum: The Art of Doing Twice the Work in Half the Time" by Jeff Sutherland and JJ Sutherland, Published by Crown Business, 2014.

- "The Phoenix Project: A Novel about IT, DevOps, and Helping Your Business Win" by Gene Kim, Kevin Behr, and George Spafford, Published by IT Revolution Press, 2013.

- Robbins, S.P., & Coulter, M. (2020). "Fundamentals of Management". Pearson.

- Cohn, M. (2020). "Succeeding with Agile: Software Development Using Scrum". Addison-Wesley Professional.

Bibliography

- Sutton, R.I. & Rao, H. (2014). "Scaling Up Excellence: Getting to More Without Settling for Less". Crown Business.

- Daugherty, P. & Wilson, H.J. (2018). "Human + Machine: Reimagining Work in the Age of AI". Harvard Business Review Press.

- Beyer, B., Jones, C., Petoff, J., & Murphy, N. R. (2016). "Site Reliability Engineering: How Google Runs Production Systems". O'Reilly Media.

- "Weapons of Math Destruction: How Big Data Increases Inequality and Threatens Democracy" by Cathy O'Neil, published by Crown in 2016.

- "Privacy and Freedom" by Alan F. Westin, published by Atheneum in 1967.

- "Bandit Algorithms for Website Optimization" by John Myles White, 2012, O'Reilly Media.

- "Python Machine Learning" by Sebastian Raschka and Vahid Mirjalili. Publisher: Packt Publishing, Year: 2019.

- "Advances in Neural Information Processing Systems" (NIPS) conference proceedings, which include various papers on reinforcement learning (published annually, with different publishers). "Team of Teams: New Rules of Engagement for a Complex World" by Stanley McChrystal, David Silverman, Tantum Collins, and Chris Fussell. Publisher: Portfolio; Published: 2015.

www.ingramcontent.com/pod-product-compliance
Lightning Source LLC
LaVergne TN
LVHW081521050326
832903LV00025B/1566